MW01199742

THE MAKING OF MISSISSIPPIAN TRADITION

Florida Museum of Natural History: Ripley P. Bullen Series

The Making of
MISSISSIPPIAN TRADITION

CHRISTINA M. FRIBERG

University of Florida Press
Gainesville

25 24 23 22 21 20   6 5 4 3 2 1

Library of Congress Cataloging-in-Publication Data
Names: Friberg, Christina M., author.
Title: The making of Mississippian tradition / Christina M. Friberg.
Other titles: Ripley P. Bullen series.
Description: Gainesville : University of Florida Press, 2020. | Series:
    Florida Museum of Natural History: Ripley P. Bullen series | Includes
    bibliographical references and index.
Identifiers: LCCN 2020016438 (print) | LCCN 2020016439 (ebook) | ISBN
    9781683401612 (hardback) | ISBN 9781683401896 (pdf)
Subjects: LCSH: Mississippian culture—Illinois—American Bottom. |
    Excavations (Archaeology)—Illinois—Cahokia Mounds State Historic Park.
    | American Bottom (Ill.)—Antiquities.
Classification: LCC E99.M6815 F75 2020 (print) | LCC E99.M6815 (ebook) |
    DDC 977.3/89—dc23
LC record available at https://lccn.loc.gov/2020016438
LC ebook record available at https://lccn.loc.gov/2020016439

UF PRESS

UNIVERSITY
OF FLORIDA

University of Florida Press
2046 NE Waldo Road
Suite 2100
Gainesville, FL 32609
http://upress.ufl.edu

For my mom, Mary Gorayeb Friberg

a first-generation American Brooklynite who put herself through college, studied anthropology, and made sacrifices so her daughters could follow in her footsteps

Contents

Figures

Tables

Acknowledgments

This book was made possible only with the support of a number of people and organizations. I would like to begin by acknowledging and honoring the Peoria, Kickapoo, and Potawatomi people, on whose ancestral Illinois Valley homelands this research was conducted. I'd like to thank my parents, Norman and Mary Friberg, and my sisters, Karen and Honor, for supporting me through years of hardship and long distance. I am forever grateful to my husband, Gerrit, for his extraordinary patience, for always believing in me, and for pushing me to do my best work.

Many thanks to the faculty and staff of the Department of Anthropology at the University of California, Santa Barbara, including Amber VanDerwarker, Lynn Gamble, and Kathe Schreiber. In particular, I owe a debt of gratitude to my mentor, Gregory Wilson, whose dedication and support have been instrumental in the success of my career thus far. I would like to thank Colleen Delaney, associate professor of anthropology at CSU Channel Islands, for her invaluable research on the early Mississippian–period LIRV, and for encouraging me to continue investigations at the Audrey-North site. I would like to extend a most heartfelt thank-you to the landowners of Haypress Falls and stewards of the Audrey site, Denny and Sherry Vetter, without whom my fieldwork at the Audrey site would not have been possible.

Thanks to the many members of the Audrey site field crew: PI Greg Wilson, Mallory Melton, Matt LoBiondo, Brian Barbier, Anna Khrustaleva, and Jenna Santy. Thanks also to Jason King and Chuck Titus of the Center for American Archaeology; Duane Esarey, Tom Emerson, Dan Blodgett, Steve Boles, Tamira Brennan, Rob Hickson, Larry Kinsella, Bob Monroe, Dave Nolan, and Jim Pisell from the Illinois State Archaeological Survey; Larry Conrad and Andrea Alveshere from Western Illinois University; and Mike Conner from the Illinois State Museum–Dickson Mounds. A number of dedicated undergraduate interns at UCSB assisted with lab analysis: Majdolene Dajani, Samantha Kretchmar, Yvonne Morado, Eddie Moua, and especially Jessica Strayer. I would like to recognize Chris Chien, graphic artist, who designed some of the detailed regional maps that appear in this book. Thanks to Brad Koldehoff for sharing his expertise on Mississippian lithic analysis. Thanks also to Bill Iseminger at Cahokia Mounds, Kelvin Sampson at the Illinois State Museum, and Larry Conrad at WIU for their information on the oversized Ramey Incised jar from Cahokia.

This research was made possible with funding from the National Science Foundation award #1614379, and in part from the UCSB Academic Senate and UCSB Department of Anthropology. Finally, I would like to thank Ed Herrmann and Indiana University Bloomington for supporting me through the process of publishing this book.

1

Introduction

Culture contact has historically been described as the phenomenon of broadscale or dramatic social, political, and economic changes that occur when different groups engage in interactions (Schortman and Urban 1998). Studies of culture contact have, with rare exception, focused on colonial encounters (Cusick, ed. 1998; Dietler 2010; Liebmann and Murphy, eds. 2011; Lyons and Papadopoulos, eds. 2002; Stein 2005). The European colonization of large portions of the Western Hemisphere is a well-studied example (Armstrong 1998; Deagan 1998, 2004; Liebmann and Murphy 2011; Lightfoot and Martinez 1995; Silliman 2005; and many others). In many of these cases, although contact ultimately resulted in a complex and diverse set of negotiations and cultural entanglements, the main catalyst for these changes was the desire of one group to expand its power over others. Postcolonial theories of culture contact emphasize the agency of indigenous individuals to either resist or actively participate in colonial efforts, yet the significance of institutionalized power differentials in these encounters cannot (and should not) be denied (Cusick 1998; Dietler 2010: 49; Liebmann and Murphy 2011: 18; Lightfoot and Martinez 1995; McGuire 1983; Silliman 2005; Stein 2002; Wernke 2011). Anthropologists have been ruminating on these issues for years, eventually substituting simplistic, top-down models of diffusion and acculturation with bottom-up approaches that capture the nuance of the human experience through negotiations of gender, ethnicity, and power relations (Cusick 1998; Emberling 1997; Silliman 2009; Smith 2007; Voss 2008).

These studies have made great strides in highlighting variation in how colonial encounters unfolded in different locales and temporal contexts, and how social relationships were forged, contested, and transformed in cross-cultural negotiations. However, less attention has been paid to expansive, intergroup social phenomena that occur in the absence (or perhaps alongside the development) of institutionalized power struggles. For this reason, archaeological studies of the emergence and expansion of complex nonstate societies leave a host of questions unanswered. How and why does one group assert its influence over others without the use of force? Why do outside groups adopt the cultural practices of these influential entities? Under what conditions and in what ways do they insert their own traditions into these asymmetrical scenarios? What are the mechanisms operating in this process and how and why do outcomes vary regionally? Investigating these questions will aid in comparative anthropological inquiries as to how and why large polities extend their influence over hinterland areas in the absence of imperial or state-level power.

The bottom-up approaches developed in studies of culture contact are beneficial for cultivating a more nuanced understanding of these historical processes. I propose that the political expansion of complex nonstate societies is best understood when identity formation and shifts in daily practice are considered in tandem with economic relations and the negotiation of political alliances. In this manner, I seek to evaluate how and why the complex Mississippian polity of Cahokia extended its influence over the North American midcontinent, and the ways in which Woodland communities negotiated identities and made new traditions by participating in this process.

Cahokia was the largest pre-Columbian polity in North America, and its inhabitants spread aspects of Mississippian culture as far north as the Red Wing locality in northwest Wisconsin and southeast Minnesota, some 800 km from Cahokia (Emerson 1991a; Emerson and Lewis, eds. 1991; Emerson and Pauketat 2008; Galloway 1989; Hall 1991; King, ed. 2007; Knight 2006; Stoltman, ed. 1991). However, little is understood about how Cahokians initiated these distant interactions, and how and why local groups participated in them. Settlements in the American Bottom region of southwestern Illinois show evidence of direct political and economic ties with the paramount center of Cahokia. Archaeological research in Cahokia's northern hinterland has further shown that the inhabitants of frontier settlements selectively adopted certain aspects of a Mississippian way of life, while maintaining a number of Woodland traditions (Bardolph 2014; Birmingham and Goldstein 2005; Delaney-Rivera 2000, 2004; Emerson 1991a; Finney 1993; Friberg 2018a; Millhouse 2012; VanDerwarker et al. 2013; Wilson 2011, 2012a; Wilson et al. 2017; Zych 2013). Interactions with Cahokia had diverse outcomes in different regions. In order to understand variation in the nature of interactions in Cahokia's hinterland, this project focuses on both political and economic interaction and the social implications for identity and daily practice.

The Lower Illinois River Valley (LIRV), located on Cahokia's immediate northern periphery, is well suited to the investigation of the Mississippianization process. This study focuses on recent excavations at the late eleventh-century and early twelfth century Audrey site village (11GE20) in order to determine the inhabitants' social, political, and economic relationships with Cahokians and how the LIRV's regional culture contact dynamic differed from that of other hinterland regions farther north. These issues will be addressed through an analysis of craft production and exchange (political and economic interaction) in addition to household and community organization (daily practices) at the Audrey site. This study's significance lies in its consideration of both the particular histories of groups in contact and the character of the broader Mississippian phenomenon through a rigorous comparative analysis of unique regional patterns.

Cahokia's Influence

Cahokia has been referred to as the nexus of the "Mississippianization of the masses" (Pauketat 1997a: 11). A network of three of the four largest pre-Columbian sites north of Mexico (Cahokia, East St. Louis, and St. Louis) comprised the central political-administrative complex of Greater Cahokia (Pauketat 1994, 2004: 71). At its zenith (AD 1050–1200, the Lohmann and Stirling phases), Cahokia's central precinct would have been home to an estimated 15,000 individuals and covered over 9 km2 of the Mississippi River floodplain (Pauketat 2003; Pauketat and Lopinot 1997: 115). People from neighboring regions and beyond would have heard tales of, and perhaps even participated in, massive gatherings where spectacular public ceremonies were performed, including feasts, elaborate mortuary rituals, and the building of massive earthen monuments, the largest of which, Monks Mound at Cahokia, stood approximately 30 m tall (Fowler 1991, 1997; Fowler et al. 1999; Iseminger 2010: 41; Pauketat 2010; Pauketat et al. 2002).

With these events unfolding at Cahokia, one might see the lure the polity would have had for some groups in outlying regions; nevertheless, we must strive to explain how and why the Cahokian lifestyle was adopted or emulated on such an impressive scale, especially by the inhabitants of distant regions (Figure 1.1). Beginning with Cahokia's coalescence, the surrounding portions of the American Bottom comprised numerous Mississippian villages, mound and village complexes, and farmsteads where Cahokian lifeways were enacted on a daily basis. Outside of the American Bottom, a number of groups were presumably Mississippianized through interactions with Cahokians. Such groups include those inhabitants of the Richland Complex in Cahokia's eastern uplands, thought to have consisted primarily of relocated immigrant farmers (Alt 2002a, 2006a; Pauketat 2003). Spanning hundreds of kilometers from the American Bottom, the twelfth-century northern hinterland regions—the Central Illinois River Valley (CIRV), Apple River Valley (ARV), and the Aztalan site in southeastern Wisconsin—are characterized as Mississippianized Woodland populations selectively emulating aspects of a Cahokian way of life (Birmingham and Goldstein 2005; Emerson et al. 2007; Emerson and Lewis, eds. 1991; Finney 1993; Friberg 2018a; Millhouse 2012; Richards 1992; Stoltman, ed. 1991; Wilson 2011, 2012a; Wilson et al. 2017; Zych 2013).

Three hundred kilometers northeast of Cahokia in east-central Illinois, inhabitants of the Collins complex also emulated Cahokian lifeways, particularly religious practices and celestial alignments of architecture, suggesting direct ties to Cahokia (Douglas 1976). Farther still, the Trempealeau site complex in west-central Wisconsin (~750 km north of the American Bottom) has been identified as a rare example of a Lohmann phase (AD 1050–1100) Cahokian colony (Pauketat et al. 2015). Cahokian "emulation" seemingly extended over 800 km to the Red Wing Locality in northwest Wisconsin and southeast Minnesota (Gibbon and Dobbs 1991; Holley 2008; Rodell 1991), although some Woodland groups in the Midwest appear to have avoided engagement with Cahokians (Benn and Green 2000: 482, Henning 1967). Until recently, little was known about the Mississippianization, or lack thereof, of portions of Cahokia's immediate northern periphery, the LIRV, just 100 km from Cahokia's central precinct.

The expansion of the Cahokia polity is thought to have been enabled by the production and exchange of important craft items and raw materials, some of politico-religious significance, and others that provided economic benefits (Kelly 1991a, 1991b; Pauketat 1997a, 1997b, 1998a). Indeed, settlements in the American Bottom and its eastern uplands show direct evidence of political and economic ties with Cahokia and are considered part of the Greater Cahokia cultural area (see Figure 1.1). This political economic dynamic was likely essential to the expansion of Cahokia's power and influence, but some scholars have suggested that there may have been limits to Cahokia's economic control in distant regions (Brown et al. 1990; Muller 1997; Pauketat 1998a). For example, in the CIRV and ARV northern

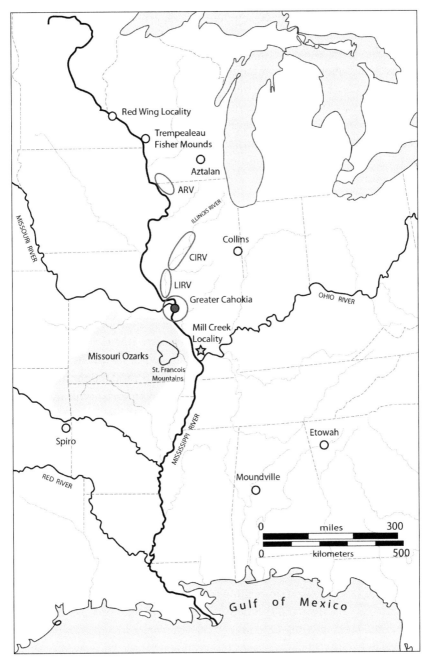

Figure 1.1. Map of study area.

hinterland regions, a scarcity of certain Cahokian craft items such as marine shell beads, basalt celts, and Mill Creek chert hoes provides limited evidence for direct political economic ties with Cahokia. Recent research also shows that these groups maintained certain local Woodland-era traditions such as methods of food preparation, serving, and storage (Bardolph 2014; VanDerwarker et al. 2013; Wilson et al. 2017). As the LIRV sits geographically between Greater Cahokia and these northern regions, it is an ideal locale through which to investigate the spread of Cahokia's influence to the north and to better develop our understanding of variability in the process of Mississippianization.

Research Questions

Theories of the Mississippian phenomenon have shifted over the years from basic culture-historical descriptions to political-economic models of Cahokian expansion and chiefly power (see Chapter 2). More recent research focuses on Mississippianization as a historical process whereby Woodland peoples had the agency to resist or participate in Cahokian practices, and did so with reference to their own identities and traditions. Within this framework, I approach the following research questions: (1) Did the LIRV's proximity to Cahokia enable certain social, political, and economic interactions with American Bottom groups that did not transpire with more distant groups? and (2) How did these interactions impact the social organization and daily practices of groups in the LIRV?

Ultimately, this study attempts to interpret what life was like for Mississippians at Audrey Village by characterizing the nature of the culture contact dynamic in the LIRV and how it differed from the Mississippianization of the northern hinterland. The proximity of the LIRV to the American Bottom may have facilitated more frequent interactions with Cahokian groups than was possible for northern hinterland groups. These interactions would have resulted in major organizational changes for Audrey villagers, whether it be through community organization, the production and consumption of pottery, or the organization of lithic tool industries.

In order to understand the nature of the relationship between LIRV and Greater Cahokian groups and how it differed from relations with northern hinterland Mississippians, it is necessary to investigate the types of interactions occurring among these groups. In the archaeological record, the consequences of these interactions are apparent in the domestic and economic activities that took place at these sites. Activities such as settlement planning and architectural construction would reflect either a Cahokia-influenced hierarchical society, or a less stratified, Woodland-era community organization. An examination of domestic activities—including the storage, processing, and cooking of food (in pit features) and the manner in which food was served (ceramic vessels used)—would illuminate the degree to which Audrey inhabitants adopted Cahokian lifeways or maintained local traditions. An evaluation of evidence for production and/or exchange of Cahokian crafts at Audrey would establish whether the site's inhabitants were tethered to the centralized Cahokian political economy, or instead conducted independent, decentralized economic activities. Finally, research has demonstrated increased interaction between northern hinterland groups from the Terminal Late Woodland (AD 800–1050) to the early Mississippian period (AD 1050–1200). These findings are essential to the current study, as they suggest Mississippian lifeways spread through these interregional networks as well as through interactions with or pilgrimages to Cahokia. If we hope to understand Mississippian culture contact dynamics, or the dynamics of any culture contact scenario, we must investigate our research questions through comparative analyses of datasets from multiple regions.

Organization of Book

Multiple lines of archaeological evidence will be evaluated to address the research questions above. Architectural, feature, ceramic, and lithic data were collected primarily from the 2016 University of California, Santa Barbara (UCSB) excavations of the Audrey-North site (11GE20) in the LIRV. Interregional analyses are presented using data from dissertations, published reports, and articles from the Greater Cahokia area, the CIRV, and the ARV in order to evaluate how the LIRV is positioned within the broader Mississippian landscape.

Chapter 2 orients the reader with a discussion of theory pertaining to culture contact and the history of research at Cahokia. As much of this theory is integrated within the Cahokia literature, I present a brief summary of Mississippian settlement systems in the Greater Cahokia area, the northern hinterland, and the LIRV to provide the regional background and theoretical focus necessary for situating the arguments made in subsequent chapters. Chapter 3 describes previous and recent archaeological investigations at the site.

In order to facilitate a rigorous interregional comparative analysis of various archaeological patterns, the remainder of the book is organized by analytical unit rather than topic. Chapter 4 addresses questions related to the impacts of Mississippianization on community organization at the Audrey site. The chapter begins with a detailed architectural analysis, and a functional and spatial analysis of pit features from the 2016 UCSB excavations. I then conduct a comparative analysis of patterns from Audrey, Greater Cahokia, and northern hinterland sites to assess whether Audrey villagers maintained a communally oriented, Woodland-era social organization or subscribed to a more hierarchically organized, Cahokian way of life.

Chapter 5 presents an analysis of ceramic artifacts collected during the 2016 UCSB Audrey site excavations. Jar rims are seriated based on established chronological sequences from Cahokia's Tract 15A (Pauketat 1998b); these patterns are considered in conjunction with AMS (accelerator mass spectrometry) dates from four features to date the site to Cahokia's early Stirling phase (AD 1100–1150). I then conduct a comparative analysis of ceramic temper, surface finish, orifice diameter, and vessel class from the Audrey site, Greater Cahokia, and the CIRV and ARV northern hinterland regions to determine the degree to which Audrey inhabitants adopted Cahokian potting practices and/or retained traditional Woodland-era potting techniques and foodways. Finally, the presence of exotic, non-Cahokian pottery in the LIRV and northern hinterland is considered as potential evidence for interregional exchange and interaction among northern groups.

Finally, Chapter 6 addresses whether the LIRV's proximity to Cahokia may have enabled access to the Cahokia craft exchange networks that were vital to the political economy of Greater Cahokia (see also Chapter 2). This issue requires a detailed analysis of the Audrey site's lithic assemblage, examining not only the production and/or exchange of Mill Creek hoes, basalt celts, or microlithic chert drills for shell-bead manufacture, but also the consumption of local Burlington chert. These patterns are compared to data from the Greater Cahokia and northern hinterland areas to assess the extent of Cahokian economic control, the organization of Mississippian lithic tool industries, and regional variation in the nature of economic activities. Finally, similarly to Chapter 5, an analysis of exotic cherts within lithic assemblages suggests interregional exchange and interaction between LIRV and northern hinterland groups.

Chapter 7 concludes the book by synthesizing the patterns presented in Chapters 4, 5, and 6 to reconstruct what life was like for the Mississippian inhabitants of Audrey Village. The chapter further discusses the implications of my findings for the limits of Cahokia's political influence and economic control and the nature of culture contact dynamics north of the American Bottom. I discuss how, as expected, the proximity of the LIRV to Cahokia did in fact resulted in more organizational changes at Audrey than we see in the northern hinterland. Audrey inhabitants nevertheless maintained certain Woodland-era conventions and they hybridized others, generating new Mississippian traditions in the process. Additionally, a discussion of exotic materials at Audrey (and CIRV and ARV sites) characterizes the spirit of exchange and interaction between and among these diverse regions that was the ultimate catalyst for the Mississippianization of the north.

Project Significance

The nature of Cahokia's level of political influence has been debated for decades as Cahokia's emergence had an undeniable impact on neighboring regions. Perhaps understandably, the Mississippian phenomenon is often examined from a Cahokia-centric (core) perspective, overlooking the particular histories of local (peripheral) communities and the power of local worldviews. I hope to avoid biased perspectives by illuminating both the nature of Cahokia's influence and the ways in which hinterland peoples negotiated the Mississippianization process. This multiscalar approach—from detailed, household-level analyses to broad interregional comparisons—helps to address the long-standing problem of identifying the inner workings of extensive cultural phenomena. More broadly, this study will facilitate a better understanding of how and why large and complex nonstate polities extend their influence over hinterland areas.

2

Culture Contact and the Cahokia Phenomenon

To say Cahokia had a significant cultural impact on the late eleventh- and early-twelfth-century Midwest is an understatement. From the lower to the upper Mississippi Valley, diverse groups of people came to share architectural and artifactual traditions, intensify agricultural production, and engage in Cahokia-inspired religious practices. As transformations were taking place, the early Mississippian period (AD 1050–1200) experienced a dramatic increase in interaction not only between Cahokia and these distant peoples, but also among hinterland groups, fueling a complex, interconnected Mississippian network (see Emerson 1991a). These interactions involved the renegotiation of identities, resulting in fundamental organizational changes to the social interactions enacted in daily life. Although Cahokia's emergence has been likened to a cultural "Big Bang" (Pauketat 1997a), these changes did not occur overnight in the American Bottom or elsewhere. Mississippianization was a complex process with diverse outcomes across a vast landscape.

Theories of culture contact have been useful in unpacking the Mississippian phenomenon. As this body of theory was being developed, Cahokia research moved in tandem. In this chapter I first present a brief review of culture contact literature relevant to Cahokia. I then discuss the history of research on the Cahokia phenomenon from the early days of defining Cahokian culture history to political-economic models of the Mississippian phenomenon. In addition, I offer a brief outline of the early Mississippian-period Cahokia settlement system and the Mississippian manifestations in the northern hinterland. Finally, I address current understandings of (1) how the Lower Illinois River Valley fits within the Mississippian phenomenon and, (2) contemporary theories of Mississippianization through which to interpret the data presented in the following chapters.

Culture Contact and the Historical Process

Social theory generated in the culture contact literature has sought to characterize the changes that take place when cultural groups interact, whether through colonization, empirical expansion, migration, or social circumscription. Early studies of culture contact, such as world systems and core-periphery theories, have exaggerated the concept of acculturation and diffusion of cultural practices from a core polity to its peripheral settlements (Champion 1989; Chase-Dunn and Hall 1991; Frank 1993; Friedman and Rowlands 1977; see also Wallerstein [1974] 1991). This emphasis on the core overlooks variation in the particular histories of local communities and the agency of individuals negotiating contact (Alt 2001; Anderson 1994: 74; Cusick 1998; Liebmann and Murphy 2011: 18; McGuire 1983; Pauketat 2007; Pauketat and Alt 2005; Wernke 2011; Yoffee 2005). Historical processualism is a framework based in a theory of practice that emphasizes the particular histories of prehistoric communities and accounts for human agency such that "history is the process of cultural construction through practice" (Pauketat 2001a: 87, 2003, 2007, 2010). Employing an historical-processual approach can facilitate moving beyond categorical and Cahokia-centric analyses toward a focus on how different local groups negotiated contact with Cahokia.

As culture contact deals with cultural practices in flux, aspects of life structured by practice—such as identity and tradition—are also subject to change. The negotiation of culture contact is a complex process whereby local peoples do not passively adopt the practices of a more powerful core polity, but may resist, or choose to participate in the active entanglement of new and local practices with reference to their own identities (Dietler 2010: 49; Lightfoot and Martinez 1995; Pauketat and Alt 2005; Silliman 2005; Stein 2002). Indeed, identities are "ways of distinguishing [that are] operationalized and embedded in the social practices that constitute daily life" (Neuzil 2008: 9). Multiple studies of pre-Columbian culture contact have observed that as local groups negotiate contact with a dominant polity, highly visible cultural practices performed in the public sphere are more quickly adopted than less visible, everyday practices (Alt 2001, 2002a; Clark 2001; Lyons 2003: 49; Neuzil 2008). Deeply ingrained practices, resistant to change through cultural interaction, include domestic foodways, household spatial organization, and storage strategies (Bardolph 2014; Dietler 2010: 231–242; Wilson et al. 2017).

Theories of identity negotiation have been useful in interpreting Cahokia contact scenarios; the selective maintenance of traditional domestic practices through the Mississippianization process has been demonstrated for both the Richland Complex (Alt 2001, 2002a, 2006a) and the northern hinterland Central Illinois River Valley (CIRV) and Apple River Valley (ARV) regions (Bardolph 2014; Wilson et al. 2017; Wilson and VanDerwarker 2015). Highly visible emulations are expressed through religious performances, construction of ceremonial architecture, and the production and exchange of objects that were used in public contexts. Recent research in the southwestern United States has found that the interplay between these acts of signaled identity and habitual practice is integral to large-scale social transformation and the development of shared identity (Peeples 2018). These practices, through which social identities are produced and reinforced, have bearing on the nature and degree of integration between groups in contact settings (Neuzil 2008: 8; Peeples 2018: 9). Therefore, comparing the innovative ways in which people retained local practices while selectively adopting Cahokian lifeways will help us understand the social, political, and economic relationships Cahokia was able to establish with these groups.

In culture contact scenarios that involve regional consolidation and political expansion, such as the case of Cahokia, it is necessary to consider the agents involved in the process. How does one group expand its influence over a vast area? The development of complex nonstate societies is often associated with elite power brokerage through the control of esoteric knowledge and distribution of cosmological symbolism (Brown 2007; Cobb 2003: 78; Emerson 1997a: 40, 1997b; Emerson and Pauketat 2008; Helms 1992; Knight 1989: 206; Pauketat 1994, 1997a; Wilson 2001: 126; Wilson et al. 2006). This process is accomplished through elite-controlled production and exchange of objects of political and religious significance; in Cahokia's northern hinterland, these symbols are often interpreted and made meaningful within local contexts (Friberg 2018a; Wilson et al. 2017). Furthermore, in studies of political expansion, it has been demonstrated that the growth of the political and economic influence of all polities is contingent on travel time and other transportation logistics (Hally 1993; Hally et al. 1990: 130; Hassig 1985; Peebles 1978: 375). Simply put, distance is a factor in the geographic scope of a polity's economic control and political influence, but it is not the only factor, and we must not underestimate the power of local worldviews in these negotiations.

Finally, when investigating culture contact scenarios, it is essential to take a multiscalar approach (Dietler 2010: 9; Lightfoot and Martinez 1995; Silliman 2005; Wilkie and Farnsworth 1999). Examining culture contact on multiple scales allows archaeologists not only to assess the particular histories of groups negotiating contact, but to consider how those historical trajectories varied between groups, the nature of interactions among groups in contact with each other, and how those interactions characterize the broader cultural phenomenon under inquiry.

Cahokia Contact

Throughout the long history of Mississippian scholarship, archaeologists have recognized Cahokia as an expansive phenomenon involving diverse social groups throughout the Midwest. From the monumental architecture of downtown Cahokia and its outlying settlements to its distant outposts and the cultural transformation of the Midwest, Cahokia archaeology has historically examined the movement of people, objects, and ideas across the landscape. In the following sections, I present a brief history of theoretical frameworks used in the study of Cahokia specifically, and the Mississippian phenomenon more broadly.

Defining Mississippian: Cahokia Culture History

Mississippian is simultaneously a time period (roughly AD 1050–1500), a cultural affiliation, and a multiregional phenomenon. In his early twentieth-century study of aboriginal pottery in the eastern United States, Holmes (1903) first identified Mississippian as a complex of stylistically similar shell-tempered pottery from the Middle Mississippi Valley (Wilson and Sullivan 2017: 4). Almost a century later, Pauketat (1994: 40) defined Mississippian as "a term used by archaeologists to identify a late prehistoric temporal period but also to identify an organizational 'adaptation' and configuration of cultural elements in the Southeast." Indeed, Mississippian has several manifestations within the midwestern and southeastern United States (Figure 2.1): Middle Mississippian (Cahokia, and later, Moundville); Caddoan Mississippian (Spiro); Fort Ancient cultures; Plaquemine Mississippian (Natchez and Emerald); and the Southeastern Appalachian Mississippian chiefdoms (Etowah). As diverse as these Mississippian historical moments were, they are linked by a set of organizational attributes and cosmologies that first converged at the city of Cahokia in AD 1050 (Wilson, ed. 2017).

Cahokia's massive mounds have interested travelers, historians, and scientists since the French began to explore the Mississippi Valley in the late seventeenth century. Following the American Revolution and the Treaty of

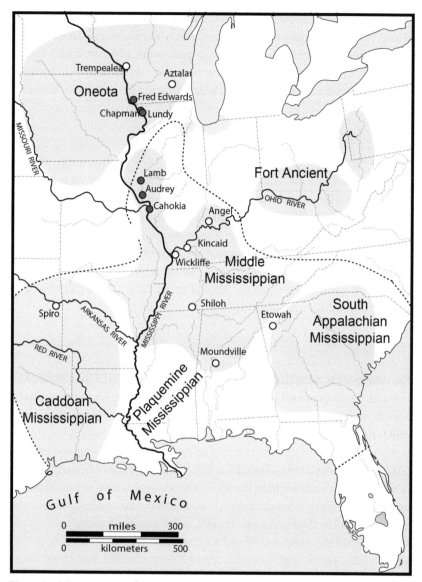

Figure 2.1. Mississippian culture areas.

Paris in 1783, Americans (and others) gained new interest in mound sites, with the goal of legitimizing the Euro-American presence east of the Mississippi; this gave way to the infamous Mound-builder Myth (Kelly 2000: 7). By the early twentieth century, Warren K. Moorehead endeavored to demonstrate that the Cahokia Mounds, east of St. Louis, were constructed by Native American peoples. He published findings from his 1921–1927 excavations at the Cahokia site and surrounding mound settlements in a descriptive account of material culture and mound stratigraphy (Moorehead [1929] 2000). Moorehead conducted the first systematic archaeological excavations at Cahokia, and his efforts highlighted the historical value of the site, leading to its eventual designation as a protected state park (Kelly 2000); Cahokia is now a UNESCO World Heritage Site. Moorehead's work remained the only substantive publication on Cahokia until the 1960s (Kelly 2000).

As interest in the archaeology of Native American sites increased through the first half of the twentieth century, and reports were published through scientific and cultural institutions, researchers began to observe connections between material culture from various sites to establish regional culture histories. Waring and Holder (1945) famously linked objects of religious symbolism from Mississippian-period sites throughout the Southeast to form what they termed the Southeastern Ceremonial Complex (SECC). The presence of these similarly themed cult objects at various sites in the Eastern Woodlands was suggestive of long-distance exchange and shared cosmology between peoples throughout the Midwest and Southeast from AD 1000–1500 (Galloway 1989; Knight et al. 2001; Lankford et al. 2011; Phillips and Brown 1984; Townsend 2004). Knight (1986) was one of the first researchers to explore the symbolic meaning of these religious objects— which he terms "sacra"—and their significance to Mississippian social organization.

Placing many of Moorehead's findings in a culture-historical framework, Griffin (1949) was one of the first archaeologists to develop a typology of Cahokia pottery. In defining the "Old Village Complex," he described and named pottery types based on vessel class, paste, and surface finish; these designations are still used today (Griffin 1949). Through their survey work in the Central Mississippi Valley, Griffin and Spaulding (1950) documented preceramic (Archaic) through Mississippian-period occupations of the region, adding to the growing picture of the geographical extent of the Mississippian pattern. In his research on the Winnebago, Griffin identified the Old Village Complex (or Mississippian Pattern) from St. Louis to the Red Wing area of northwest Wisconsin and southeast Minnesota (Griffin 1960: 822). He further suggests that the Mississippian pattern, which varied notably from the Woodland pattern, originated in the south-central portion of the Mississippi Valley (southern Illinois and Missouri, near the American Bottom).

Continuing the investigation of long-distance exchange and regional interaction, Hall (1967) drew inferences on the extent and nature of the Mississippian phenomenon based on both archaeological data and ethnographic records. He claimed that while Cahokian lifeways may have been influenced by groups from the south, the polity's influence spread northward, like "a gateway on the northern frontier of the Mississippian heartland," and that remnants of this process were apparent in cultural practices of historical Plains Indian groups (Hall 1967: 176). A lasting impact of Hall's (1967: 80) work is his suggestion that it is wrong to assume Cahokia was the center of all cultural diffusion in the Mississippian-period Midwest when it is more likely that "ideas were being received as well as disseminated" throughout the region.

These early studies identified similarities in material culture and began to contemplate Mississippian sociopolitical complexity and the political expansion of Cahokia. However, the research relied mostly on general observations and ethnographic analogy. These interpretations were not tested until archaeologists began to conduct more rigorous analyses, beginning with the documentation primarily of mound architecture and mortuaries at Cahokia and other nearby Mississippian centers in the 1960s and 1970s (Fowler 1978; Gregg 1975; Hall 1975; Porter 1974; Vogel 1975). In the late 1970s and 1980s, the FAI-270 Highway Mitigation Project paved the way for systematic excavations of the Cahokia site and other Mississippian settlements in the path of the construction project. The excavations were instrumental in providing a well-defined baseline of archaeological data (Bareis and Porter 1984; Emerson and Jackson 1984; Esarey and Pauketat 1992; Finney 1985; Fortier 1985; Jackson and Hanenberger 1990; Jackson et al. 1992; Kelly et al. 1990; McElrath et al. 1987; Milner et al. 1984).

Defining Chronologies

One of the basic contributions of the University of Illinois FAI-270 project was the development of an American Bottom chronology from the Late Woodland through the Mississippian periods. Early investigations established cultural phases, which were then calibrated with radiocarbon assays gathered in the FAI-270. The dates were ultimately applied to seriations of Cahokia pottery, tightening date sequences into subphases as short as 17 years (Figure 2.2).

Hall (1975, 1991) was the first to suggest a cultural phase existed in the American Bottom between the Late Woodland, Patrick phase (AD 600–800),

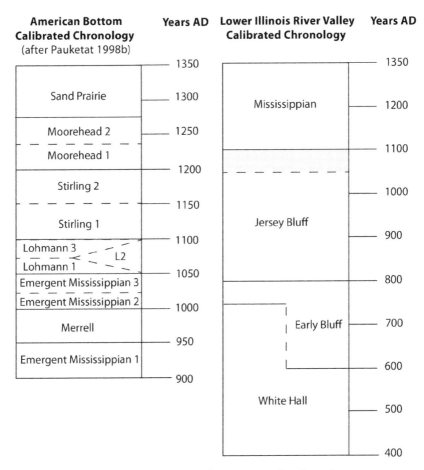

Figure 2.2. American Bottom and Lower Illinois River Valley chronology.

and the early Mississippian–Lohmann phase (AD 1050–1100) during which the Mississippian way of life appeared to be emerging: Emergent Mississippian (AD 900–1050). Kelly and colleagues later corroborated Hall's phase assignment with additional data from Emergent Mississippian American Bottom settlements (Kelly et al. 1984a, 1984b; Kelly et al. 1990). Following the Emergent Mississippian phase in the American Bottom are the Lohmann (AD 1050–1100), Stirling (AD 1100–1200), Moorehead (AD 1200–1275), and Sand Prairie Mississippian phases (AD 1275–1350) (see Pauketat 1998b for a detailed discussion and additional citations on Cahokia chronology).

Holley (1989) documented detailed and quantifiable diachronic stylistic changes in jar rims at Cahokia's ICT-II tract. Pauketat (1998a: 137–253) subsequently operationalized these principles at Cahokia's Tract 15A to seri-ate jar rims into 10 distinct subphases from Emergent Mississippian through the Moorehead phases. Pauketat's distinction between early- and late Stir-ling–phase pottery has been particularly helpful in dating the Mississippian occupation of the Audrey site (see Chapter 4). Cahokia ceramic seriation has since been used as a reliable relative dating technique for American Bot-tom and CIRV pottery (Wilson et al. 2018).

Cahokian Political Economy

With broadly shared material culture traditions observed throughout the Mississippian-period Midwest and Midsouth, Cahokia archaeologists began to consider the mechanisms at play in the spread of Mississippian cultural practices. Political alliances between Cahokia and these distant settlements are thought to have been brokered by elite exchange of specific politico-religious objects such as flint clay figurines, Long-Nosed God earpieces, and Cahokia-style chunkey stones or discoidals (Pauketat 2004: 121). These ob-jects are rare, but have been found in ceremonial and elite contexts at select Mississippian sites from Wisconsin to Oklahoma, which some research-ers suggest is evidence of political ties with Cahokia (Emerson 1989, 1997b; Hall 1991; Kelly 1991b). Flint clay figurines were produced in the Cahokia area from Missouri flint clay (Emerson and Hughes 2000; Emerson et al. 2002) and reference Mississippian cosmological narratives (Alt and Pauke-tat 2007: 243; Emerson 1989; Farnsworth and Emerson 1989). Some of the statuettes depict the mythological hero Red Horn, or "He-Who-Wears-Hu-man-Heads-as-Earrings," who defeated underworld giants in a ball game, possibly the game of chunkey (Hall 1997; Pauketat 2004: 116–118). Further-more, Long-Nosed God earpieces (or maskettes), made of shell or copper, are thought to be a reference to Red Horn's "human heads," as depicted in the Spiro Mounds Resting Warrior figurine (Hall 1991: 31).

The production and exchange of these items is ultimately related to the emergence of sociopolitical complexity in the American Bottom. For this reason, a number of Mississippian archaeologists adopted political eco-nomic perspectives on chiefly power and interregional exchange (Brown et al. 1990; Cobb 2000; Muller 1997; Pauketat 1994, 1997a, 1998a; Trubitt 2000; Welch 1991; Yerkes 1983, 1989). In his foundational book, Muller (1997) dis-cussed the anthropological concept of political economy as it relates to the Mississippian phenomenon. Muller (1997: 2) used Ingram's (1885) definition of political economy as the "theory of social wealth," and the "science of production, distribution, and consumption of wealth." He operationalized this theory as a means to understand Mississippian social organization and complexity such that hierarchy is produced through the religious and ideological control of the economy. However, his investigations left him skeptical, suggesting Mississippian societies relied primarily on a household-level mode of production rather than elite-sponsored craft specialization; he concluded that the relationship between domestic production, community production, and the development of elites needed to be further investigated (Muller 1997: 352).

Other researchers embraced political economic frameworks, particularly the prestige-goods economy model, to explain the origins and operation of hierarchical Mississippian societies. The prestige-goods economy model rests on the principle that the development of chiefly societies (where status is ascribed rather than achieved) began with the achievement of political power by those who controlled the production and exchange of wealth items within a community (Wilson and Sullivan 2017; *sensu* Frankenstein and Rowlands 1978; Friedman and Rowlands 1977). Within the context of Cahokia, researchers made an effort to substantiate the emergence of chiefly power through the identification of centralized production of prestige goods and objects of politico-religious significance (Emerson 1989, 1997a, 1997b; Pauketat 1994, 1997a; Pauketat and Emerson 1991; Yerkes 1983, 1989).

In the process of demonstrating elite control of political and religious symbolism, Cahokia archaeologists began to focus on the study of craft production, both of prestige goods and economically important, utilitarian items. When considered together, the various craft production studies support a broader narrative of the political economy that fueled the development of Greater Cahokia. As Pauketat (1997b: 30) asserts, a Cahokian political economy "encompasses the local and supralocal configurations of human interactions and ideologies as these formed the historical landscape of the American Bottom and beyond." The expansive distribution of politico-religious objects—statuettes, maskettes, chunkey stones, and so on—is associated with the spread of Cahokian influence across a vast area. However, other items, such as Mill Creek hoes, Crescent Hills Burlington chert, marine shell beads, and basalt celts, seem to have a more restricted distribution associated with economic activity within the American Bottom (Pauketat 1998a).

While the inhabitants of the American Bottom region were heavily involved in Cahokian craft industries and exchange networks, the same cannot be said for hinterland groups. Settlements in the American Bottom and its eastern uplands are considered to be within Cahokia's inner sphere of influence (Pauketat 1998a: 50), as they show direct evidence of political and economic ties with the paramount center of Cahokia through the production and/or exchange of certain crafts (Alt 2002a; Emerson and Jackson 1984; Hanenberger 2003; Kelly 1991a, 1991b; Pauketat 1994: 73–80, 1997a, 2003, 2004: 96–97; Pauketat et al. 2012; Wilson et al. 2006). These craft industries—which included Mill Creek hoes, St. Francois basalt celts, and marine shell beads—were probably integral to Cahokia's rise to power (Cobb 2000; Emerson 1989, 1997b; Kelly 2008; Koldehoff and Kearns 1993; Muller 1997; Pauketat 1994, 1997a; Pauketat and Alt 2004; Wilson 2001, Yerkes 1983, 1989). In addition to these crafts, Cahokians organized their lithic tool industry to specifically exploit the Crescent Hills Burlington chert quarries (~50 km from Cahokia's central precinct) such that production was centralized at the source, and finished tools and raw materials were distributed throughout much of the region (Kelly 1984b; Koldehoff 1987: 178, 1995: 58).

American Bottom craft industries were ultimately linked to Cahokia's agricultural economy. Pauketat (1994, 1998a, 2003) has suggested that in order to sponsor public events and sustain the large populations at Cahokia, elites provided access to Cahokian craft networks to outlying settlements in exchange for reciprocal provisions in the form of agricultural surplus. Mill Creek hoes are named for the chert quarries in the Mill Creek locality in far southern Illinois (Koldehoff 1985), where the hoes were manufactured and later exchanged in finished form (Cobb 1989, 1996, 2000). Although the hoes were not produced at Cahokia, Cahokians appear to have been major consumers of the tools. Mill Creek hoes were economically significant to Cahokians as they facilitated the intensification of agriculture (Hammerstedt and Hughes 2015; Koldehoff 1985); for this reason, some have suggested that Cahokia elites perhaps exerted control over the distribution of Mill Creek chert within the American Bottom and eastern uplands (Brown et al. 1990; Pauketat 1998a: 68–69).

Cahokians also produced finely made celts (hafted woodworking tools) almost exclusively using basalt from the St. Francois Mountains in the Missouri Ozarks (Kelly 2008; Koldehoff and Wilson 2010; Pauketat 1997a: 6). An uneven distribution of celt production debitage at Cahokia and other sites has been interpreted as evidence that this industry was under some level of elite control. Caches of these celts have been found at several sites throughout the American Bottom (Butler 2014; Pauketat and Alt 2004). Access to these implements would have greatly facilitated the clearing of agricultural fields and the collection of building materials. Finally, the production of shell beads using microlithic chert drills was restricted primarily to a subset of the residential groups at Cahokia, likely linked to elites (Holley 1995; Mason and Perino 1961; Pauketat 1997a; Trubitt 2000; Yerkes 1983, 1989). Some American Bottom settlements also engaged in bead production, but most did not. The economic significance of marine shell beads is not fully understood, but their political significance in the Cahokian sphere is demonstrated in the famous beaded burial in Cahokia's Mound 72, where a high-status male was buried atop a bed of approximately 20,000 marine shell beads (Fowler 1991, 1997; Fowler et al. 1999).

To summarize, Cahokian political economy operated on multiple scales related to regional consolidation, political expansion, and the far-reaching Mississippian phenomenon. The same politico-religious objects that helped legitimize chiefly power at Cahokia were also integral to the spread of Cahokian ideology and lifeways across the Midwest through long-distance exchange networks. Concurrently, the expansion of Cahokia's political control—underwritten by the intensification of maize agriculture—was fueled by a complex network of craft production and exchange that may have been restricted to settlements within the American Bottom and eastern uplands.

The LIRV is located in the immediate periphery of Greater Cahokia (100 km north of Cahokia's central precinct), separating the northern hinterland from the American Bottom proper. How then does the LIRV fit within the broader Mississippian political economy? The presence of flint clay figurines, marine shell maskettes, and Cahokia-style chunkey stones at various sites in the LIRV suggests political ties with Cahokia groups similar to those observed in the northern hinterland (Cook 1983; Farnsworth and Emerson 1989; Farnsworth et al. 1991). Regarding economic ties, although one Mill Creek hoe, 13 celts, and a cache of 120 marine shell beads have been recovered at the Audrey site, the degree of Audrey inhabitants' involvement in these Cahokian craft exchange networks remains unclear. Chapter 6 investigates these issues and their potential impacts on the broader social organization of Audrey Village.

Cahokia's Regional Settlement System

The movement of people and objects across the landscape of the American Bottom floodplain fueled the urbanization of Cahokia and its development as a regionally consolidated polity (Betzenhauser 2017; Emerson 1997c; Emerson et al. 2008; Pauketat 1998a). The Cahokia site itself was part of the broader phenomenon of social, political, and economic development in the surrounding landscape (Brown 2006: 198). Greater Cahokia can be broken down into three settlement areas (Figure 2.3): Cahokia's central political-administrative complex, the surrounding American Bottom, and the eastern upland Richland Complex settlements. Settlement patterns in the northern hinterland suggest that this same phenomenon of urbanization and complex settlement hierarchy did not unfold outside of Greater Cahokia (Emerson 1997c: 172; Wilson et al. 2017), highlighting organizational differences essential for understanding the nature of the Mississippian process in these disparate regions.

Cahokia's Central Political-Administrative Complex

The central political-administrative complex (Pauketat 1994), located in the northern American Bottom floodplain, is made up of three of the largest pre-Columbian political centers in North America: the Cahokia (11MS2), East St. Louis (11S706), and St. Louis (23SL4) multimound complexes (Kelly 2005; Pauketat 2004: 71, 2005). The Cahokia site covers 1,300 ha and has a minimum of 104 circular, ridge-top, and platform earthen mounds of various sizes (Fowler 1997). The largest of these, Monks Mound, is a thrice-terraced quadrilateral platform mound measuring 30 m tall and 294 × 320 m north to south at its base (Fowler 1997: 87; see also Schilling 2010 for a detailed analysis of Monks Mound's construction). Monks Mound sits on the northern edge of Cahokia's 20 ha grand plaza, which is surrounded by smaller mounds, mortuaries, nucleated household groups, and additional plazas and mounds (Pauketat 2004: 78–84 Wilson et al. 2006). A variety of public events were held around Cahokia's grand plaza, including large-scale feasting and depositional events (Pauketat et al. 2002; Wilson 1996) and elaborate mortuary ceremonies at Mound 72 (Alt 2008; Fowler 1991, 1997). At its height, during the early Mississippian period (AD 1050–1200), Cahokia is estimated to have had a population of between 8,000 and 15,000 people (Pauketat and Lopinot 1997).

The East St. Louis site, 8 km west of downtown Cahokia, was a civic-ceremonial precinct of the Greater Cahokia polity (Pauketat et al. 2013). The site included a minimum of 45 mounds, domestic and special-purpose buildings, and monumental post features extending approximately 1 mile (1.6 km) from southwest to northeast (Kelly 1997). During the late Stirling phase (AD 1150–1200), a compound of small storage huts was burned in one large conflagration, possibly for ritual purposes (Pauketat 2005; Pauketat et al. 2013). This event coincided (perhaps meaningfully) with the restructuring

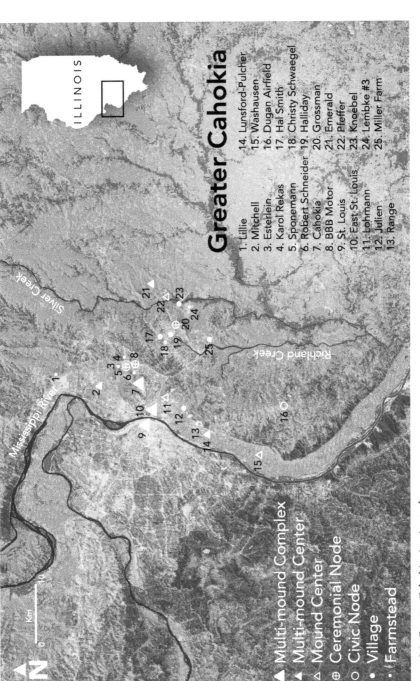

Figure 2.3. Greater Cahokia sites in study.

of social, political, and religious life and decreasing population density across the region from the Stirling into the Moorehead phase (Pauketat et al. 2013: 223).

Finally, the St. Louis site, the smaller of Cahokia's civic-ceremonial precincts, is located approximately 12 km from the Cahokia precinct on the western side of the Mississippi River. The known limits of the site spanned 30 ha and included 26 mounds. However, the site was destroyed by historic construction, leaving archaeologists with only its legacy as an expansive early Mississippian multimound center (Marshall 1992; Williams and Goggin 1956; Wilson et al. 2006).

The Surrounding American Bottom

The civic-ceremonial centers of Cahokia's central political-administrative complex were connected by a continuous series of mound centers, ceremonial nodes, and small habitation and farming sites (see Figure 2.3) (Emerson et al 2008). These settlements are found throughout the American Bottom floodplain—within about 25 km of Cahokia—and can be further divided into the northern and southern American Bottom around two major multimound centers: Mitchell (Porter 1977) in the north and Pulcher (11S40) (Kelly 2002) in the south (Wilson et al. 2006). Mitchell and Pulcher likely acted as subsidiary (rather than paramount) chiefly centers, with direct control over their immediate areas (Anderson 1997: 251). Although Mitchell emerged in the late Stirling phase (AD 1150–1200), the Lohmann- and early Stirling–phase northern American Bottom settlement pattern includes eight single-mound centers; the Lohmann site (11S49) (Esarey and Pauketat 1992) is perhaps the best-known example of these. The close proximity of these sizable nucleated centers illustrates the unique complexity of the American Bottom settlement hierarchy (Wilson et al. 2006).

Cahokian ceremonial nodes function both as habitation sites and centers of religious activity and are marked by temple architecture, special-purpose buildings, council houses, and mortuary features that include religious pottery and iconography (Emerson et al. 2008: 223). Wall screens (isolated walls) and marker posts were also important features of ceremonial nodes, and likely acted to demarcate and/or separate sacred and profane spaces or to provide privacy or restriction of access (Emerson et al. 2008: 225). Ceremonial nodes were also part of the early Mississippian settlement pattern in the CIRV to a lesser extent (see discussion of the CIRV and the Eveland site below). If we hope to characterize the Audrey site beyond the category of a large village, it is important to consider all types of Mississippian settlements. Data from two northern American Bottom ceremonial nodes will be used in comparative analyses in the coming chapters of this book: the BBB Motor (11MS595) site (Emerson and Jackson 1984) and the Sponemann site (11MS517) (Jackson et al. 1992).

The early Mississippian, northern American Bottom floodplain was also dotted with farmsteads and other small outlying sites. These small sites are generally considered single-family settlements and lack the special-purpose buildings and other features that define Cahokia's ceremonial nodes. Fortunately, an archaeological survey in the state of Illinois has yielded useful comparative data from a number of these sites, including: Julien (11S63), a multifamily village (Milner 1984), Robert Schneider (11MS1177) (Fortier 1985), Esterlain (11MS598) (Jackson 1990), Karol Rekas (11MS1255) (Hanenberger 1990), and most recently the Lillie site (11MS662) (McCullough et al. 2017).

The Pulcher Area of the southern American Bottom is a less densely populated settlement system of single-mound centers, ceremonial nodes, and outlying settlements surrounding the Pulcher mound complex (Barrier and Horsley 2014; Kelly 2002). The Lunsford-Pulcher site was an Emergent Mississippian and early Mississippian multimound center 25 km south of Cahokia that likely influenced the nucleation of several smaller village settlements in the area (Kelly 2002). The pottery of the Pulcher tradition is known for its limestone tempering, an attribute of the famous Cahokian Monks Mound Red bowls and seed jars; these vessels likely came into the northern American Bottom from the Pulcher area during the Emergent Mississippian and early Lohmann phases (Kelly 2002: 141).

Data from three Pulcher area sites are used in comparative analyses in later chapters of this book. Washausen (11MO305) is a mound-and-plaza center 15 km south of Pulcher (Barrier and Horsley 2014; Betzenhauser 2011). Range (11S47)—an isolated site with Late Woodland, Emergent Mississippian, and early Mississippian components—is a small nucleated village by most standards, but Emerson and colleagues (2008: 223–225) consider it a ceremonial node due to the presence of a large ritual deposit between the site's two Mississippian-period structures (see also Kelly 2002; Kelly et al. 1990). Finally, Dugan Airfield is a civic node in the southern uplands of the American Bottom (Skousen, ed. 2018; analysis of Dugan's ceramic assemblage suggests the site was populated by both potters of the Pulcher tradition and immigrants from the Cairo Lowlands area of southeast Missouri (Wilson 2018: 134–135).

The Archaeology of Power in Cahokia's Countryside

Research on Cahokia's settlement system has made clear that economic, political, and religious movements in, around, and outside of Cahokia were simultaneous and codependent. Indeed, Cahokia's complex settlement hierarchy was sustained by an intensified agricultural economy (supported by Cahokian craft industries) that sponsored the public and ritual events that were in turn used to elevate and/or maintain the political status of the Cahokian elite. While these broader patterns are vital in understanding the achievement and maintenance of chiefly power, a more agent-based approach would consider the social consequences of hierarchical community organization.

Studies of rural community organization and settlement patterns in Cahokia's countryside considered the impacts of these changes on the everyday lives of Cahokian peoples using community and household-level units of analysis (Emerson 1997a; Mehrer 1995; Pauketat and Emerson, eds. 1997; Wilson 1998). Major patterns of power in community organization were recognized in the variety, type, and size of architecture (Emerson 1997a; Mehrer 1995). Emerson (1997c) suggests the organizational changes that resulted from status differentiation in the Cahokia area coincided with the introduction of special-purpose architecture, such as sweat lodges, large community buildings, and L- and T-shaped temples; he refers to these shifts in community organization as the "architecture of power" (Emerson 1997c: 171). Access to these special-purpose buildings would have been restricted to certain members of the community, perhaps through the use of isolated screen-walls (Emerson et al. 2008: 224). Another significant organizational change was an increase in house size over time thought to be related to the privatization of domestic activities (evidenced by interior storage and processing features) (Mehrer 1995: 146; Pauketat 1994; see also Bardolph 2014; Kelly 1990). Conceptualizing the architecture of power has been useful in understanding community-level changes to social organization in Cahokia's countryside. Subsequent research on the Richland Complex settlements in Cahokia's uplands has highlighted marked differences in community organization with important implications for the negotiation of culture contact on the fringes of the Cahokia polity.

The Richland Complex

The third Cahokian settlement area was established in the eastern uplands above the American Bottom floodplain (see Figure 2.3), where a suite of early Mississippian settlements became known as the Richland Complex (Alt 2001; Pauketat 2003). Research in this area has become important in understanding the social and spatial dimensions of Cahokian cultural influence and political economy, and also the implications for organizational changes and identity negotiation among these nonlocal Cahokia peoples. During the Lohmann phase (AD 1050–1100), the uplands experienced an influx of people from the American Bottom and the Varney culture area of northeastern Arkansas and southeastern Missouri (Alt 2002a, 2006a; Pauketat 2003; Wilson 1998). Site types vary from nodal farmsteads and villages to lesser and major mound centers. Evidence suggests that the inhabitants of the region engaged in Cahokian craft industries; the arrangement likely involved Cahokia's central political-administrative complex provisioning these groups with Mill Creek hoes, basalt for celt manufacture, and marine shell for bead production in exchange for agricultural surplus (Pauketat 1997a, 1998a, 2003). This political-economic system—which some suggest was perhaps even more emphasized in the Richland Complex than at American Bottom floodplain settlements—was the foundation of a centralized political economy of Greater Cahokia (Pauketat 1994; 2003).

While each of these settlements appears to be affiliated with Cahokia socially, politically, and economically, there is nevertheless variation in the ways Cahokian lifeways were incorporated by the rural farmers who occupied them (Alt 2006a, 2018; Pauketat 2003). For example, Woodland-era single-post architecture was retained in the uplands after the widespread adoption of the wall-trench technique in the American Bottom (Alt and Pauketat 2011; Wilson 1998). A hybrid architectural technique (using single-set posts in wall trenches) has been observed at the Halliday, Knoebel, and Hal Smith sites (Alt 2001: 149, 2002: 226; Pauketat and Alt 2005). These unique patterns make the Richland Complex difficult to define as the settlements seem to straddle the line between (1) direct involvement in Cahokia's fundamental economic activities, and (2) the negotiation of contact with Cahokia—two scenarios that distinguish patterns of lifeways between the American Bottom and northern hinterland Mississippian traditions. Because the LIRV geographically straddles Greater Cahokia and the northern hinterland, Richland Complex patterns will be essential for comparative analyses of craft production, architecture, and community organization.

Data from several Richland Complex sites will be used in comparative analyses in the following chapters. The largest, and perhaps most complex, of these is the Emerald site (11S2, or Emerald Acropolis), a multimound center that recently has been interpreted as a shrine complex (Pauketat et al. 2017). In addition to its numerous conical mounds and main platform mound, the site includes rectangular buildings with prepared yellow clay floors and a number of water-laden features, including a monumental post pit with a sacrificial burial at its base. With a lack of evidence for long-term domestic occupation, the clay-lined houses are thought to be shrine houses, serving both as temporary shelters for pilgrims and as spaces in which these Cahokian religious practitioners conducted rituals (Alt 2016; Pauketat and Alt 2015, 2017; Pauketat et al. 2017). The Pfeffer site (11S204) is a smaller Lohmann/Stirling-phase mound center about 22 km east of Cahokia with ample evidence of ritual activity (Alt 2006b).

The Grossmann site (11S1131), 17 km southeast of Cahokia, is a large, Lohmann-phase ceremonial node with more than 100 domestic and ceremonial buildings arranged around a central plaza, mimicking the quadrilateral organization of American Bottom mound-and-plaza sites (Emerson et al. 2008: 223). Architecture and material culture from the site—including the site's famous cache of 70 basalt celts (Pauketat and Alt 2004)—were used for religious, administrative, and civic activities (Alt 2018: 123). Halliday (11S24) is a large Lohmann/Stirling-phase (AD 1050–1150) Greater Cahokia village, only 16 km east of downtown Cahokia (Alt 2006b); unlike Grossmann, the settlement was organized into Woodland-era courtyard groups, but includes Cahokia-style ceremonial architecture and a cemetery (Alt 2006b; Wilson 1998). Knoebel (11S71) is a Lohmann-phase village 22 km southeast of Cahokia with domestic and ceremonial Cahokia-style architecture and evidence of basalt celt manufacture (Alt 2006b; Kruchten 2012).

The Richland settlement complex also includes smaller farmsteads and nodal sites. The Hal Smith site (11S885) is a small village 15 km east of Cahokia with an occupation dating to the Lohmann phase (Alt 2006b). Miller Farm is another small Mississippian village (Wilson and Koldehoff 1998). The Lembke #3 site (11S87) is a small early Mississippian farmstead located on Scott Air Force Base (Holley et al. 2001). Finally, the Christy Schwaegel site (11S1588), 11 km southeast of Cahokia, is a Stirling-phase nodal farmstead with a T-shaped religious structure thought to be a medicine lodge (Pauketat et al. 2012).

Richland Complex research has established a series of expectations for the ways in which groups on the fringes of Greater Cahokia may have been organized. Although upland groups appear to have been closely tied to Cahokian religious, political, and economic activities, the maintenance of certain Woodland-era traditions and aspects of community organization suggest inhabitants of Richland Complex sites negotiated the Cahokia phenomenon differently from the majority of the inhabitants of the American Bottom floodplain. This research has also made important theoretical contributions (see below) to the Cahokia literature with a focus on agency, identity, and tradition in the process of Mississippianization (Alt 2001, 2006a; Alt and Pauketat 2011; Pauketat, ed. 2001; Pauketat 2003; Pauketat and Alt 2004, 2005).

Cahokia's Hinterland

While some archaeologists were addressing questions of Cahokia's expansion and sociopolitical complexity, others began to grapple with how and why Cahokia's influence spread to distant regions. Researchers from the lower through the upper Mississippi valleys brought their research together in an effort to explain the panregional Mississippian phenomenon. This large-scale academic pursuit is marked by the publication of two foundational edited volumes: *New Perspectives on Cahokia: Views from the Periphery* (Stoltman, ed. 1991) and *Cahokia and the Hinterlands* (Emerson and Lewis, eds. 1991). Both volumes were focused primarily on providing evidence of long-distance exchange by identifying exotic pottery, lithic raw material, and Cahokian prestige goods at hinterland sites. While these efforts were inherently political-economic in nature, researchers also highlighted variation in the adoption of Cahokian practices (pottery, architecture, religion, and so on) and how closely tied these various regions may or may not have been to Cahokian groups (Conrad 1991; Goldstein 1991; Harn 1991). Several of the papers also posited the importance of interaction between northern groups (independent of Cahokia) (Claflin 1991; Emerson 1991a; Finney and Stoltman 1991: 243; McConaughy 1991: 120). Emerson (1991a: 232) made perhaps the most insightful statement for future research in his concluding chapter of the Hinterlands volume:

> I am struck by the very strong relationship that seems to exist between the Apple River and Central Illinois. In fact, this relationship is much stronger than anything I can envision between either of these areas and Cahokia. Do these northern sites, perhaps, form a cultural unit? I suggest that it would be worth our while to look more closely at these northern Mississippian groups and less at the Cahokia connection.

Looking past the power and influence of Cahokia is a challenge in Mississippian archaeology, but this approach has become essential in studies outside the American Bottom. I focus here on two hinterland regions, the CIRV and the ARV, because in the journey north from Cahokia to northern Illinois and southern Wisconsin, one would have to travel through the LIRV; thus the CIRV and ARV are most likely to have evidence of interaction with LIRV groups. Furthermore, substantial research has been conducted in both regions since the early 1990s, resulting in rich datasets for comparative analysis (Bardolph 2014; Bardolph and Wilson 2015; Emerson et al. 2007; Finney 1993; Millhouse 2012; VanDerwarker and Wilson 2016; VanDerwarker et al. 2013; Wilson and VanDerwarker 2015; Wilson 2011, 2012a; Wilson et al. 2017, Wilson et al. 2018).

Central Illinois River Valley

Adjacent to the LIRV, data from the CIRV set an important baseline of patterns for the ways in which more distant groups negotiated contact with Cahokia. The CIRV is a 210 km section of the Illinois River floodplain and bluff tops extending from Meredosia, Illinois, in the south, north to Hennepin, Illinois (Figure 2.4) (Conrad 1991). Prior to the Mississippian period, the region was occupied by two Late Woodland groups: Bauer Branch in the south and Maples Mills (and later Mossville) in the northern CIRV (Esarey 2000; Green and Nolan 2000); while these groups were contemporaneous, there is little evidence for interaction between them (Green and Nolan 2000: 369). Bauer Branch pottery is characterized as grit-tempered, cord-marked jars with distinct shoulders and squared-off orifices; Maples Mills pottery is similar, but the vessels occasionally feature cord-impressed designs (Wilson et al. 2017: 104). The Mossville phase (AD 1050–1160; Wilson et al. 2018: Table 5) is considered the Terminal Late Woodland (TLW) period in the CIRV.

The first evidence of Mississippian material culture in the region appears around AD 1050 (Cahokia's Lohmann phase) at the Mossville-phase Rench site (11P4) (McConaughy 1993). The domestic site included two structures built using Woodland/Mississippian hybrid architectural techniques. Excavations at Rench yielded both late Late Woodland, grit-tempered, and Mississippian shell-tempered pottery; Lohmann-phase Cahokia pottery has been recovered at other sites in the CIRV as well (Wilson et al. 2017: 104). In the following Eveland phase (AD 1130–1240; Wilson et al. 2018), settlements in the CIRV included mostly small farmsteads clustered around ceremonial

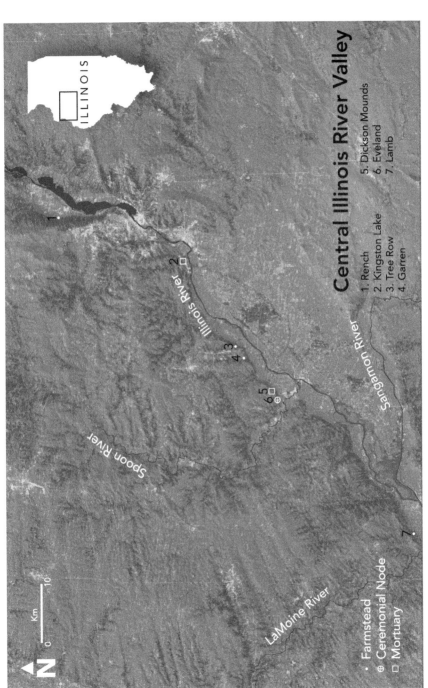

Figure 2.4. Central Illinois River Valley sites in study.

complexes, such as the Eveland site (11F353) (Conrad 1991; Harn 1991). The Eveland ceremonial complex sits below the Dickson Mounds mortuary complex (11F10) and includes four Cahokia-style ceremonial buildings in addition to two domiciles (Conrad 1991). Kingston Lake (11P11) is another mortuary site in the CIRV (Conrad 1993); both Dickson Mounds and Kingston Lake include burials that are closely reminiscent of the headless and handless individuals buried in Mound 72 at Cahokia.

More characteristic of early Mississippian settlements in the CIRV is the Lamb site (11SC24), a small habitation site in the southern portion of the region; while no structures were encountered during excavation, a number of features were identified, including a large communal earth oven—a Woodland-era cooking convention (Bardolph 2014, 2015; Wilson and VanDerwarker 2015). The Lamb site provides evidence in the region of the selective adoption of certain aspects of Mississippian lifeways, and the retention of local, Woodland-era traditions (Wilson and Bardolph 2015). Two additional Mississippian farmsteads, the Tree Row site (11F53; Meinkoth 1993) and the Garren site (11F920), are considered in comparative analyses in later chapters of this book.

Apple River Valley

Data from Mississippian ARV sites are valuable for comparative analysis as they represent manifestations of Mississippian within a distant geographical region populated by Late Woodland cultural groups and emerging Oneota groups; patterns of Mississippian lifeways in the ARV should contrast with the LIRV, which is on the immediate periphery of Greater Cahokia. The ARV comprises the floodplains and bluffs surrounding the winding 90 km Apple River from southern Wisconsin southwest to its confluence with the Mississippi River near Arnold, Illinois (Figure 2.5). The majority of settlements from the Woodland through Mississippian periods are found within a few kilometers of the mouth of the river (Wilson et al. 2017). Descendant from the Woodland-period effigy-mound builders to the north, ARV Mississippians may have had kinship connections with groups in southwest Wisconsin (Millhouse 2012: 63, 99, 140). The Terminal Late Woodland occupants of the ARV produced Grant series pottery, which are grit-tempered, cord-impressed, collared jars with castellated rims (Wilson et al. 2017: 106).

Mississippian material culture first appears in the ARV after AD 1050 as a result of contact with Mississippian groups from the south (Bennett 1945; Emerson 1991b; Griffin 1961). At the time, the region was inhabited

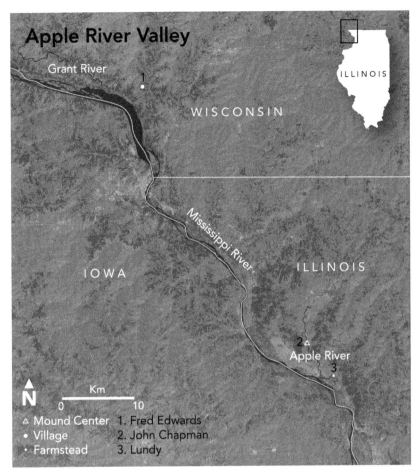

Figure 2.5. Apple River Valley sites in study.

by TLW farmers in bluff-top settlements, some of which were potentially multiethnic (Benn 1997; Finney and Stoltman 1991). The Mississippian occupation of the region was relatively brief and overlapped with culturally Woodland groups: AD 1100–1300 (Emerson 1991b; Emerson et al. 2007). The Mississippian settlement pattern in the ARV consists of two mound centers and surrounding hamlets and farmsteads (Millhouse 2012: 81).

Archaeological research in the ARV has resulted in two sites with datasets that can be used for comparative analysis. The John Chapman site (11JD12) is a Mississippian mound center located adjacent to a large Woodland mound group; excavations of the single-post, semisubterranean houses at John

Chapman village yielded primarily shell-tempered Cahokia-style pottery with some Woodland-style jars resembling Grant series ware (Millhouse 2012; Wilson et al. 2017: 110). The Lundy site (11JD140) is a small farmstead 3.5 km from the confluence of the Apple and Mississippi Rivers; excavations revealed both wall-trench (Mississippian) and single-post (Woodland-era) architecture and shell-tempered Cahokia-style pottery with hybridized Woodland-era attributes (Emerson 1991b; Emerson et al. 2007). Finally, the Fred Edwards site (47GT377) in southwestern Wisconsin (~60 km north of the ARV Mississippian settlements) is a Mississippian village that likely had kin and exchange ties with ARV groups (Finney 1993, 2013; Finney and Stoltman 1991; Millhouse 2012: 63, 99, 140). Fred Edwards differs from other ARV sites in that the village is surrounded by a palisade wall, but it is similar in that excavations also revealed evidence for Woodland/Mississippian hybridity (Finney 2013). All three of the sites in the ARV comparative sample have evidence of interaction with both Late Woodland and Mississippian cultural groups in the surrounding regions. These movements of people and objects in the Upper Mississippi Valley have important implications for the cultural climate of the broader region negotiating Mississippianization.

Mississippian in the Lower Illinois River Valley

The Lower Illinois River Valley—the region of focus for this study—comprises the lower section of the Illinois River floodplain from its confluence with the Mississippi River north to Meredosia, Illinois, including the secondary tributary valleys cut through limestone bluffs (Figure 2.6) (Adler 1983: 9–10). The Late Woodland period in the LIRV is made up of three phases: the White Hall phase (AD 400–750), the early Bluff (AD 600–800), and the Jersey Bluff phases (AD 800–1050) (see Figure 2.2) (Delaney-Rivera 2004; Farnsworth and Emerson 1989; Farnsworth et al. 1991; Studenmund 2000). The early Bluff and Jersey Bluff phases are both considered late Late Woodland to distinguish them from the Late Woodland White Hall phase, as they represent a cultural shift coinciding with the Late Woodland and Emergent Mississippian phases in the American Bottom (Studenmund 2000: 304). White Hall–phase settlements clustered around the mouth of Apple Creek and at bluff bases with close access to streams; White Hall pottery includes primarily sand-tempered jars with notched lips and cordmarking on vessel bodies and rims (Studenmund 2000: 317, citing Struever 1968: 169). Little is known about the early Bluff phase, but settlements are located in the extreme southern portion of the LIRV (Studenmund 2000: 323). Yet Jersey

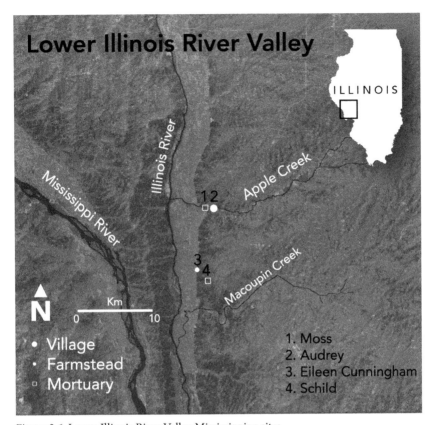

Figure 2.6. Lower Illinois River Valley Mississippian sites.

Bluff settlement patterns were more extensive; base camps and isolated sites spanned the length of the LIRV (Farnsworth et al. 1991; Studenmund 2000: 326). Jersey Bluff pottery includes both grit-tempered bowls and jars with either plain or cordmarked surfaces (Farnsworth et al. 1991). Farnsworth and colleagues (1991; see also Farnsworth and Emerson 1989) argue that Jersey Bluff populations continued to occupy settlements in the LIRV as late as AD 1250. However, these observations were admittedly not well supported, and thus more research is warranted to test the contemporaneity of Jersey Bluff and early Mississippian settlements (Farnsworth and Emerson 1989: 27)

The early Mississippian settlement pattern in the LIRV consists of a number of small Mississippian farmsteads, two small villages, and associated mortuary mounds clustered around creek and river bottom areas (Delaney-Rivera 2000: 149, 2004, 2007; Farnsworth et al. 1991; Goldstein

1980: 22–23; Perino 1971). The most prominent archaeological evidence of Cahokia contact in the LIRV dates to the early twelfth century, corresponding with the early Stirling horizon in the American Bottom. LIRV artifact assemblages are generally characterized by an intermixture of both Jersey Bluff–phase and Mississippian material culture (Clafflin 1991; Farnsworth and Emerson 1989; Farnsworth et al. 1991: 83; Studenmund 2000). Excavations at the Audrey-North site (11GE20) in the late 1970s/early 1980s began to test Woodland-Mississippian interaction and challenge the concept of a limited Mississippian presence in the region (Cook 1981, 1983; Delaney-Rivera 2000; 2004).

The Audrey site is located in Eldred, Illinois, on the Apple River, a tributary of the Illinois River. Excavations uncovered portions of a large Stirling-phase Mississippian village with an earlier, White Hall–phase component, including two Late Woodland (single-post) and six Cahokian-style (wall trench) structures, one circular sweat lodge, 75 pit features, and possible palisade segments (Cook 1983). Delaney-Rivera's (2000, 2004) subsequent analysis of the Audrey site ceramic assemblage identified both White Hall- and Stirling-phase pottery with some hybrid examples, concluding that, on the whole, the Mississippian assemblage was typical of American Bottom assemblages. These archaeological investigations will be discussed in more detail in the following chapter.

Moss cemetery (11GE12) is located on an ancient sand dune 800 m from the emptying point of Apple Creek into the Illinois River floodplain; the cemetery may have served the inhabitants of the Audrey site, which is only 800 m to the southeast (Goldstein 1980: 29–30). The burial deposit was placed in a natural wash depression, and a row structure of burials suggests a kin-based social structure (Goldstein 1980: 32,136). Material culture recovered from the Moss cemetery burials are indicative of Mississippian mortuary ceremonialism. However, in addition to Cahokia-style jars (some of which may be Cahokian imports), some burials included Late Woodland–style, grit-tempered jars and Woodland/Mississippian hybrid jars (Delaney-Rivera 2000: 236–237).

The Schild cemetery (11GE15) is located 13 km south of Moss on the eastern edge of the Illinois River floodplain (Goldstein 1980: 38). The cemetery site has both a Late Woodland and Mississippian component consisting of two deposits on natural knolls, and likely represents populations from more than one community; the cemetery may also be associated with the nearby Whiteside site (Delaney-Rivera 2004: 49; Perino 1971). The mortuary structure of the Schild cemetery represents a higher degree of organizational complexity than the Moss cemetery, including charnel structures and multiple temporal episodes in addition to row structures (Goldstein 1980: 236). Material culture recovered from burials also included Late Woodland–style, Mississippian-style (and Cahokia imports), and hybrid pottery (Delaney-Rivera 2000: 241, 2004, 2007). The Mississippian components of both the Moss and Schild cemeteries correspond with the Stirling phase (AD 1100–1200) (Delaney-Rivera 2007: 307; Goldstein 1980; Perino 1971).

Eileen Cunningham (11GE630) is a multicomponent habitation site located at the mouth of Cole Creek in Greene County (Fishel 2018). The majority (n=43) of features identified at the site date to the early Bluff phase (AD 600–800); four Mississippian pit features were excavated but no structures were uncovered (Fishel 2018: 30). Ceramic analysis of Mississippian feature fill found Stirling-phase jars, including Ramey Incised and Powell Plain types (Fishel 2018: 50–51).

Biodistance analysis and ancient DNA studies of the Illinois Valley found that skeletal populations from this era suggest a continuity in local population genetics with a possibility that smaller groups or individuals from Cahokia migrated north (Droessler 1981; Reynolds et al. 2015; Steadman 2001). However, there is also emerging evidence in the form of several eleventh-century (Lohmann phase) rim sherds that there was a small-scale Cahokian presence in the region that immediately preceded the broader Mississippianization of the region. Apart from the contemporaneity of Woodland and Mississippian-period deposits and the lack of evidence for Cahokian migration into the region, the possibility of early Cahokian interactions and similarities in foodways distinguish the LIRV from northern hinterland regions. Therefore, the LIRV is an ideal region in which to investigate variation in the process of Mississippianization as a result of regular interaction with Cahokian groups.

The LIRV's proximity to Cahokia distinguishes it from the northern hinterland regions, including the CIRV, ARV, and areas of Wisconsin, which are a considerable distance from the American Bottom. However, proximity to Cahokia should also be considered as proximity to a Cahokian node, such as the far-off settlement complexes of Trempealeau (Pauketat et al. 2015) and Collins (Douglas 1976). Proximity to Cahokia may have enabled certain interactions for inhabitants of the LIRV that were less practical at farther distances. Thus, the ease of traveling from Cahokia to the LIRV—whether the travelers were Cahokians, local LIRV inhabitants, or migrant groups settling in the LIRV—raises the possibility that LIRV groups had closer social, economic, and political ties with Cahokians than those in the more distant hinterland. Indeed, on the eastern edge of the Cahokia polity, Richland Complex groups closely emulated Cahokian lifeways while retaining aspects of local identity, yet were directly tied into the Cahokian economy and religious ceremonialism (Alt 2002a; Pauketat 1998a, 2003); this example stands in contrast to the northern hinterland where there is generally less Cahokian emulation and little evidence for involvement in Cahokian craft industries (Wilson 2011).

Currently there is tentative evidence to suggest that LIRV groups had closer socioeconomic ties to Cahokia than did more distant hinterland groups. For example, early Mississippian assemblages from the LIRV include elaborate Cahokia-style fineware vessels; these are absent from hinterland sites in the CIRV and ARV. The assemblages also include more serving-ware in general (like Cahokia) than those from the more distant hinterland regions; this suggests that the LIRV and American Bottom shared broadly similar foodways and serving/ceremonial practices (Delaney-Rivera 2000; Wilson et al. 2017). Nevertheless, these questions need to be investigated further through an examination of architecture, community organization, and Audrey's lithic tool industry, in addition to a re-examination of Audrey's Mississippian ceramic assemblage that uses data from controlled contexts.

Contemporary Theories of Mississippianization

Thus far, I have discussed culture contact theories and the history of thought related to the Cahokia phenomenon, and briefly outlined the current understanding of Mississippian life in the American Bottom, Richland Complex, and northern hinterland regions. This information is vital as a baseline of comparative data and a framework through which to evaluate the Mississippianization of the LIRV and implications for a better understanding of the broader Mississippian world.

Let us return to the research questions presented in Chapter 1: Did the LIRV's proximity to Cahokia enable certain social, political, and economic interactions with American Bottom groups that did not transpire with more distant groups? How did these interactions impact the social organization and daily practices of groups in the LIRV? The first question can be addressed through the framework of Cahokian political economy. An interregional comparative analyses of craft production will help assess the degree to which Audrey's inhabitants engaged in Cahokia's craft exchange networks. But how do we conceptualize the implications of these and other interactions for the broad-scale cultural changes in the LIRV and the more fundamental changes to social organization at the Audrey site? Some contemporary theories of Mississippianization, stemming from research in the Richland Complex and northern hinterland areas—and influenced by the culture contact literature—are useful for situating Audrey and the LIRV into a broader Mississippian context.

Identity and Tradition

Inherent in the historical process of culture contact is the negotiation of identities and traditions. There are multiple forms of identity—individual, gender, social, national, racial, ethnic, and so on—but as this study deals with groups in contact, I choose here to focus on social identities, or ways of distinguishing group membership (*sensu* Neuzil 2008). Social identities are produced and reinforced through daily practices, and the continued enactment of these practices results in the formation of traditions. I define tradition as the enculturated practices and ways of doing that are both structured by and reinforce identity. Traditions, like identity, are not static; they are constantly made and remade (Pauketat 2001b: 255). These concepts are important to consider because in the process of Mississippianization, people selectively adopted aspects of Cahokian lifeways, making sense of a rapidly changing landscape within their existing worldviews, and renegotiating identities, social relationships, and traditions in the process (Bardolph 2014; Friberg 2018a; Pauketat 2001b; Wilson et al. 2017).

Betzenhauser has suggested that in the American Bottom a shared Mississippian identity was constructed through participation in communal events (Betzenhauser 2017). Others have highlighted the maintenance, and in some cases assertion, of local traditions during the Mississippian transition (Alt 2002a; Bardolph 2014; Bardolph and Wilson 2015; Friberg 2018a). Alt (2016) has more recently suggested that in the eastern uplands, the specific local tradition of vernacular architecture was the most effective locus for ideological change, combining the familiar with the novel to transform traditional local architecture into Cahokian religious shrines. This concept could be easily applied to Ramey Incised jars. These domestic cosmograms (Friberg 2018a) were everyday utilitarian vessels, yet they also embodied the cosmos, and interacting with one was tantamount to holding the cosmos in one's hands (Alt and Pauketat 2007: 241; Emerson and Pauketat 2008: 179).

Some Cahokia contact archaeologists have interpreted identity maintenance as hybridity where the adoption of certain aspects of Cahokian lifeways and the maintenance of other local traditions can be observed within a particular practice (architectural techniques) or object (pottery) (Alt 2001, 2006a; Delaney-Rivera 2004; Wilson et al. 2017). These tangible remnants of identity negotiation have also been considered entanglements, accounting for the complementarity of the process, that both groups in contact were negotiating change (Bardolph and Wilson 2015; Dietler 2010; Hodder 2012; Pauketat et al. 2015). But we should be careful not to overlook the differing scales of contact scenarios, the active agents involved, and the power differentials at play (Wilson and Sullivan 2017: 12). With both human and nonhuman agents at the forefront of her argument, Alt (2018) considers hybridity a process enacted at Cahokian settlements where material culture and practices were syncretized to produce both individual and collective identities. Evaluating the concept on a global scale, Deagan (2013: 274) recognizes an overarching pattern: hybridity in various contexts of culture contact eventually transitions to normativeness. Although this observation seems simplistic, the implication is compelling, that new practices incorporated into local ways of life (hybridized) ultimately become tradition.

Where in the archaeological record do we look for the negotiation of identity and the making of tradition? The culture contact literature has broadly demonstrated that highly visible (public) cultural practices are more quickly adopted in the negotiation of contact than less visible, everyday (domestic) practices (Alt 2001, 2002a; Clark 2001; Dietler 2010: 231–242; Lyons 2003: 49; Neuzil 2008). Enculturated practices through which identities are structured—domestic foodways, household spatial organization, and storage strategies, for example—are resistant to change in culture contact scenarios; therefore, analysis of community organization and the consumption of pottery may reveal the maintenance of local traditions. I argue that the presence of hybridity in these practices would then indicate the making of new traditions.

Migration, Diaspora, and Interaction

Issues of identity and tradition become complicated when we consider the role of immigrants and the movement of people throughout the Mississippian world. The question of whether the process of Mississippianization was fueled by migration into and out of Cahokia has been a topic of debate for many years (Alt 2006a, 2008; Fowler 1971; Hall 1991; Harn 1975; Kelly 1982; Pauketat 2003; Vogel 1964). More recently, rather than using a perspective of movement from Cahokia outward, scholars consider movement of people throughout the Mississippi Valley and interaction between and among all Mississippian groups as integral to the phenomenon (Wilson 2012a; Wilson et al. 2017; Wilson et al. 2020).

Political economic theories of Mississippianization made a significant contribution to our understanding of the spread of Cahokian influence through the exchange of objects (and ideas by association). But other archaeologists began to consider the concept of pilgrimage, that the movement of people and interaction between people, things, and other entities was a mechanism through which ideas were exchanged and ideologies adopted. For example, the Emerald site has been described as a Cahokia shrine complex populated by brief occupations of religious practitioners making their way to or from Cahokia (Pauketat et al. 2017; Skousen 2016). These places of pilgrimage brought together diverse groups of people (asserting diverse identities) to engage in religious practices and make new traditions (Alt 2001, 2006a).

Recent bioarchaeological[1] analysis has confirmed that immigrants comprised a large portion of Cahokia's population, and thus certainly played a role in the beginnings of the broader Mississippian phenomenon (Emerson and Hedman 2016; Slater et al. 2014). The Mississippianization of the northern hinterland may have roots in pilgrims returning from Cahokia to their people in distant lands to sow the seeds of change (Wilson et al. 2017: 117). A number of Cahokia researchers are beginning to consider this movement of people as a Cahokian diaspora (Baltus and Baires 2017; Emerson et al. 2017; Skousen 2016; Pauketat et al. 2017; Wilson et al. 2020). An important distinction is made between a simple diasporic model—migration out of Cahokia and into the hinterland—and one that acknowledges the homelands of Cahokian pilgrims; individuals returning to northern regions from Cahokia would have negotiated complex identities incorporating their knowledge and experience from Cahokia, and perhaps a deeper connection to their ancestral homelands (Wilson et al. 2020). The negotiation of these complex identities is ultimately tied to both the maintenance of tradition and the production of new traditions.

Conclusion

Who were the inhabitants of Mississippian-period Audrey Village? What was the nature of their relationship with Greater Cahokia? How did interactions with Cahokians and other Mississippians impact the organization of daily life? How were Audrey villagers situated within the broader Mississippian world? I believe the answers to these questions can be found in the process of tradition making.

Tradition is identity in practice. Through the process of Mississippianization, Audrey inhabitants renegotiated social identities, altering ingrained daily practices and the social interactions determined by community organization. In these negotiations, aspects of traditional lifeways certainly may have been maintained, but major organizational changes that altered daily practice would ultimately result in the production of new traditions. During the eleventh and twelfth centuries, traditions were in transition throughout the Mississippian world, and these processes were simultaneously fueled and complicated by movements of people and interactions between and among Cahokians and northern hinterland Mississippians. Ultimately, the Cahokia phenomenon ushered in a new era of cooperation, of belonging, and of both collective and unique (Mississippian) tradition making. I demonstrate the complexity of this process in the following chapters.

3

Archaeological Investigations at the Audrey-North Site (11GE20)

The Audrey-North site is located in the Lower Illinois River Valley (LIRV), approximately 100 river kilometers north of Cahokia on a sand dune formation along Apple Creek in Eldred, Illinois (Delaney-Rivera 2000). Audrey is one of two known Mississippian village sites in the LIRV, with a predominantly early Stirling horizon occupation (AD 1100–1150), but it is unclear whether there was also a smaller, earlier Lohmann phase occupation (AD 1050–1100). The site was first excavated from 1973 to 1985 (Cook 1983), but the research was not well documented and never officially published.

Center for American Archaeology (CAA) Excavations 1973–1983

Following a deep-plowing episode in the 1960s that revealed concentrations of archaeological materials, landowner Denny Vetter contacted the CAA in Kampsville, Illinois, for a professional archaeological assessment. Alice Berkson was the first archaeologist to investigate the Audrey site in 1973. Berkson conducted a controlled surface collection of the cultivated portion of the site, identifying Archaic, White Hall phase, Late Woodland–Jersey Bluff phase, and Stirling phase Mississippian scatter areas (for more detail, see Delaney-Rivera 2000).

Dr. Thomas Cook, director of research and education programs at the CAA, began excavations in 1975, starting a multiyear extensive excavation project. Cook opened a 1,400 m^2 area, exposing 2 Late Woodland (single-post) and 6 Cahokian-style (wall-trench) structures, 1 circular sweat lodge, 75 pit features, and possible palisade segments (Figure 3.1). One of the structures was significantly (four times) larger than the others and is associated with a screen trench, a single wall separating the building from the rest of the settlement (Delaney-Rivera 2004: 44). Cook (1983) noted features lined with burnt, reddened limestone that are likely Woodland-style earth ovens (see Wilson and VanDerwarker 2015). Excavations also found one Mill Creek chert hoe, fragments of a flint clay figurine, a cache of marine shell beads, and an unknown quantity of celts and discoidals (Delaney-Rivera 2004: 45).

While Cook's CAA excavations have been discussed in more detail elsewhere (Cook 1981, 1983; Delaney-Rivera 2000), I provide a brief overview here. The first areas to be excavated were Blocks 1, 2, and 3, which uncovered Mississippian pit features, the corner of a rectangular wall-trench building in Block 3, and a circular single-post structure with an internal hearth, a likely sweat lodge in Block 2. The excavation of Block 4 uncovered a small rectangular wall-trench building (Structure 4), from which a Holly Fine Engraved vessel was recovered, and what Delaney-Rivera (2000: 156) describes as a single-post feature. The feature appears to be a rectangular structure of some kind, although, without more detailed excavation notes, it is difficult to know whether it is a true single-post structure or whether the nature of the sandy soil at Audrey made it difficult to confidently define wall trenches.

Block 5 excavations recovered both Woodland and Mississippian period features, the most significant of which was a row of postmolds measuring 20–30 cm in diameter which continued into Block 10. The feature is considered by Cook (1983) and Delaney-Rivera (2000: 156) to be a segment of a palisade wall; unfortunately, a later gradiometer survey was unable to find further evidence of this palisade. Block 6 excavations encountered Woodland and Mississippian features and two rectangular wall-trench structures oriented to the same azimuth (Structures 2 and 3), one of which (Structure 3) was burned and included a Mill Creek hoe and a cache of 120 marine shell beads (Cook 1983). Block 7 included several large pit features with pottery and faunal remains, and, perhaps more notably, a clay pipe, spindle whorl, and a bird effigy bowl (Delaney-Rivera 2000: 157).

Trench 1 and Block 8 (connecting Block 5 to Block 6) uncovered a number of features, mostly Woodland period, containing large quantities of burnt limestone; some of these features may be similar to the earth ovens used by Late Woodland and early Mississippian individuals in the CIRV (Wilson and VanDerwarker 2015). Another Mississippian wall-trench building was identified in Block 9 in addition to a Mississippian pit feature and an undefined series of postmolds.

Excavation of Block 11 exposed a large wall-trench structure (Structure 4), four times the size of the other Mississippian buildings at the site. The building, described as double-walled (Delaney-Rivera 2000: 158), measures

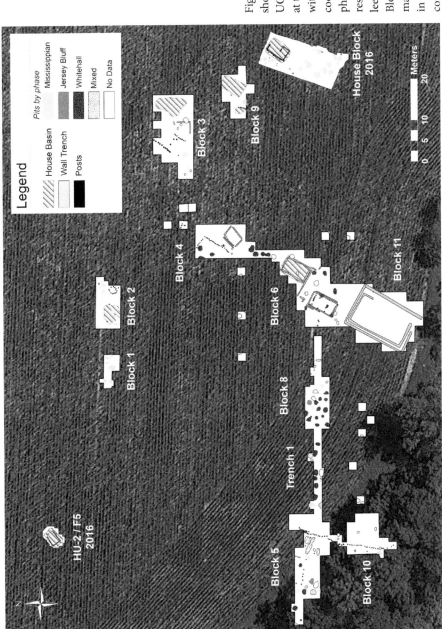

Figure 3.1. Map showing CAA and UCSB excavations at the Audrey site with pit features coded by cultural phase, based on research by Colleen Delaney. Block 7's approximate location is in the southeast corner of the field.

13.5 × 7 m on the interior. It is unclear whether the building was excavated partially or completely. As Delaney-Rivera (2000: 172) notes, field notes and site maps from the CAA excavations at Audrey are incomplete, which unfortunately makes it unclear to which structures Cook is referring when he discusses the eight Mississippian structures and two Late Woodland single-post structures. For these reasons, my analysis of architecture at the Audrey site will only include the five clearly defined wall-trench structures in Blocks 4, 6, 9, and 11.

Delaney-Rivera's Ceramic Analysis 2000

The most significant contribution to the archaeology of the Audrey-North site is Delaney-Rivera's (2000) dissertation research; she concluded that the LIRV was colonized by nonlocal Mississippians around AD 1050, influencing local Jersey Bluff populations to incorporate aspects of a Cahokian way of life (see also Delaney-Rivera 2004, 2007). Delaney-Rivera encountered hybrid pottery at Audrey, in addition to both White Hall–phase (AD 400–600) pottery and mostly late early Stirling phase (AD 1100–1150) pottery; overall, the Mississippian ceramic assemblage was typical of American Bottom assemblages, including Cahokian-style fineware vessels. A small-scale petrographic analysis of these assemblages revealed nonlocal Mississippian, local Mississippian, and locally produced hybrid pottery (see also Stoltmann 1991, 2001). Furthermore, Delaney-Rivera asserts that the presence of Cahokian-style architecture suggests there were close ties with Cahokia, and that American Bottom individuals may have lived at Audrey (2000: 260). The results of her ceramic analysis are discussed in more detail in Chapter 5.

Another important contribution to the archaeological investigations of the Audrey site is Delaney-Rivera's later assessment of cultural phases for the site's numerous pit features. In her analysis of the pottery from various features at the site, she was able to assign cultural components to a number of the features; her notes were critical for the data used to produce a distribution map in ArcGIS. Figure 3.1 shows the distribution of all extant White Hall, Jersey Bluff, and early Stirling–phase Mississippian pit features identified at Audrey. As she previously suggested (Delaney-Rivera 2000), the Mississippian occupation of the site exists primarily to the north and east, whereas the White Hall phase occupation lies primarily to the south and west. Jersey Bluff–phase features are scarce and scattered across the site.

UCSB Gradiometry Survey 2014

In April 2014, UCSB professor Gregory Wilson and I conducted a magnetic survey at the Audrey site using a Bartington Grad 601 magnetic gradiometer (a sensitive instrument used to detect changes in magnetic fields as small as 1 nT [nano Tesla]). The systematic survey covered approximately 2 ha of the site, revealing previous excavation units and magnetic anomalies representing buildings and pit features.

Methods

Data Collection

Before the gradiometer survey could be conducted, it was important to establish a grid of 30 × 30 m survey blocks using a Topc on total station for easy georeferencing in ArcGIS. Twenty-four survey grids were staked over the cleared field area. The survey was conducted by running a Bartington Grad 601 magnetic gradiometer in 50 cm, zig-zag transects within the 30 × 30 m grids, collecting data every 0.125 m for a total of 240 data points per transect and 7,200 data points per grid.

Processing Gradiometry Data

The data were downloaded using Bartington Grad 601 Communication Application Version 3.16. Each 30 × 30 m grid's file was then imported into ArchaeoFusion, a free software tool for creating maps from various types of remote sensing data. Raw data grids were dragged in place to form the map. First the data were clipped so a small range of data remained (-10 to 10 nT), eliminating any magnetic outliers (such as historic metals) that might skew the data. Then a series of processing steps—destripe, despike, zero mean traverse, and so on—were used to interpolate data, smoothing out the map and bringing out subsurface anomalies.

Results

When the resulting gradiometer map is paired with maps of the CAA excavations (Figure 3.2), it becomes clear that the Audrey site is a large nucleated Mississippian settlement with organized rows of rectangular wall-trench structures. A clear example is the line of four rectangular anomalies extending from southwest to northeast, parallel to the line of structures excavated by Cook in the 1970s and 1980s (Area 1 in Figure 3.2); a possible plaza, free of structures, separates these two areas. Given their orientation, shape, and even spacing, these anomalies likely represent a row of Mississippian houses.

Area 2, in the northwest portion of the survey area, contains multiple anomalies of interest. These strong monopolar anomalies (represented in black) are less clear in shape than the houses in Area 1, yet they also appear to be arranged in rows, possibly with linear anomalies connecting them. The long linear anomalies oriented at 90 degree angles are intriguing, especially considering the presence of a possible palisade wall Cook identified in his excavation of Block 10. However, previous excavations of Block 8 and Trench 1 left a strong magnetic signature blurring any connection between the Area 2 anomalies and the palisade.

The gradiometer survey also revealed important insights into the limits of the Audrey site. While there are fewer anomalies to the east, the presence of features at the top edge of the map suggests that the Mississippian settlement extends to the north, beyond the Vetter property. Without further testing, it is impossible to know the full extent of the site, but it is safe to say the Audrey site is larger than the 2 ha surveyed and certainly larger than originally thought. As with any remote sensing survey, Audrey's magnetic anomalies need to be tested, or ground-truthed, before making any definitive conclusions.

UCSB Excavations 2016

In the summer of 2016, based on the results of the gradiometer survey, we targeted two areas for excavation (see Figure 3.2): the first was a large area over the two northernmost anomalies in Area 1, the probable row of houses, to investigate both domestic architecture and domestic activity areas; the second area included two of the small anomalies from Area 2 (in the western portion of the site) over which 2 × 2 m hand excavation units were placed. The larger block excavation, referred to as House Block, was machine-scraped to the base of the plow zone, revealing one rectangular house basin, 19 pit features, and some isolated posts. We were able to excavate eight of the pit features in the House Block area. Excavation of the first of the two hand excavation units (HU-1) had to be abandoned due to repeated flooding, but HU-2 excavation encountered a dense midden. Once excavation was expanded, it became clear the anomaly was in fact a small rectangular wall-trench structure.

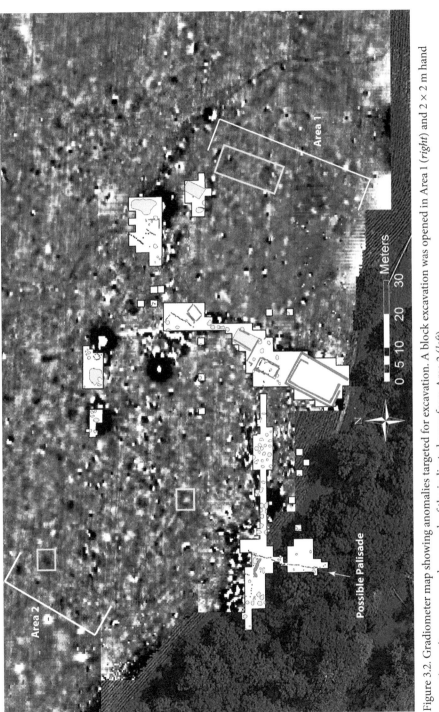

Figure 3.2. Gradiometer map showing anomalies targeted for excavation. A block excavation was opened in Area 1 (*right*) and 2 × 2 m hand excavation units were opened over each of the indicated areas from Area 2 (*left*).

Methods

Excavation procedures followed Illinois State Archaeological Survey (ISAS) guidelines to produce data comparable with published ISAS site reports. All contexts below the plow zone were dry-screened with ¼-inch mesh, and all materials were saved for later sorting and washing in the lab; the only material not screened was the 10 L flotation samples collected during feature excavation. Excavation areas and features were mapped with a Topcon total station, an electronic survey instrument. Detailed unit- and feature-level paperwork were kept, mapping point-provenienced objects in plan; elevations were measured extrapolating from line levels. Plan view photos were taken at each level of excavation, and feature profiles were drawn and photographed. A drought early in the field season made it necessary to "water" the site before covering up with Visqueen at the end of each day; this method saturated the soil, making subsurface features easier to see. Upon completion of excavation, exposed profiles were lined with black Visqueen and the excavated portions backfilled by hand. Both excavation areas were machine-backfilled by the landowner.

Backhoe Scraping and Feature Identification

The northern portion of Area 1 was mapped out using the total station to locate coordinates on the site's established grid (Figure 3.3). The 8.5 × 20 m House Block area was scraped with a backhoe in 3–5 cm increments to remove the disturbed plow zone. Machine-scraped areas were shovel-skimmed to flatten and begin the process of feature identification.

Drought conditions made the soil chalky and shovel scraping challenging, adding to the difficulty of identifying feature fill in dry sandy soil. Feature identification required dampening the House Block with over 50 gal of water each evening. The moisture helped bring out soil color, although feature identification was still challenging. After shovel skimming the entire House Block, areas with apparent feature fill were carefully troweled to define the edges of each feature; this same method was used to define the edges of Feature 5 in the northwest portion of the site as well. Once a feature was defined, it was numbered, logged, and photographed. Features included one rectangular house basin, 19 pit features, and ~10 isolated posts; the southern anomaly, originally thought to be a house, appeared instead to be a series of pit features. Throughout the process, ceramic and lithic artifacts were collected when encountered, although material was not screened.

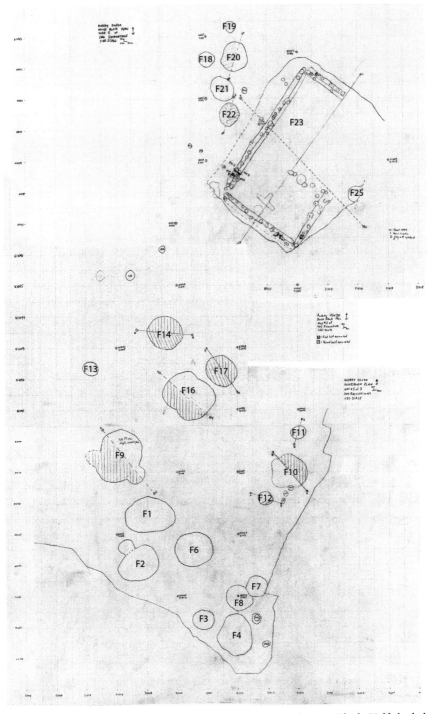

Figure 3.3. Plan maps of features identified in machine-scraped House Block. Half-shaded features were bisected. Both halves were excavated on fully shaded features.

Hand Excavation Units

Two 2 × 2 m hand excavation units were opened, one over each of the two western anomalies of interest. The locations of the units were mapped using GIS, recording the arbitrary grid coordinates, and finding the points with the total station in the field. These units were oriented north-south, and shovel-skimmed to remove the plow zone (approximately 25 cm of deposit). When excavation of HU-2 began to encounter dark fill and a large number of lithic flakes, the area was expanded with additional units (see Figure 3.1). After HU-1 was flooded multiple times, efforts were concentrated on other units and features instead. Plow zone contexts were not screened and no flotation samples were taken.

Feature Excavation

Prior to excavation, all features were tested with a soil probe to estimate depth of feature fill. This method was useful in (1) determining which features to prioritize, and (2) for those that couldn't be excavated, providing an impression of feature function (that is, storage pit, basin, or hearth) and whether the deposit was ephemeral or represented a true feature.

Ten circular/ovoid features were bisected along the widest diameter. Bisection nails (A and B nails) were mapped in plan and shot in with the total station (see Figure 3.3). The first half of each feature was excavated in arbitrary 10 cm levels and all material screened through ¼-inch mesh, recovering all screened artifacts. For features that were not excavated completely, 10 L flotation samples were collected from each level of the excavated half. Photos were taken at the bottom of each completed level. When sterile soil was reached, the features' profiles were cleaned and photographed, stratigraphy was scribed using a nail or trowel, and the profiles were drawn using a level line. For the three pit features that were excavated in entirety, the second halves were excavated in natural levels, zones identified in profile. A 10 L flotation sample was collected from each zone.

Feature 5 and Feature 23, both house basins, were excavated in the same manner, although more flotation samples were collected throughout excavation of the houses. Also, in the interest of time, after the first half of Feature 23 was excavated, only the northwest quarter was excavated in natural levels, leaving the northeast quarter intact. Following house basin excavation, the floors of the houses were trowel-scraped clean for photographs, mapping, and drawing of wall trenches, posts, and internal features. Select posts were bisected and drawn in profile.

Flotation

The flotation samples collected in feature excavations were processed in the field using the bucket method, dried, and packed for later lab sorting and analysis. Each sample was separated into two buckets and mixed with water and a mild detergent to aid in deflocculation. Once all soil clods were dissolved, the mixture was manually agitated and the water was slowly skimmed off the top onto chiffon mesh; this process produced the light fraction of each flotation sample. The remaining material was water-screened through chiffon mesh; these remains, including botanicals, fauna, ceramics, and lithic artifacts, comprised the heavy fraction of each flotation sample. Heavy and light fractions were hung to dry completely before packaging, labeling, and shipping.

Features

House Basins

Feature 5: The 2 × 2 m unit opened over our second area of interest uncovered what appeared to be a dense midden deposit. Once the excavation was expanded, it became clear that the circular anomaly represented a dense fill zone in a small rectangular structure basin. The basin was bisected along its shortest axis, and the northeast half was excavated first. The second (southwest) half was excavated according to natural levels identified in the profile. The rich, dark fill of Feature 5 included three fill zones, densely packed with chert flakes, shell-tempered ceramic sherds (similar to Stirling phase pottery at Cahokia), burnt limestone, and faunal remains, including deer, small mammals, fish, birds, and large amounts of turtle shell. The building is a small (2 × 3 m) rectangular semisubterranean wall-trench structure, the floor of which was lined with a thin layer of yellow clay. A smudge pit feature was discovered on the floor of the house (Feature 29), and excavation through the floor of the house revealed an early Late Woodland, Jersey Bluff–phase pit feature (Feature 28). The original Mississippian-period excavation of the house basin intruded into this feature, explaining the limited presence of grit-tempered pottery throughout the basin fill.

Feature 23 is a rectangular Mississippian wall-trench structure (3 × 4.65 m) with two building episodes. The basin fill contained shell-tempered pottery stylistically similar to Stirling phase Cahokia pottery. Also present were lithic tools and debitage, faunal remains, and a high density of burnt limestone. During excavation of the 40 cm deep basin, a distinct linear deposit of artifacts paralleled the south wall. Moreover, wall trenches were visible at higher elevations all the way to the floor, suggesting that the walls were left standing when the basin was filled. The floor of the house also appeared to be lined with a thin layer of yellow clay, distinct from the sandy subsoil, although the deposit was sufficiently thin to disappear with a few trowel scrapes. Although no formal hearths were found, a large cobble of burnt basalt was deposited on the floor of the house. Interestingly, bisected postmolds show that the walls of the house were inward-leaning and the posts extended through the wall trenches. Finally, the profile revealed the presence of another set of wall trenches, from a later construction episode, for a structure superimposed on top of Feature 23. The floor of this later structure was indistinguishable from basin fill during excavation.

Pit Features

With the exception of Features 27, 28, and 29, which were identified on or below the floor of Feature 5, all features were identified at the machine-scraped surface of the House Block. Ten features were excavated and documented; three were partially excavated and were determined not to be features (Features 12 and 24 were tree roots, and 27 was a rodent burrow). Those that could not be excavated were mapped and tested with a soil probe to estimate depth and nature of fill.

Feature 9 is a pit measuring 125 cm in diameter with a maximum depth of 67 cm. The feature was adjacent to Feature 26, so the two were bisected together. The south half was excavated first and the north half was left intact. The pit has straight walls and a flat bottom with five zones of fill consisting of mostly silty sand, at times clayey. Feature fill was representative of typical Mississippian domestic refuse, including ceramic sherds, Burlington chert artifacts, faunal remains, and a large amount of burnt limestone. Two geode crystals and the rim of a duck head effigy bowl were recovered from the feature. Excavators noted red sterile sand just below the base of the feature which could represent in situ burning, or more likely a leach zone from the burned material in the zone above.

Feature 10 is a shallow basin-shaped pit, 110 cm in diameter with a maximum depth of 18 cm. The feature was bisected by excavating the southwest half, leaving the northwest half intact. The basin has a flat bottom and sloping sides with one fill zone of silty sand containing flecks of charcoal and shell-tempered pottery sherds.

Feature 14 is a pit measuring 112 cm in diameter with a maximum depth of 22 cm. The feature was bisected and excavated according to above described methods. The pit has straight walls and a flat bottom with two fill zones of silty sand, at times clayey. Feature fill was representative of typical Mississippian domestic refuse, including lithics, shell-tempered pottery, faunal remains, and burnt limestone.

Feature 16 is a pit measuring 134 cm in diameter with a maximum depth of 41 cm. The feature was bisected, excavating the southern half, leaving the northern half intact. The pit has straight walls and a flat bottom, with six zones of fill consisting of silty sand. Feature fill was representative of typical Mississippian domestic refuse, including dispersed lithics, ceramics, faunal remains, charcoal, and burnt limestone. Notably, a body sherd of a red-slipped, thin-walled beaker was recovered from the pit.

Feature 17 is a pit measuring 107 cm in diameter with a maximum depth of 39 cm. The feature was bisected and excavated according to the above-described methods. The pit has straight walls and a flat bottom with three zones of fill consisting of silty sand. Feature fill was representative of typical Mississippian domestic refuse, including lithics, ceramics, faunal remains, and burnt limestone. At the base of the feature, excavators encountered two freshwater mussel shells and multiple sherds from a large Ramey Incised vessel (vessel 17.1).

Feature 20 is a basin-shaped pit just west of Feature 23 measuring 100 cm in diameter with a maximum depth of 25 cm. The feature was bisected, excavating the western half, leaving the eastern half intact. The pit has a flat bottom and insloping walls with three zones of fill consisting of silty sand. Feature fill contained shell-tempered pottery, scattered chert, and a large amount of limestone. There is no evidence of in situ burning.

Feature 22 is a basin-shaped pit just west of Feature 23 measuring 71 cm in diameter with a maximum depth of 15 cm. The feature was bisected and excavated according to methods described above. The pit has a round bottom and insloping sides with one fill zone consisting of silty sand and Mississippian domestic refuse. Several large pieces of burnt limestone were recovered in excavation.

Feature 26 is a small basin-shaped pit, 75 cm in diameter with a maximum depth of 15 cm. The feature was identified at the machine-scraped House Block surface and bisected with the adjacent Feature 9, leaving the north half intact. The basin has a flat bottom and sloping sides, with one fill zone of silty sand containing scattered charcoal, and little cultural material, including shell-tempered pottery.

Feature 28 is a pit measuring 95 cm in diameter with a maximum depth of 14 cm. The feature was encountered below the clay-lined floor of Feature

5, bisected, and the entire second half was collected as a flotation sample. The pit has a flat bottom and straight walls with one fill zone consisting of silty sand, chert flakes, a large quantity of limestone, and grit-tempered cordmarked ceramics. Notably, no evidence of Mississippian occupation, such as shell-tempered pottery or maize (Dana Bardolph, personal communication 2017), were recovered from the feature. The feature represents a Jersey Bluff storage pit that was superimposed by the Feature 5 structure basin, a Mississippian-period feature.

Feature 29 is a small bell-shaped pit measuring 22 cm in diameter with a maximum depth of 29 cm. The feature was encountered on the floor of Feature 5 and was bisected. The first half was excavated and the second half collected for flotation. The pit has a round bottom and insloping sides that bell out slightly just a few centimeters below the top of the pit. Feature fill included two zones of silty sand with abundant charcoal, and occasional chert and ceramic artifacts. The carbonized material consisted of large pieces of wood charcoal, complete corn cobs, and other plant remains, leading excavators to identify Feature 29 as a smudge pit.

Unexcavated Features: The remaining 14 features could not be excavated due to time constraints and a small field crew. After difficulty defining features in the southern portion of the House Block (an area we originally targeted as a possible house based on a magnetic anomaly), a soil probe survey was able to confirm feature fill in Features 1, 2, and 8. Unfortunately, Features 3 and 4 became flooded from heavy rainfall and could not be investigated. The soil probe survey was inconclusive for Features 6 and 7, which were either ephemeral or nonexistent. Features 11, 13, 15, 18, 19, and 21 were all small and shallow, and thus were not prioritized for excavation. Finally, Feature 25 was identified as either a single pit or two superimposed posts at the top layer of basin fill in the northwest quarter of Feature 23; Feature 25 was left intact along with the entire northwest quarter of Feature 23.

4

Architecture and Community Organization

The Mississippian period in the American Bottom began with the political consolidation of the region, marked by an increase in population and nucleated settlement patterns. In the first 50 years of settlement at Cahokia proper (AD 1050–1100, the Lohmann phase), a massive labor force was mobilized for the construction of mounds, leveling of plazas, and the building of houses and other special-purpose buildings. In the surrounding American Bottom floodplain and eastern uplands, a hierarchy of settlements emerged, including lesser mound centers, large and small administrative villages, hamlets, and farmsteads (Barrier and Horsley 2014; Emerson 1997c; Fowler 1978; Pauketat 1994). Studies of architecture and community organization have been integral in recognizing this pattern and shaping our understanding of the broader Cahokian settlement system. Mound centers and administrative villages show evidence of communal and ritual activities in addition to participation in Cahokian craft industries and large-scale maize agriculture (Barrier and Horsley 2014; Betzenhauser 2011: 412), possibly for provisioning Cahokia's large population (Lopinot 1997). Indeed, agricultural and craft production at American Bottom settlements and, on a smaller scale, rural hamlets and farmsteads was likely integral to the Cahokian economy (J. Kelly 1997; L. Kelly 1997; Pauketat and Lopinot 1997: 120). This complex network of settlements, referred to here as the Greater Cahokia area (Pauketat 1998a), represents a major organizational shift away from identities and social relations structured by communally oriented Woodland-era traditions and toward those negotiated through a more privatized, hierarchically organized way of life.

Contemporaneous Mississippianized groups to the north tended to maintain aspects of traditional Woodland-era community organization.

Northern hinterland regions generally lack the settlement hierarchy and sociopolitical complexity observed at even rural sites in the American Bottom (Emerson 1997c: 172; Wilson et al. 2017). Current evidence suggests settlement patterns in the early Mississippian Central Illinois River Valley (CIRV) consisted of mainly hamlets, farmsteads, and ceremonial nodes (Conrad 1991; Wilson 2011). While the Apple River Valley (ARV) Mississippian settlements include some large villages and mound centers, the region has been described as a frontier, with Mississippian settlements surrounded by local Woodland sites (Finney 1993; Millhouse 2012: 68). Within these settlements, inhabitants continued to store, process, cook, and serve food according to local traditions. Whereas Cahokians kept storage and cooking facilities inside and nearby the home, hinterland groups conducted domestic activities outside the home, in communal locations (Bardolph 2014; Wilson and VanDerwarker 2015). Furthermore, while Cahokians incorporated a certain level of ceremonialism in their foodways, northern groups rarely used the formal servingware common at Greater Cahokia sites, instead favoring plain jars (Wilson et al. 2017).

To what degree did the inhabitants of the Audrey site adopt the complexity of Cahokian lifeways and which, if any, aspects of local Woodland community organization did they maintain? These questions are addressed through a comparative analysis of architecture and community organization at the Audrey site, the Greater Cahokia area, and the northern hinterland (CIRV). Audrey was a large nucleated Mississippian village, occupied for 15 to 36 years, with multiple types of structures of varying sizes and functions, all oriented to a similar azimuth. The planning of the village suggests a certain level of social hierarchy among Audrey inhabitants, and a Cahokian manner of asserting and maintaining these status differences. First, Audrey's architects constructed special-purpose buildings, including sweat lodges and large communal structures. They also built screen trenches to divide elite or sacred space from the rest of the village. In addition to these Cahokian architectural features, two small structures—one of which was lined with yellow clay, similar to the Cahokian shrine houses identified at multiple Richland Complex sites (Alt 2016; Alt and Pauketat 2017; Pauketat et al. 2017)—may be part of a larger special-purpose compound. A gradiometer map of the Audrey site suggests additional buildings of this size may be clustered in the northwestern portion of the site. If there are indeed a number of these small rectangular wall-trench buildings with plastered clay floors at Audrey, this would be the first evidence of a special-purpose (possible shrine) compound observed outside of the Greater Cahokia area.

By all indications, Audrey was a sizable nucleated Cahokian village. For example, a functional and spatial analysis of pit features excavated in the House Block suggests domestic activities occurred near the house rather than in communal areas, in contrast to Late Woodland settlements and some early Mississippian sites in the CIRV (Bardolph 2015). Feature analysis also found no evidence (at present) of earth oven features, a Woodland-era cooking convention that was maintained by Mississippian groups in the CIRV (Bardolph 2015; Wilson and VanDerwarker 2015). In general, Audrey inhabitants do not seem to have organized their domestic activities in a communal manner, which is indicative of a more Cahokian community organization. A detailed architectural analysis further complicates these patterns. Bisections of several posts in the wall trenches of the two houses excavated in 2016 show that while Feature 5 was built using a Cahokia-style wall-trench technique, Feature 23 was constructed using Woodland-Mississippian hybrid architecture observed in Cahokia's eastern uplands (Alt and Pauketat 2011; Pauketat and Alt 2005).

Overall, the evidence presented in this chapter characterizes the Audrey site as a planned Mississippian village with a noted level of social hierarchy, where inhabitants also retained certain communally oriented Woodland ways of life. These patterns will be outlined in detail in the coming pages. The chapter begins with an overview of Cahokian architecture and community organization. I then present a detailed analysis of architecture, followed by a functional and spatial analysis of pit features from the Audrey site. Finally, I compare Audrey site data with patterns from Cahokia, the eastern uplands of the American Bottom, and northern hinterland sites.

Greater Cahokia Architecture and Community Organization

In order to understand the relationship between architecture, spatial organization, and domestic activities at the Audrey site, these patterns must be interpreted within the context of hierarchical community organization in the Greater Cahokia area. Thus I begin with a background on architecture and community organization at Cahokia and surrounding settlements to situate Audrey in relation to the complex settlement system immediately to its southern border.

Data are used from various sites in the immediate Cahokia vicinity: including Tract 15A (Pauketat 1998b), the ICT II Tract (Collins 1997), and the Spring Lake Tract at Cahokia (Baires et al. 2017), in addition to the East St. Louis site, a multimound civic ceremonial precinct 8 km west of Cahokia's central precinct (Pauketat 2005; Pauketat et al. 2013). Several early Stirling–phase, Richland Complex settlements in the eastern uplands of the American Bottom are also included in this discussion: the Christy Schwaegel site (11S1588), which is a nodal farmstead (Pauketat et al. 2012); four village settlements including the Halliday, Knoebel, Hal Smith, and Grossmann sites (Alt 2001, 2002a, 2006b); the Pfeffer site, a lesser mound center (Alt 2002a, 2006b); and finally the Emerald Acropolis, a site that is a mound center and has been interpreted as a Cahokian shrine complex (Pauketat et al. 2017).

Settlement Orientation

The Mississippian cosmological model, aligning with oral traditions from multiple Native American groups with related belief systems (Edwards 2010: 16), includes upper (sky) and lower (earth/water) worlds represented in multiple levels around a central axis, or axis mundi (Emerson 1989: 58–59; Lankford 2004: 208, Lankford 2007; Pauketat 2004: 111; Pauketat and Emerson 1991: 929). The four corners of the cosmos, or cardinal directions, were guarded by Upper World thunderer or birdman deities (Brown 2003: 94–95; Brown 2007; Brown and Kelly 2000; Emerson 1989: 78–80; Knight et al. 2001: 134–136; Lankford 2004: 209–210). Depictions of the cosmos often feature four birdmen (or related motifs) oriented around the axis mundi (represented by a central cross, or perhaps the orifice of a ceramic vessel) in a quadripartitioned manner (Emerson 1997b: 222; Lankford 2004; Lankford 2007; Pauketat 2004: 111; Pauketat and Emerson 1991: 929; Reilly 2004: 131). In the Greater Cahokia area, the "centered quadripartite world view" (Emerson 1997b: 222) is even embodied in community organization, as seen in villages oriented to cardinal directions, with mounds and houses (many of which are four-sided) surrounding a plaza with a central pole, or axis (Emerson and Pauketat 2008: 173–175).

Indeed, the distribution of architecture, mounds, and the plaza at Cahokia's central precinct is highly ordered along a shared axis (Betzenhauser 2017: 81; Collins 1997; Fowler 1997; Pauketat 2013), made even clearer by the construction of an elevated causeway connecting Rattlesnake Mound northward across the site to the Grand Plaza at the base of Monks Mound (Baires 2014). Recently, Pauketat and colleagues (2017) have argued that the alignment of planned Cahokian settlements may have deeper cosmological meanings. The Emerald Acropolis has been interpreted as a Cahokian pilgrimage site in the eastern uplands of the American Bottom based in part on scant evidence of long-term occupation. The site's 12 rectangular and circular earthen mounds, and hundreds of wall-trench houses, T-shaped medicine lodges, square temples and council houses, and small shrines (in addition to circular rotundas and sweat lodges) were collectively oriented to an azimuth that aligns with the northern maximum moonrise or southern maximum moonset. Pauketat et al. (2017) argue that these lunar alignments—along with the presence of water-washed features and a natural spring at the site—suggest religious practitioners at Emerald focused on underworld cosmological themes linking the moon and water.

Wall-Trench Architecture

The wall-trench style of architecture, thought to be related to the planned construction of the massive Cahokia central precinct, was rapidly implemented at Cahokia and in much of the American Bottom in the Lohmann phase (AD 1050–1100) and early Stirling phase (AD 1100–1200) (Pauketat and Alt 2005). This method of digging trenches beneath the floor of a semi-subterranean house basin for the setting of posts is a variation on Woodland-era architectural techniques. Rectilinear single-set post buildings were common domestic structures in the Terminal Late Woodland Greater Cahokia region (Emerson and Jackson 1984). These houses were built using flexed-pole walls, the posts of which were bent over the top of the structure and tied together to form an arbor roof. A truss built with more substantial posts on the interior of the house supported the incurving walls and arbor roof, keeping them from collapsing (Alt and Pauketat 2011: 112, Figures 6,9).

The wall-trench form was introduced as a new Mississippian architectural technology for the purpose of inserting prefabricated walls (Pauketat and Alt 2005, 2011; Sullivan 2007 citing Lidberg 1940). This method would have allowed for the mass production of standard-sized house walls that could be easily set in place by one or two people; the walls could likewise be easily replaced individually as needed, rather than rebuilding an entire structure. These freestanding "curtain walls" were likely tied together at the corners and either an arbor or gabled roof placed over them, supported by an interior truss (Alt and Pauketat 2011: 117–119). Contemporary Richland Complex groups in the eastern uplands of the American Bottom continued to build houses and temples using Woodland-style single-post architectural techniques a generation after they had been phased out in the floodplains (Alt 2001: 148; Alt and Pauketat 2011; Wilson 1998). Additionally, Alt (2001: 149) describes examples of what she considers hybrid wall-trench structures at the Halliday and Hal Smith sites in the eastern uplands; the buildings appear to be of wall-trench construction, but they were actually built with individually set posts within ephemeral wall trenches.

Special-Purpose Buildings

The Lohmann and Stirling phases at Greater Cahokia settlements witnessed an increase in the variety of architecture. Emerson (1997c: 176) sees these organizational changes as coinciding with the appearance of status differentiation: in other words, the "architecture of power." As Emerson (1997c: 171) states, the architecture of power is "one of the strongest measures of hierarchical variation and political power."

The diverse types of architectural features found at Greater Cahokia settlements highlight the variety of domestic, ceremonial, and administrative activities that occurred on a daily basis. For example, nonresidential wall-trench structures may have served as temple or charnel structures, while larger buildings were used as communal buildings or council houses. More specifically, circular structures are often inferred to be sweat lodges, T-shaped and cross-shaped structures likely served as temples, and L-shaped and small rectangular structures may have been used for storage (Betzenhauser 2011: 405).

Sweat Lodges

The sweat lodge is an important Mississippian special-purpose building as it bridges the gap between political and ritual practices. Emerson (1997c: 182) suggests that these circular structures were a key marker for rural American Bottom nodal settlements and that they represent a shift in meaning of local leadership to include religious practice, rather than being defined solely by differential access to stored and exotic goods. Sweat lodges are thought to have been used for ritual purification practices and are often associated with elite individuals (Emerson 1997a: 78; Mehta 2007). Historically in the southeastern United States, sweat houses were found among the households of local leaders (Swanton 1946); this notion is corroborated by archaeological evidence of sweat lodges correlated with elite structures at Cahokia (Pauketat 1993).

Religious Buildings

Several other types of buildings were also used for ceremonial purposes in the Greater Cahokia area. These include rectilinear structures such as

T- and L-shaped buildings. T-shaped buildings—rectangular wall-trench buildings with small T-extensions or entrances—likely served as residences for important people or priestly medicine lodges in which the T-extensions were used as alcoves for the storage of sacred objects (Alt 2006b; Collins 1990; Pauketat et al. 2012). One such medicine lodge was excavated at the Christy Schwaegel site in the eastern uplands of the American Bottom; the building, which was ritually burned, featured paired internal hearths and an alcove aligned to the winter solstice sunrise (Pauketat et al. 2012: 19).

The function of L-shaped structures is not well understood, but their scarcity at most sites suggests that they also served a special religious or political function (Collins 1990). Similarly to the T-shaped buildings, the L-extensions may have also served as alcoves for storing ceremonial bundles or other objects. Little is written about the rarely encountered cross-shaped building. These structures are made up of four chambers connected by a central hearth area; this configuration is likely evocative of the axis mundi and four corners (cardinal directions) cosmological themes.

Finally, small rectangular structures were also used as religious buildings at some sites. For example, investigators at the Emerald Acropolis in the eastern uplands uncovered a number of small rectangular single-post and wall-trench structures that showed scant evidence of long-term habitation; however, the houses showed signs of multiple rebuilding episodes, and basin fills were laminated with layers of yellow clay and water washing (Pauketat et al. 2017). Pauketat et al. (2017) interpret these structures as "shrine houses" that were occupied by pilgrims to the Emerald Acropolis, who upon arrival would repair the walls and plaster the floors with yellow clay, leaving the houses open for water to wash in and renew structures before their next visit. Shrine houses, usually identified by their yellow-plastered floors and interior features or offerings, have also been discovered at other Richland Complex and American Bottom sites, normally as isolated occurrences (Alt and Pauketat 2017). Recently, Alt and Pauketat (2017: 2) have asserted that shrines—"regularly used place[s] or object[s] of prayer and offering"—may take many forms such as monuments, features, architecture, or personal religious bundles themselves. Alt (2016: 142–143) further suggests that Cahokian shrine houses in particular drew on vernacular architecture to appeal to memory, tradition, and the familiar in a rapidly changing social and political climate, and that these buildings were integral to the creation of a new Cahokian religion.

Storage

In addition to subterranean storage pits, Mississippians in the Greater Cahokia area also built architecture for storage of food and other items. Excavations at the East St. Louis site uncovered a cluster of 25 small, rectangular semisubterranean wall-trench and single-post buildings oriented to the same azimuth (Pauketat 2005: 152; Pauketat et al. 2013). The buildings ranged in size from 2.2 to 3 m in length and 1.6 to 2.4 m in width, some of which had inward-leaning walls (Pauketat 2005: 164). Too small to be domiciles, these small structures are found at multiple Lohmann and early Stirling–phase villages in the Greater Cahokia area and seem to represent storage huts (Alt 2006b; Collins 1990; Emerson and Jackson 1984: 157; Mehrer 1995: 129). At the Halliday site in the eastern uplands, each courtyard group included at least one small rectangular storage hut (Alt 2002a: 223, 2006b). Importantly, in the late Stirling phase, the huts at East St. Louis were burned in one large conflagration, and evidence suggests this act was done intentionally as a ritual offering (Pauketat et al. 2013); other examples of burnt offerings from Mississippian sites include maize, flint clay figurines, pots, pipes, palettes, and crystals (Alt 2006a; Emerson 1997a; Emerson and Jackson 1984; Jackson et al. 1992).

Structure Size

Domestic buildings tend to increase in size from the Late Woodland through the Mississippian periods, with the earlier, smaller buildings lacking interior pits, and the larger, later buildings (beginning in the Stirling phase and increasing through the Moorehead and Sand Prairie phases) including a variety of interior features for food storage and processing (Mehrer 1995: 127–129); the increase in house size over time may correlate to a trend for increasingly complex societies to privatize their domestic activities (Mehrer 1995: 146; see also Bardolph 2014 and Kelly 1990). Baires and colleagues (2017) tested this well-known trend through a statistical analysis of rectangular structures identified in a magnetic survey of the Spring Lake Tract at Cahokia. Their comparison of estimated length-to-width ratios and floor areas of rectilinear anomalies with existing architectural data from Greater Cahokia settlements showed the Spring Lake structures clustered by size with identified Terminal Late Woodland (TLW), Lohmann, Stirling, and Moorehead–phase houses; ground truthing of a sample of the anomalies confirmed their results and substantiated the claim that temporal affiliation can be estimated based on structure size and shape (Baires et al. 2017).

Structure size can also be indicative of function. Mississippian settlements tend to have a modal size distribution of rectangular wall-trench structures, with large structures distinct from average-sized domiciles, and occasionally small structures (Mehrer 1995). As mentioned above, structures too small for use as domiciles were likely used for storage or as shrines (Alt 2006b; Collins 1990; Mehrer 1995; Pauketat 2005; Pauketat et al. 2017). The average-sized rectangular structures at a residential site represent domestic structures (Baires et al. 2017). A number of these domiciles and other buildings may be arranged in close proximity to form household clusters (Emerson 1997c; Mehrer 1995; Pauketat and Lopinot 1997: 106).

Returning to Emerson's (1997c: 171) "architecture of power" theme, larger buildings often served a public function, or were used as elite houses and had increased storage space (Pauketat and Lopinot 1997); this distinction is more easily verified by the identification of internal features, such as benches, hearths, and storage pits, in addition to the presence or absence of status items such as exotic goods and specialty craft items. Trubitt (2000: 673) tests the relationship between household size and status or wealth by correlating house floor areas to density of status-based artifacts; she finds that larger Stirling-phase houses tend to have a higher density of status items while smaller houses tend to have a lower density, suggesting larger houses were occupied by higher-status individuals.

Spatial Organization and Domestic Activities

Community organization is also reflected in the types of activities occurring at a settlement and whether those activities are open to the community or restricted to a select few. Archaeologically, these patterns are represented in the spatial distribution of buildings and features. Emerson (1997c: 171) asserts that the "architecture of power" not only includes large elite structures, monumental constructions, and special-purpose buildings, but also considers increasing segmentation of space as a function of elevated sociopolitical complexity. Indeed, even before the building of palisade walls within and around settlements at the end of the Stirling phase, Cahokians organized their communities by neighborhoods or activity areas. For example, Pauketat (1998b: 112) identifies the segregation of buildings by size and shape at Cahokia Tract 15A where large rectangular buildings were located in a separate area from small rectangular and L-shaped buildings. Craft production may have also been spatially segmented. For instance, In Yerkes's (1989: 97) work on the production of shell beads in the American Bottom, he notes the presence of production areas (perhaps workshops) for microlithic tools used for drilling beads at the Cahokia site. Similarly, the uneven distribution of basalt celt production debitage at Cahokia and surrounding sites suggests that this activity was also spatially controlled at these settlements (Pauketat 1997a).

In addition to segmenting activity areas, Cahokians also used architecture to restrict access and control movement of community members. While plazas provided designated communal spaces for public events and ritual performances, special-purpose buildings were likely restricted or mediated by power holders within the community, such as priests, administrators, and elites (Emerson 1997c; Knight 1986: 681; Pauketat 1994). Stirling-phase households at Cahokia were made up of multiple buildings, and these household clusters were arranged around large public plazas (Collins 1997: 128; Mehrer 1995). Freestanding screen-walls were constructed presumably to provide privacy or restrict passage to certain residents (Alt 2006b: 120; Pauketat 1998b, 2005). In this same vein, the increase in house size from the TLW to the Mississippian period is also likely associated with segmentation of space and the use of architecture to assert and maintain power structures.

Domestic practices are structured by the types of social interactions individuals have on a daily basis (Bardolph 2014: 84). Woodland groups—with less sociopolitical complexity than observed in Mississippian societies—were more communally oriented, and thus cooked, processed, and stored food in public, shared spaces (Bardolph 2014: 25–27, and VanDerwarker 2015). Mississippianized hinterland groups tended to retain these Woodland-era domestic traditions, conducting such activities in communal outdoor locations (Bardolph 2014: 25–27). Furthermore, hinterland groups in the CIRV often used communal earth oven features, a Woodland-era subsurface cooking technology that had been largely discontinued in the Mississippian American Bottom (Wilson and VanDerwarker 2015: 165). In contrast, Mississippian groups in the Greater Cahokia area, negotiating hierarchical social relations, increasingly privatized their domestic activities, conducting a greater number of food-processing and storage tasks in or near their houses (Bardolph 2014; Kelly 1990: 339). Mehrer (1995: 133) describes this pattern as an "architectural trend ranging from relatively little variation and lack of interior bulk storage in the earlier phases to more variation with abundant interior storage in Stirling phase times."

Audrey Site Architecture

Excavations and a magnetic gradiometry survey have revealed the Audrey site was a large, planned, nucleated Mississippian village site, with organized rows of wall-trench buildings arranged around a plaza. The buildings include one large structure that may have served an administrative function or belonged to an elite individual, one elite domestic structure, and at least one small sweat lodge. Based on previous excavations (Cook 1981) and identified anomalies from the gradiometer survey, the site measures at least 2.5 ha and appears to extend northward beyond County Road 1750 N. In this section, I present the analysis of Audrey site architecture (both general patterns and architectural details) to consider architectural diversity (that is, building types, building sizes, and architectural styles), site orientation, and site occupation. Due to the scarcity of excavation records, certain architectural details are only available for the two structures excavated by UCSB in 2016.

Architectural Analysis

Six complete wall-trench structures and one circular sweat lodge have been identified at the Audrey site (Figure 4.1). Features 5 and 23, both anomalies identified in the gradiometer survey and targeted for excavation, were confirmed to be rectangular wall-trench pole and thatch structures. The sweat lodge and four other wall-trench buildings were documented during Cook's excavations with the CAA (1981, 1983). Unfortunately, few architectural details were provided in the excavation reports. In addition to the single-post circular sweat lodge, Cook's (1983) report discusses eight wall-trench structures and two Late Woodland single-post rectangular structures. From the digitized excavation maps, I identify two areas with rows of single posts, one in Block 4 and one in Block 3; however, it appears the full extent of these structures was not identified. As excavators in 2016 encountered difficulties identifying features in the well-draining silty sand at the site, it is possible the wall trenches for these two buildings went undocumented and that they, too, represented Mississippian houses; the post walls also seem to be in line with the Mississippian village grid which further supports this assessment. Regarding the fifth and sixth Mississippian wall-trench structures Cook identified, these both refer to the building corner identified in Block 3 and the basin illustrated in Block 9, respectively; these two buildings were not fully exposed, and thus lack the necessary data to be fully considered below.

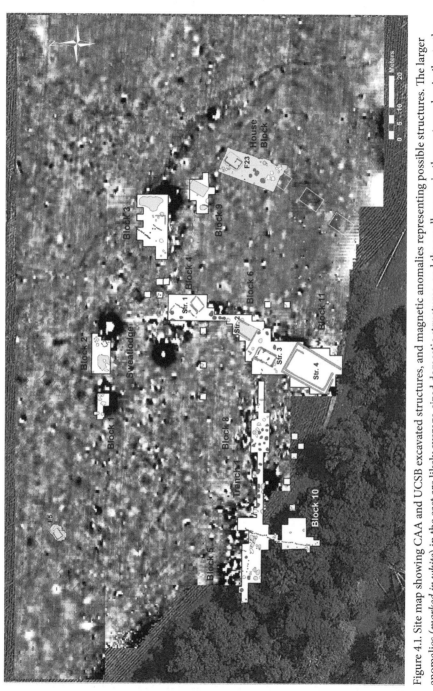

Figure 4.1. Site map showing CAA and UCSB excavated structures, and magnetic anomalies representing possible structures. The larger anomalies (*marked in white*) in the east are likely average-sized domestic structures, and the smaller ones in the west may be similar to the smaller Feature 5- and Structure 1–type buildings.

Table 4.1. Rectangular wall-trench buildings at the Audrey site

Structure #	Project	Length (m)	Width (m)	L to W Ratio	Area (m2)	Azimuth
Feature 23	UCSB	4.65	3	1.55	13.95	33.25°
Feature 5	UCSB	3	2.1	0.7	6.3	53.9°
Structure 1	CAA	4.03	2.43	1.66	9.79	49.42°
Structure 2	CAA	6.04	3.12	1.94	18.84	30.75°
Structure 3	CAA	6.43	3.18	2.02	20.45	29.5°
Structure 4	CAA	13.58	6.85	1.98	93.02	29.95°

Source: Compiled by author.

I have assigned structure numbers to the CAA buildings for the purposes of discussion (see Figure 4.1 and Table 4.1).

Structure Orientation

Mississippian settlements in the American Bottom were planned communities, usually organized around a central axis. The axis often measured close to the cardinal directions, but occasionally the axis was oriented to mark a specific celestial event, such as the summer or winter solstice, or lunar maximum moonrise or moonset, as was the case at the Emerald Acropolis (Pauketat et al. 2017). The Audrey site settlement was aligned to a specific grid system, and all of the recovered rectangular structures are oriented generally in the same direction. Given the cosmological significance of the Emerald axis discovered by Pauketat et al. (2017) discussed above, it seems worthwhile to consider Audrey's own axis.

I calculated the azimuths of the architectural features at Audrey using ArcMap 10.4.1. This was accomplished by drawing lines parallel to the long axes of the houses, right-clicking, and selecting "Direction/Length," which provides an azimuth and length based on your provided grid system; it should be noted that north on the ArcGIS map was measured as 90° and east as 0°, so all resulting azimuths were subtracted from 90 to produce accurate azimuths on a 0° N grid. As the gradiometer grid was set to magnetic north, I then corrected the values for Features 5 and 23 (excavated by UCSB in 2016) to a true north orientation so they could be compared with other sites; it is unknown whether the various CAA excavations were set to a magnetic or true north grid, so these azimuths were not adjusted. I found official declination for Eldred, Illinois, in 2014 (the year the gradiometer survey was conducted) as the earth's magnetism shifts every year. The National Oceanic and Atmospheric Administration's Magnetic Field Calculator (https://www.ngdc.noaa.gov/geomag-web/#declination) uses the WMM 2015 model for calculating declination of true north. In 2014, the declination at a latitude of 39° 14′ 30″ N, and a longitude of 90° 32′ 46″ W, was 1° 4′ W ± 0° 22′, changing by 0° 5′ W per year. For the sake of simplicity, I interpreted this as 1° west of magnetic north, and subtracted a degree from the azimuths for Features 5 and 23 to correct them to true north.

Results range from 29.5° to 53.9° east of north,[1] but these measurements seem to fall into two groups: houses oriented between 29.5° and 33.35°, and those oriented between 48.42° and 53.9°. The former group includes Feature 23 and Structures 2 and 3 (all of which are similar, average-sized early Mississippian houses) and Structure 4, the large rectangular wall-trench structure. The latter group includes Feature 5 and Structure 1, both of which stand out as smaller structures. These bimodal azimuths may represent early (small houses) and later (larger houses) village planning episodes at the site, respectively. More importantly, the azimuths of Feature 5 (48.42°) and Structure 1 (53.9°) are similar yet distinct from the larger structures at the site, suggesting that these buildings may have been planned to align to a different celestial event from that for the rest of the site. In fact, that event may have been the lunar maximum moonrise and moonset, as the azimuth of the Emerald site's mounds is exactly 53°. These azimuths would need to be more accurately measured, and more of these smaller structures excavated to draw any definitive conclusions.

Structure Size and Function

Fortunately, the Mississippian wall-trench buildings excavated by the CAA were mapped in plan, so all six identifiable structures from the Audrey site can be compared in terms of size. The Audrey site's architecture includes three sizes of rectangular wall-trench structures (Table 4.1). The smallest structures are represented by Feature 5 and Structure 1, both of which have floor areas under 10 m²; Baires et al. (2017: 746) suggest buildings of this size are too small to be domiciles. The second size group overlaps the average Stirling-phase house at Audrey and includes Feature 23 and Structures 2 and 3. Although Feature 23 has a smaller length, these three houses all measure 3 m wide and have floor areas of between 13.95 and 20.45 m². Lastly, Feature 4 measures 6.85 × 13.68 m with a floor area of 93.02 m², more than four times larger than the average-sized Stirling-phase house.

These size disparities are likely indicative of structure function. The mid-range-sized buildings likely represent domiciles (Baires et al. 2017). Given its large size, Structure 4 may have functioned as either an administrative or community building, or alternatively as an elite residence. As for the smallest structures, it is unclear whether these are indeed too small to have functioned as domiciles, but there are some important distinctions other than size, between these and the other structures at the Audrey site that will be discussed in greater detail below.

The circular, single-post structure uncovered by CAA excavations in Block 2 is interpreted to be a sweat lodge due to its shape and the presence of a central hearth (Delaney-Rivera 2000: 160). The building measures approximately 4.5 m in diameter and appears to have an entrance ramp oriented generally in the same direction as the rectangular buildings.

Internal Features and Status Items

In addition to structure size, remains encountered on house floors can be useful in determining structure function and/or the status of the occupants. For example, Structure 3 stands out among the average-sized domiciles due to the fact that the structure was burned with the contents of the house intact. The house had interior features, including a hearth and a pit with a cache of 120 marine shell beads; no such caches or evidence of bead production have been found elsewhere at the site, suggesting that these beads were rare and highly valued. In addition, the only intact Mill Creek hoe recovered from the site was found in the corner of this burned structure. Delaney-Rivera (2000: 164) has suggested that Structure 4 was home to an elite family and posits that a possible screen feature (isolated wall-trench wall) was used to separate this house from the rest of the site (see Figure 4.1). Perhaps the proximity of this large and elaborate building to Structure 4 supports the affiliation of the two buildings (see Figure 4.1); these two buildings could make up part of an elite household complex. Unfortunately it is unclear whether Structure 4 was excavated as there is a lack of information regarding the contents of its floor.

Another interesting consideration is the floor contents of the smaller buildings, Feature 5 and Structure 1. Excavators recovered portions of a Holly Fine Engraved bottle that originates from the Caddo region of northeast Texas (Delaney-Rivera 2000: 162, 225) just outside of Structure 1. As will be discussed in Chapter 5, there are few exotic ceramic vessels at the Audrey site, so this finely made foreign bottle was likely an important possession. Nothing quite as elaborate or unusual was recovered from the excavations of Feature 5, but the building did stand out as special. One internal feature, a smudge pit (Feature 29), was identified on the floor of Feature 5; smudge pits were likely used for producing smoke (possibly for smoking fish or meat, or for curing hides), though it is not known in this case what the purpose of smoke production would have been on the interior of Feature 5 (Binford 1967). Additionally, the floor of Feature 5 was plastered in a layer of yellow clay. This is significant because yellow clay floors (and post holes lined with clay) have been identified at Mississippian sites in the Cahokia uplands where they are associated with renewal rituals (Alt 2002a; Pauketat and Alt 2005: 22–223; Pauketat et al. 2017). It is unknown whether the floor of Structure 1 was also plastered with yellow clay in the same manner as Feature 5.

Summary

The large size of the settlement at Audrey, the ordered site layout, and the variety of architecture differentiate Audrey from the nucleated Mississippian farmsteads that Farnsworth and others have suggested were most representative of Mississippian settlement patterns in the LIRV (Farnsworth and Emerson 1989; Farnsworth et al. 1991; Studenmund 2000). Subsequent research at Audrey (for example, Delaney-Rivera 2000, 2004) suggests a more robust Mississippian occupation in the region than was characterized by these early scholars, and the current analysis furthers that assertion. Moreover, the Audrey site may have had a more complex village organization than previously thought. The two small buildings (Structure 1 and Feature 5) may not be the only examples of small structures at the site; indeed, the gradiometer survey tentatively suggests that there may be a complex of small structures in the northwestern portion of the site, representing either a special-storage compound or a cluster of shrine buildings (see Figure 4.1). This pattern needs to be verified with excavation, but it would fundamentally change our understanding of the site.

Architectural Technique

Wall-trench architecture is considered a hallmark of Mississippianization. Yet, as research on architecture of Richland Complex settlements has demonstrated, the Cahokian wall-trench style of architecture was not immediately adopted outside the Greater Cahokia area, and the technique was implemented in varying ways (Alt and Pauketat 2005; Pauketat and Alt 2011). With the exception of the single-post circular sweat lodge, all of the fully exposed architecture at the Audrey site appears to use the Cahokia wall-trench technique. However, controlled and well-documented excavations at the Audrey site have revealed architectural details that show two different construction methods were used at the site. These details are de-rived primarily from the 2016 excavations of the Feature 5 and Feature 23 house basins.

Feature 5

This feature may be small, but its architecture matches the profile of a tradi-tional Cahokian wall-trench building. When excavations reached the house floor, wall trenches were visible on three sides; the fourth side, the northeast-ern wall, is marked by two rows of posts (Figure 4.2). Excavators bisected four posts in the northwest, northeast, and southeast walls to investigate the angle and depth of posts and wall trenches (Figure 4.3). Three of the four posts excavated were rigid, straight posts from 8 to 10 cm in diameter and 23 to 25 cm deep. The northwest post (PH-2) was neatly set into a 15 cm wide wall trench that extended 34 cm below the house floor. Wall trenches were not visible for either post on the northeast wall (PH-3 and PH-4); it may be the case that this wall was built with single-set posts, or the trench may have been difficult to distinguish in the dry silty sand. PH-1, a post outside the

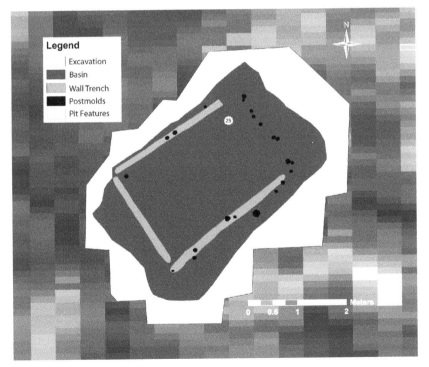

Figure 4.2. Plan map of Feature 5.

Feature 5 Post Profiles

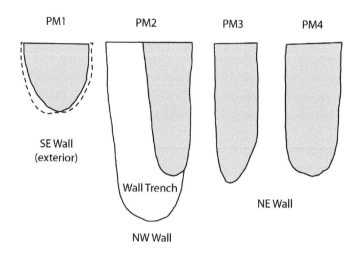

PM1

SE Wall
(exterior)

PM2

Wall Trench

NW Wall

PM3

PM4

NE Wall

Feature 23 Post Profiles

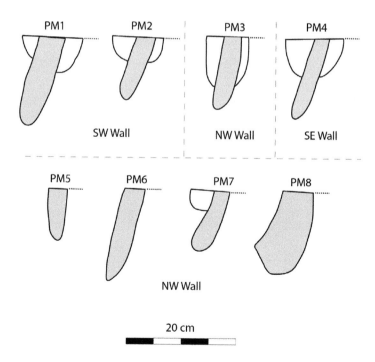

PM1   PM2   PM3   PM4

SW Wall   NW Wall   SE Wall

PM5   PM6   PM7   PM8

NW Wall

20 cm

Figure 4.3. Figure 5 bisected posts (*top*). Feature 23 bisected posts, profiles showing inward-leaning angles (*bottom*).

southeast wall trench, appears to be slightly inward-leaning. This post was the largest of those excavated, at 12 cm in diameter, and only extended 12 cm below the floor of the house. Perhaps this post was used to provide external support to the rigid wall of Feature 5, acting as a buttress of sorts; indeed, Alt and Pauketat (2011: 114) note tilted exterior support posts outside the large rotunda at Cahokia Tract 15B.

The roof of Feature 5 would have been constructed through either a bent-pole technique or a gabled construction, latched onto horizontal beams of the structure's walls. In either case, the roof would not have required the support of internal posts (Alt and Pauketat 2011). The only internal feature is a small smudge pit (Feature 29). Another important choice made in the construction of Feature 5 is that the floor of this building was plastered with yellow clay. Additionally, a lump of this clay was identified on the floor on the southeast side of the building, although the lump was likely created from rodent activity in the Late Woodland period refuse pit immediately below it. The yellow clay floor of Feature 5 is significant as the treatment is usually associated with ceremonial or special-purpose buildings, such as the shrine houses at the Emerald Acropolis (Pauketat et al. 2017). However, it should be noted that Feature 5's clay floor treatment differed from that observed at Richland Complex sites; the layer of clay was rather thin and did not extend into the postmolds as was the practice at Emerald, Halliday, Grossman, and Pfeffer (Alt 2006b; Pauketat et al. 2017). Despite these differences, Feature 5's clay floor nevertheless may have been analogous to the yellow clay floors of Mississippian shrines. With the exception of one possible single-post wall, Feature 5 is a traditional, rigid-wall, Mississippian pole-and-thatch structure that may have served a ceremonial purpose.

Feature 23

The larger of the two houses excavated in 2016, Feature 23, is also a rectangular wall-trench building (Figure 4.4). Even before reaching the floor, wall trenches were visible at higher elevations of the house basin; three distinct sets of wall trenches are also visible in the feature's profile. Once excavation reached the floor, two sets of wall trenches were visible on three of the four walls, each filled with posts. The northwestern wall also had posts just outside of it. Eight of these posts were bisected: PM 1 and PM 2 in the southwest wall, PM 3 in the northeast wall, PM 4 in the southeastern wall, and PMs 5–8 in the northwestern wall (see Figure 4.3). Seven of these posts slanted inward and ranged from 7 to 12 cm in diameter, set 21 to 35 cm below the house floor. The exception was PM 5 which was a straight-set post

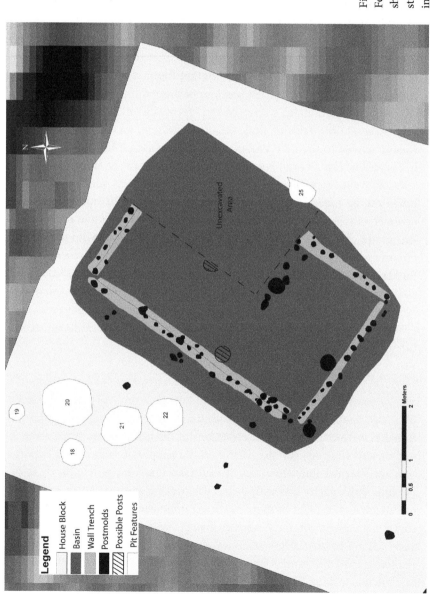

Figure 4.4. Plan map of Feature 23 house floor showing multiple construction episodes and internal support posts.

Legend
- House Block
- Basin
- Wall Trench
- Postmolds
- Possible Posts
- Pit Features

Unexcavated Area

Meters
0   0.5   1   2

N

that only extended 17 cm below the floor. Importantly, where wall trenches were visible in these profiles, we can see the posts extended through the wall trenches on all four walls of the house. This pattern indicates the posts were set into individually dug post holes at the bottom of prepared wall trenches at an inward-leaning angle. The inward-leaning posts further suggest the house was built using bent poles, which would have been joined at the top to form an arbor roof. Single-set posts and arbor roofs are both typical Late Woodland architectural techniques (Pauketat and Alt 2005; Alt and Pauketat 2011).

Larger support posts (~30 cm in diameter) were also set into the floor of Feature 23, although not in the prescribed locations normally identified as representing an interior roof support structure (Alt and Pauketat 2011). Interestingly, Structure 3, the elite house from Block 6, does appear to have the four interior posts associated with interior roof support, although it is unknown whether that building featured inward-leaning or rigid walls due to lack of documentation. No additional interior features were identified on the floor of Feature 23. However, it bears noting that the floor of Feature 23 may have also been lined with yellow clay, although the evidence for this was not as strong as for Feature 5. The yellow floor was encountered during excavation, but photos indicate this effect appears to be more prominent toward the center of the house; given the central location of the yellow floor, and the fact that, when scraped, the deposit appeared to be less than 1 cm thick, this effect may be the result of compaction of the domestic building's living surface.

Summary

Feature 5 and Feature 23 represent two distinct architectural techniques. Feature 23 appears to have been a bent-pole-and-thatch house built with inward-leaning walls using single-set posts within the wall trenches, forming an arbor roof with interior support posts. In contrast, Feature 5 does not have inward-leaning walls or interior roof support posts, but rather straight posts set neatly into the prepared wall trenches. The floor of Feature 5 is also plastered with yellow clay; while Feature 23 did seem to have a yellow floor, the "deposit" was ephemeral and could possibly represent compaction of the living surface. The architectural technique used in the construction of Feature 23 differs significantly both from Feature 5 and from the Cahokia style of prefabricated, rigid walls slipped into prepared wall trenches.

Estimating Site-Occupation Span

Architectural analysis can be used to estimate site-occupation span. Research on the longevity of Mississippian buildings suggests a range of 5 to 12 years between house-rebuilding episodes (Milner 1998; Pauketat 2003; see also Pauketat and Lopinot 1997). Feature 23 exhibits three (possibly more), and Feature 5 exhibits a maximum of two building episodes, both of which would suggest a relatively short-term Mississippian occupation of the site, at 15 to 36 years. However, if Feature 5 and Structure 1 represent an earlier configuration of the Audrey Village (as their size and different azimuth may suggest), then the occupation estimate increases to 35 to 60 years. A larger sample of houses at the site is necessary for a more accurate estimate. In addition, the relative lack of superimposed features also suggests a shorter site occupation. The more conservative estimate of 15 to 36 years fits the narrative of a dynamic and rapidly changing cultural landscape in the northern hinterlands. Furthermore, the ceramic seriation presented in Chapter 5 indicates the site was occupied during the late Stirling phase (1100–1150), with no evidence of either a Lohmann- or late-Stirling–phase component; thus, the ceramic evidence suggests the Mississippian period occupation of the Audrey site did not last longer than 50 years.

Audrey Site Domestic Activities

In addition to architectural evidence, the 2016 excavations at Audrey revealed a notable density of cultural materials identifying the settlement as primarily a residential site. The basin fill of both houses shows a rich array of domestic refuse, including a variety of terrestrial, aquatic, and avian faunal remains, discarded charcoal and burnt limestone from cooking features, a large quantity of pottery sherds, and impressive evidence of all stages of chipped stone tool production. Feature fill, however, is rarely representative of primary deposits, and thus is seldom indicative of feature function. Using data from pit features excavated by UCSB[2] in 2016, we can investigate the types of activities occurring at Audrey and how those activities were organized in terms of communal versus private space.

Feature Function

A morphological analysis of pit feature dimensions is useful for determining feature function. This analysis is based on a culmination of developed technomorphological methods and ethnohistoric and experimental archaeological studies of feature function (Binford et al. 1970; DeBoer 1988; Fortier et al. 1984; Harris 1996; Hastorf 1988; Holt 1996; Jackson and Millhouse 2003: 71–79; Kelly et al. 1987; Stahl 1985). Researchers in the Mississippi and Illinois River valleys have identified three basic types of circular and ovoid subterranean pit features based on profile shape: basin-shaped pits with inslanting walls and round bottoms, inslanting/flat-bottomed pits, and vertical-walled/flat-bottomed pits (Bardolph 2015; Fortier et al. 1984; Holt 1996: 60; Jackson and Millhouse 2003: 71, Figure 5.16). Based on their broad, shallow profiles, basin-shaped pits may have functioned as multipurpose/food-processing features as they lack sufficient volume for storage; such activities likely included shelling maize, washing and leaching of nuts, grinding and milling, and so on (Bardolph 2015: 160; Hastorf 1988: 125).

Vertical-walled/flat-bottomed pits are typically classified as storage facilities based on their profile shapes, depths, and large volumes (DeBoer 1988; Stahl 1985). These deep, rather than broad, pits were ideal for protecting stored foods against animal intrusion and extreme weather (Bardolph 2015: 163; Stahl 1985). The cylindrical pits stand in contrast to the bell-shaped storage pits found in the American Bottom that have restricted orifices and wide bases; bell-shaped pits likely also functioned as storage facilities, but their narrow openings may have functioned to conceal from others the true volume of material being stored beneath the surface (Bardolph 2015: 163; DeBoer 1988).

Inslanting/flat-bottomed pits are often identified as cooking features as their broad orifices and flat bottoms provided ample surface area and an ideal oxygen-rich environment for cooking; they were heated using either open fires (hearths) or preheated rocks (such as in earth ovens). Soil oxidation is often observed beneath and around the bases of cooking features in addition to large amounts of burnt limestone within the feature fill (Binford et al. 1970: 44; Holt 1996: 67; Stahl 1985; Wilson and VanDerwarker 2015). Occasionally, cooking features can be large, deep vertical-walled/flat-bottomed pits, which were most likely used as communal earth ovens for steam cooking (Bardolph 2015: 162; Holt 1996: 67). An earth oven uncovered at the late Mississippian C. W. Cooper site in Fulton County, Illinois, provides an in situ example of earth oven cooking technology (Wilson and VanDerwarker 2015). The inslanting/flat-bottomed pit included the remains of a failed corn roast, where cobs of corn were placed on top of a thin layer of vegetation and capped in clay, over which a fire was built (Wilson and VanDerwarker 2015: 169–170); it should be noted that the C. W. Cooper earth oven did not use rocks as a heating element.

During UCSB's 2016 excavations at the Audrey site, 10 pit features were excavated (Figure 4.5): 8 in the House Block area, 1 on the floor of Feature 5 (Feature 29), and 1 Late Woodland–period pit feature that was superimposed by Feature 5 (Feature 28). As Feature 28 includes exclusively Jersey Bluff–phase pottery, it will be excluded from this discussion of Mississippian domestic activity. Basic metrics of diameter and depth were recorded for all pit features and volumes calculated using Fortier et al. (1984: Figure 22) and Kelly et al.'s (1987) formulae. Within the House Block area, all three morphological feature types were identified. Three deep, vertical-walled/flat-bottomed pits range in size from 1.07 to 1.25 m in diameter and 39 to 67 cm in depth, with volumes between 0.35 and 0.93 m³. Four shallow, inslanting/flat-bottomed pits range from 0.75 to 1.12 m in diameter and 16 to 25 cm in depth, with volumes of 0.05 to 0.16 m³. Finally, one round-bottomed, basin-shaped pit was found just outside of the Feature 23 house basin, 75 cm in diameter, 15 cm deep, with a volume of only 0.03 m³.

In addition, Feature 29, identified on the floor of Feature 5, was described by excavators as a small bell-shaped smudge pit (see Figure 4.5). The presence of carbonized plant remains (including maize cobs) and the pit's restricted orifice (providing an oxygen-reducing environment) suggests this feature was used for producing smoke inside of Feature 5 (Jackson et al. 2003: 76). The purpose of this smoke-producing pit to the inhabitants of Audrey Village is unknown, but Binford's (1967) ethnohistoric research suggests smudge pits were used for smoking deer hides; alternatively, he suggests, the pits might simply have been used to repel mosquitos and other pests.

I assign feature function to these pits using a combination of morphological attributes, contextual details, and an analysis of orifice area-to-volume ratios. Harris (1996: 89) suggests that in addition to profile shape, feature function can be gleaned from an analysis of the area of the pit opening relative to the volume of the pit. For example, on one hand, pits with narrow openings relative to their volumes are ideal for storage, providing ample space while also restricting the orifice to protect its contents. On the other hand, broad pits with small volumes would be better used for food-processing activities. Bardolph (2015: 163) demonstrates the use of orifice area-to-volume ratios to classify pit features from the early Mississippian Lamb site in the Central Illinois River Valley (CIRV) into one of three categories, from highest to lowest ratio: food processing, cooking, and storage.

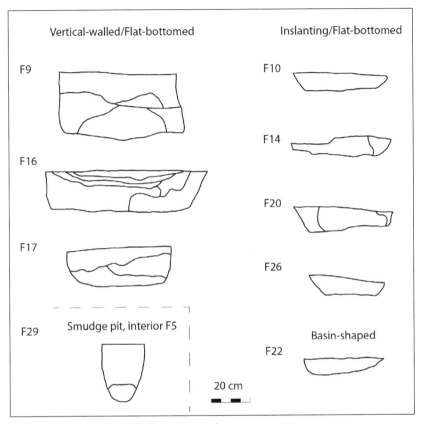

Figure 4.5. Pit feature profiles from 2016 Audrey site excavations.

Figure 4.6 shows a graph of the orifice area-to-volume ratios for the Audrey site pits. The three vertical-walled/flat-bottomed pits have the smallest orifice area-to-volume ratios, providing additional support for their use as storage facilities. Feature 29, the smudge pit from the Feature 5 house floor, also has a relatively low orifice area-to-volume ratio, resulting in a feature that contained smoldering vegetation in an oxygen-reduced environment, producing the desired smoky effect. Feature 22, the basin-shaped pit, has the highest orifice area-to-volume ratio, fitting Bardolph's description of broad and shallow food-processing pits. The pattern for the inslanting/flat-bottomed pits (Features 10, 14, 20, and 26) is less clear. Bardolph (2015) defines these pits as cooking features (likely earth ovens) broad enough for easy access, but deep enough to cook a large volume of food. However, none of the inslanting/flat-bottomed pits from the Audrey site showed evidence

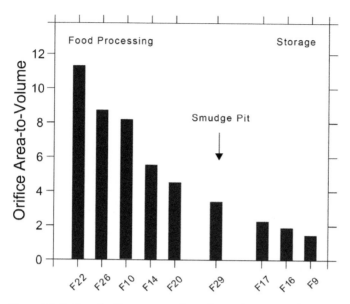

Figure 4.6. Ratios of orifice area to volume for Audrey site pit features.

of in situ burning (in the form of oxidized soil) as was found for the cooking features at Lamb. For this reason, I classify these pits as food-processing features.

Feature 20, with the smallest orifice area-to-volume ratio of the inslanting/flat-bottomed pits, was located adjacent to Feature 23 (house basin), and its feature fill included large quantities of burnt limestone, usually associated with cooking features; however, this material could have been a secondary deposit of limestone from a cooking feature elsewhere at the site. Many of the other features also contained burnt limestone (sometimes in large quantities), including the two house basins and Features 9, 14, 16, 17, and 22. In fact, Cook's (1983) CAA excavations found "kilogram after kilogram of reddish, burnt, crumbly limestone" in both Late Woodland and Stirling-phase pits, but the material was not associated with either of the identified hearths (one from the sweat lodge in Block 2, and the other on the floor of Structure 3, the burned house in Block 6). Despite encountering massive quantities of burnt limestone and abundant evidence of habitation at the Audrey site, excavators have only recovered two hearths and no convincing evidence of in situ burning within features. Wilson and VanDerwarker (2015: 168) suggest that shallow cooking features tend to lack in situ evidence of soil oxidation, but often have fill layers including deposits of heat-altered materials. Perhaps the lack of evidence for oxidation in Audrey's features is related to

Figure 4.7. Feature 9 profile showing possible oxidation in the bottom-right corner of the pit.

the well-draining silty sand at the site that made it difficult to identify and define features, with any evidence of oxidation leached out of the soil. This is, of course, a speculation, but a possibility I think is worth considering.

It is important to note that excavators described the soil beneath a portion of Feature 9, the deepest of the storage pits, as a reddish sterile sand that could have resulted either from leaching of the dark deposits above or from oxidation due to in situ burning (Figure 4.7). Bardolph (2015) identified a large communal earth oven at the Lamb site that also had the profile of a traditional storage pit, but soil oxidation and fire-cracked rock (FCR) identified the pit as a cooking feature. Feature 9, however, differs from the communal earth oven at Lamb in a few important ways. First, while Bardolph (2015: 161) suggests that the presence of FCR may indicate a cooking feature and burnt limestone was present in Feature 9, feature fill included relatively small quantities of burnt limestone compared to other features in the House Block. To demonstrate this, I calculated the density of limestone per feature by dividing the total weight of burnt limestone for each feature by the feature's volume (volume was divided by two for features that were halfway excavated). Feature 9's limestone density is in the upper 50 percent of these features, but the density is more than five times smaller than the next-densest feature. The second difference between Feature 9 and the communal earth oven at Lamb is that the reddened soil is unevenly distributed (only on the right side of the profile) and does not extend up the sides of the pit; in fact, the reddish soil only appears below the dark deposit of charcoal and burnt limestone, which supports the hypothesis that the stain as an effect of leaching.

Additional research may shed light on whether Feature 9 was used for cooking. For example, in their analysis of the C. W. Cooper earth oven, Wilson and VanDerwarker (2015: 171) identified nutshell, grass seeds, and weedy seeds that were likely used for kindling on top of the clay-capped oven; as archaeobotanical analysis of the Audrey site flotation samples is ongoing, the presence or absence of these taxa in the Feature 9 fill is currently unknown. At present, the feature will remain assigned as a storage pit since convincing evidence of cooking activity in the feature remains to be seen.

Spatial Distribution of Features

How are these food-processing and storage features spatially arranged at the site? Are these activities occurring in open, communal areas, or in more private spaces closer to domestic structures? I consider these questions using a subset of features (excavated features) and the one house (Feature 23) identified in the House Block from the 2016 Audrey site excavations. Figure 4.8 shows the excavated pit features in the House Block coded by feature function: storage pits are marked with dark shading and food-processing pits with light shading. The feature distribution map shows that food-processing pits are scattered across the site, but generally located adjacent to the house. Meanwhile, storage features are slightly farther from the house but, without more exposed features and houses (and a more quantitative spatial analysis), it is difficult to say whether these storage pits are in a private or communal location. It should be noted that no pit features were encountered on the floor of Feature 23, inside the house, which is consistent with late Lohmann-, early Stirling–phase, American Bottom household organization (Mehrer 1995). It is possible that Feature 23 and its surrounding food-processing and storage features represent a household cluster, with multiple domestic structures sharing storage and processing features between them.

Discussion: Mississippian Community Organization at Audrey

The Audrey site is a sizable nucleated village with rectangular wall-trench architecture, including elite and special-purpose buildings, built in rows (and oriented roughly to the same azimuth) around what appears to be a

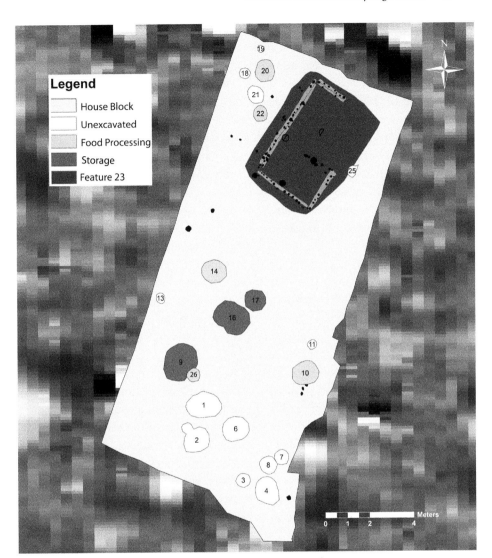

Figure 4.8. Distribution of House Block pit features by functional type.

central plaza; archaeological investigations also identified a possible isolated small-structure complex in the western portion of the site. This type
of planned settlement is consistent with Mississippian settlement patterns
in the American Bottom. Abundant domestic refuse and 2 to 3 building
episodes of Audrey site structures suggest a 15- to 36-year period of Stirling-
phase occupation. But what processes led to development of this Mississippian settlement pattern in the LIRV?

For LIRV groups in direct proximity to the American Bottom, regular political, economic, and social interaction with groups in Cahokia's inner sphere would have entailed important organizational changes in a series of everyday practices that did not occur with northern hinterland groups. In addition to building a Mississippian village, Audrey site inhabitants were fundamentally renegotiating social identities through alterations to in-grained daily practices, such as food processing and storage, and the social interactions determined by community organization. Such organizational changes would have meant a shift away from identities structured by com-munally oriented Woodland-era traditions and toward those negotiated through a more privatized, hierarchically organized Cahokian way of life. But to what degree did the inhabitants of the Audrey site adopt this Ca-hokian way of life? Which, if any, aspects of local Woodland community or-ganization did they maintain? These questions will be addressed through a comparative analysis of architecture and community organization between the Audrey site and the Greater Cahokia area.

Mississippian Architecture

The six rectangular wall-trench structures excavated at the Audrey site are set in rows of additional, similar-sized structures, oriented to the same azi-muth around a central plaza forming a planned Mississippian village. A large community building, an elite structure with associated screen walls, and a sweat lodge indicate some degree of social hierarchy and level of so-ciopolitical complexity closer to the American Bottom than is observed for contemporary early Mississippian hinterland settlements to the north (Em-erson 1997c: 182). However, excavations of the Audrey site have so far failed to recover other types of Cahokia-style special-purpose buildings, such as L-shaped, T-shaped, and cruciform structures; the gradiometer survey also did not detect any anomalies resembling special-purpose buildings. The absence of these buildings suggests that social relations at the Audrey site were not generated by the same types of status-laden ritual institutions and practices that contributed to Cahokia's complexity. Without further excava-tion, the Audrey site architectural data are limited for answering questions of complexity. But the existing rectangular structures can still be compared to those from other Mississippian settlements to determine the degree to which Audrey inhabitants adopted Cahokian architectural techniques and to explore the possibility of rectangular, special-purpose buildings at the site. These questions will be addressed through a comparative analysis of house size and architectural details.

House Size

As discussed above, the size of a rectangular wall-trench structure can be suggestive of function. Larger structures may have functioned as community buildings or elite structures, and small buildings may have been used as storage or temporary shrine houses, but the average-size buildings at a Mississippian settlement likely functioned as domiciles. Mississippian house size increased over time from the Lohmann through the Moorhead phases in the American Bottom. Also, in terms of shape, house width increased over time, shifting from small, narrow Lohmann-phase houses toward larger, square-shaped structures by the Moorehead phase. Research by Baires and colleagues (2017) at Cahokia's Spring Lake Tract provides statistically significant evidence of this long-observed trend.

The Spring Lake Tract is a residential area west of Cahokia's main precinct that had been largely untested prior to the magnetic gradiometry survey conducted by Baires et al. (2017), leaving this portion of the site's chronology unknown. The survey identified rectilinear anomalies representing 79 potential rectangular structures, although 2 of these had floor areas too small (< 10 m^2) to be considered domestic structures; circular anomalies, likely representing either pit features or circular structures, were excluded from the study, as neither was easily assigned a temporal affiliation (Baires et al. 2017: 746). First, the authors tested the statistical validity of house size-shape trends among structures from the Greater Cahokia area using k-means cluster analysis of the area versus length-to-width (L:W) ratios of Terminal Late Woodland (TLW) through Moorehead phase structures;. With acknowledged overlap, TLW-, Lohmann-, Stirling-, and Moorehead–phase buildings formed separate clusters, and the Lohmann-phase cluster showed a statistically significant difference in area and L:W ratio from all other structures (p = 0.0263) (Baires et al. 2017: 748–749). The authors then estimated length and width of the rectilinear anomalies from the Spring Lake Tract survey and compared metrics with the existing Cahokia data to predict temporal affiliation of the structures represented by the anomalies. Ground truthing of a sample of the anomalies confirmed their results, substantiating the claim that temporal affiliation can be estimated based on structure size and shape (Baires et al. 2017: 757).

If house size and shape are predictive of temporal affiliation, and the

Audrey site is indeed a Stirling-phase Mississippian village, we would expect the site's houses to be similar in size and shape to Stirling-phase wall-trench buildings from Cahokia. Using data from Baires et al. (2017: Table 2), I compare the L:W ratios and floor areas of five of the rectangular wall-trench structures from the Audrey site to the Lohmann- and Stirling-phase structures from the Cahokia Spring Lake Tract survey, standardizing the areas to log10; I exclude Structure 4 from this analysis as its area of over 93 m² would skew the graph. A scatterplot of size (area) versus shape (L:W ratio) shows that the three midsized buildings from the Audrey site fall confidentally in the Stirling-phase cluster (Figure 4.9). However, both Feature 5 and Structure 1 have areas smaller than either the Stirling- or Lohmann–phase houses at the Spring Lake Tract. In fact, in Baires et al.'s (2017: 746) study, these two buildings would not have been included as their floor areas measure smaller than 10 m², and are considered by the authors as too small for living quarters. We know from excavation that both of these smaller structures contained Stirling-phase refuse, so their temporal affiliation is not in question. But if these buildings were too small to be houses, what function did they serve to the inhabitants of the Audrey site?

Storage Huts or Shrine Houses?

Feature 5 and Structure 1 are smaller than the average-sized Stirling-phase domestic structure at Audrey, and are more similar in size to other small structures found at Cahokia and surrounding areas. These small structures have been identified as either storage huts or shrine houses, depending on context, content, and floor treatment. If structure size is suggestive of function, then Audrey's small structures also may have served a similar purpose. Pauketat (2005) identified a cluster of 25 small rectilinear wall-trench buildings at the East St. Louis mound center that were intentionally burned in a single ritual conflagration event (Pauketat et al. 2013). The buildings were identified as storage huts, too small for an individual to sleep in. Collins (1990; 1997) interpreted one such building at Cahokia's ICT II as a granary, built adjacent to a marker post. Similar buildings were identified at the Halliday and Grossmann sites in the eastern uplands, where courtyard groups were composed of one or two domestic structures; small, square-shaped storage huts; and surrounding pit features (Alt 2002a: 227; 2006b).

If the small buildings at the Audrey site also functioned as storage structures, they should be more similar in size to Cahokian storage huts than domestic structures. To investigate this assertion, I compared length and width data for Audrey's house floors to storage huts from the East St. Louis

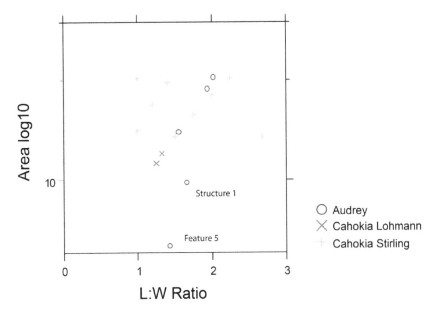

Figure 4.9. Scatterplot of L:W ratios versus floor area, standardized to log10 for Audrey site wall-trench structures and Cahokia Spring Lake Tract (Baires et al. 2017: Table 2).

(Pauketat et al. 2013) and Grossman sites (Alt 2006b: Appendix 1) and Lohmann- and Stirling-phase domestic structures from Cahokia's Tract 15A (Pauketat 1998b: Table 6.8). Figure 4.10 shows a scatterplot of length and width for these buildings. While there is some overlap between the smallest houses and the largest storage huts, Audrey's Feature 5 plots neatly among the storage huts. Structure 1 remains on the cusp of the early Mississippian domestic structures. Both are smaller than all but one of the Cahokia domiciles, with which the other three Audrey houses sit quite comfortably.

Storage Huts

Small Mississippian storage structures have additional attributes that distinguish them from other types of buildings. For example, Mississippian storage structures tend to be more square in shape than the typical rectangular early Mississippian house (Alt 2002a; Alt 2006: 128; Emerson 1997c; Mehrer 1995; Pauketat et al. 2013: 215). They also tend to lack interior features, such as pits, hearths, or support posts (Alt 2006b: 134). And, with the exception of the cluster at East St. Louis, storage structures are usually associated with household clusters that include domestic buildings (Alt 2006b; Mehrer

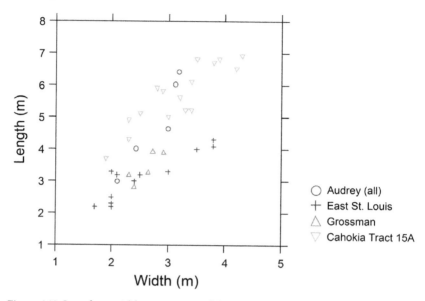

Figure 4.10. Length-to-width comparison of the Audrey site rectangular buildings with "storage huts" from East St. Louis (Pauketat et al. 2013: Table 2) and the Grossmann site (Alt 2006b: Appendix 1); and Lohmann- and Stirling-phase houses from Cahokia Tract 15A (Pauketat 1998b: Table 6.8).

1995; Pauketat et al. 2013). However, the small buildings from the Audrey site differ from these traditional storage structures in a few important ways. First, both Feature 5 and Structure 1 are more rectangular than square in shape, although this fact does not seem to exclude them from clustering with other storage huts in Figure 4.10. Furthermore, Feature 5 does include an interior feature, although perhaps the smudge pit's smoke would have been beneficial in keeping pests out of a storage facility. Finally, and perhaps most significantly, the floor of Feature 5 was plastered with yellow clay. While Alt (2006b: 109) did observe two small, possible storage structures with yellow clay floors at the Grossmann site, more recent research associates this treatment with shrines and special-purpose buildings (Alt 2016; Alt and Pauketat 2017; Pauketat et al. 2012; Pauketat et al. 2017).

Shrine Houses

Pauketat and colleagues (2017) uncovered a series of small, wall-trench buildings with prepared clay floors at the Emerald Acropolis. The floors, post holes, and interior pits of these "shrine houses" were plastered with yellow clay, and offerings were made in clay-lined features; at the end of their use, the houses were left open to the elements, allowing water to wash in. This process was repeated for every building episode, ritually closing and reopening the shrine house. Similarly, at the Halliday site in the uplands east of Cahokia, the house floors of some single-post structures and post holes were lined with yellow clay for each reconstruction (Pauketat and Alt 2005: 223); this phenomenon was also observed at the Pfeffer site, a few kilometers east of Halliday, where the floors and post holes of a large public structure and surrounding buildings had prepared clay linings (Alt 2002a: 222). In contrast, the clay floor of Feature 5 at Audrey is rather mottled in places and does not line either the posts or the smudge pit. Additionally, there is no evidence of formal hearths or ceremonial offerings, yet there is abundant evidence for domestic activity, likely representing year-round occupation of the village. However, it is interesting to note that the azimuths of Feature 5 (49.42°) and Structure 1 (53.9°) are close to the Emerald axis of 53°, which sets them apart from the other structures at Audrey, which were oriented from 29° to 33°. Metrics for the Emerald shrine houses have not yet been published for comparative analysis of size; yet Pauketat and Alt (personal communication 2018) suggest that the yellow-plastered floors are more indicative of shrine houses than structure size is.

Special-Purpose Compound?

While the function of Feature 5 (and Structure 1 by association) remains unclear, its size, the treatment of its floor, and the presence of an interior smudge pit are suggestive of a ceremonial function. There appears to be a large cluster of these small structures in the western portion of Audrey Village. UCSB's 2014 gradiometer survey identified a series of similarly sized magnetic anomalies that appear to be evenly spaced in rows; a test unit placed atop of one of these anomalies revealed Feature 5's house basin. Applying this postexcavation knowledge back to the gradiometer map, there appears to be a number of these possible house-basin anomalies, with Structure 1 as the easternmost small, wall-trench structure of the cluster (see Figure 4.1). If all these anomalies in fact represent small, wall-trench buildings, they may be part of some kind of a special-purpose compound. Further excavation is necessary to confirm the presence of additional small, wall-trench structures and to investigate their functions as either storage huts or ceremonial structures. Either scenario—a shrine or special-storage compound—would represent an unusual settlement pattern. A storage compound would be similar to the East St. Louis cluster of storage structures. Another possibility is a segregation of buildings by size, as was observed at

Cahokia Tract 15A (Pauketat 1998b: 112). Or perhaps additional excavations would reveal a complex of yellow-plastered shrine houses such as those from Emerald (Pauketat et al. 2017).

Hybrid Architecture

The Audrey site's Feature 23 is an average-sized Stirling-phase, semisubterranean wall-trench domicile. The house was part of a highly ordered, planned village settlement, where it stood in a row of similarly sized houses around a central plaza. Excavation of the house basin recovered an abundance of Stirling-phase domestic refuse. Considered alone, these attributes qualify Feature 23 as a typical, early Stiring–phase, Cahokia-style house. Architectural details, however, suggest the builders of this house combined aspects of Woodland-era and Mississippian styles of construction methods.

After a basin was dug, wall trenches were prepared for the house, at which point the builders placed single-set posts within the trenches. The posts were then set at an inslanting angle for the purpose of creating a bent-pole arbor roof that was supported by a structure of internal posts. The overall product would have been similar to a Late Woodland, single-post rectangular house. Single-post structures with inward-leaning walls are occasionally found in early Mississippian contexts in the Greater Cahokia region, but they are rare; for example, only 7 percent of rectangular structures at East St. Louis (n=2) used single-post construction (Pauektat 2005: 162). Perhaps more importantly, this type of construction is almost never employed in conjunction with wall trenches (Alt and Pauketat 2011). This unusual hybrid architectural technique was first identified at the Halliday and Knoebel Richland Complex sites, where inhabitants were also late in adopting the wall-trench style of architecture in general (Alt 2001, 2002a: 226; Alt and Pauketat 2011; Pauketat and Alt 2005). Alt (2002a, 2006a) considers this practice a hybrid form of architecture, combining both traditional, Woodland methods of constructing homes with newer, Cahokian ways of creating space. In other words, for Audrey inhabitants, Feature 23 was a Cahokian house built on a foundation of local traditions.

Domestic Activities

Through the LIRV's interactions with Greater Cahokian groups, inhabitants were not just adopting selected Cahokian practices and emulating material culture; their close ties with Cahokia meant that identities were renegotiated to incorporate aspects of Cahokian lifeways down to the basic level of community organization. Audrey site inhabitants may have deviated from communally oriented social organization of Woodland-era traditions in favor of a more hierarchical community organization emphasizing social differentiation. The transition from communal to hierarchical community organization originally occurred at Cahokia, where Woodland-era communal patterns of domestic activities were still practiced during the Emergent Mississippian and into the Lohmann phase; Collins (1997: 139) suggests "this order was supplanted during the later occupations . . . when, by all indications, status distinctions, subgroup solidarity, and household autonomy became increasingly important at the local level." These organizational changes resulted in the privatization of domestic activities, concealing storage, food-processing, and cooking features inside or adjacent to the house (Kelly 1990: 339). This pattern stands in contrast to the early Mississippian settlements in the CIRV, where food-processing, storage, and cooking activities (using Woodland-era earth ovens) appear to have been a collaborative, communal effort among residents (Bardolph 2014: 82; Wilson and VanDerwarker 2015).

If Audrey's inhabitants were more connected to Cahokia than northerners were, it would likely be represented in the organization of their domestic activities involving a combination of both exterior, communal food-processing, cooking, and storage features and features either inside or immediately adjacent to the home. A spatial analysis of pit features in the Audrey site's House Block area remains inconclusive regarding whether storage features were placed in communal locations or within a household cluster. However, there are no interior pit features on the floor of Feature 23, suggesting the majority of food processing, cooking, and storage took place outside the home. This pattern suggests Audrey inhabitants did not feel compelled to conceal their food resources from other members of the community and that foodways at Audrey were not hierarchically organized, as we might expect at Cahokia. It should be noted that while the American Bottom pattern of privatized, interior storage features began during the Stirling phase (Mehrer 1995: 127), this practice was much more prevalent in the following Moorehead and Sand Prairie phases, when house sizes continued to increase, and the broader Middle Mississippian region experienced an escalation in violence and competition. Notably missing from the Audrey site archaeological record is convincing evidence of hearths or cooking features. While Cook's CAA excavations discovered evidence of possible earth ovens at Audrey, these features, and a number of others, have not been dated and may in fact be Late Woodland–period cooking features. The lack of earth ovens at Audrey stands in direct contrast with Mississippian settlements in the CIRV, where people continued to use the Woodland-era method of communal food preparation. Current evidence suggests the Audrey site community was less concerned with privatization of domestic activities than was normally practiced in Cahokian communities, but they engaged in more privatized activities than Mississippian peoples in the CIRV.

Community Organization and Differential Access

While Audrey site inhabitants appear not to have adopted a hierarchical organization of domestic activities, certain other resources and spaces may have been restricted within the community. Interactions, political affiliations, and social relations with Cahokians would have entailed important changes that did not occur with northern hinterland groups, such as alterations to the everyday social interactions determined by community organization. Whereas Woodland identities were structured by communally oriented traditions, Cahokian identities were negotiated through a more privatized, hierarchically organized way of life. As a result of these organizational changes, access to certain spaces and buildings may have been restricted on a village-wide scale. Indeed, excavations at Audrey identified a disparity in house size, with multiple screen trenches (isolated walls) separating certain buildings from the rest of the site. One protected building, Structure 3, was burned, perhaps ritually, while its valuable contents remained inside (a cache of 120 marine shell beads and a Mill Creek hoe). While the occupants of Feature 23 and the House Block area of the village stored and processed food outside the home, the occupants of Structure 3 concealed their highly prized, exotic agricultural tool and their nonlocally produced marine shell beads. In summary, food at Audrey seems to be a resource less affected by hierarchical organizational changes than items associated with wealth and status. An expanded view of the site's layout is necessary to fully understand this pattern.

Conclusions

Frequent interactions with nearby Greater Cahokia groups led to important organizational changes for the inhabitants of the LIRV. The Audrey site was built on an organized Cahokian blueprint of wall trenches outlining domestic structures, elite structures, a community building, small structures, and some special-purpose buildings such as sweat lodges. Access to elite buildings containing status items (such as marine shell beads) was restricted to the community through the use of wall screens. These aspects of community organization reflect a Cahokian architecture of power, where certain members of the community used the construction of private household clusters and the segmentation of space to maintain their power (Emerson 1997c).

Beneath the surface, however, Audrey inhabitants continued to practice lifeways influenced by local Woodland traditions. Feature 23, an average-sized Stirling-phase domestic structure, was constructed in a semisubterranean house basin with wall trenches; yet the posts were set individually within the wall trenches and bent over to form an arbor roof supported by interior posts, a Woodland-era architectural technique. Furthermore, Audrey inhabitants may have privatized storage of wealth items, but food-storage and -processing activities were conducted outside the home rather than in interior, private locations as was the practice at some early Stirling–phase Mississippian settlements (Mehrer 1995).

Overall, the Audrey site community organization is characteristic of a planned Mississippian village with marked sociopolitical complexity whose inhabitants maintained some aspects of a communally oriented Woodland way of life. To date, it is unclear if all of the domestic structures were built using hybrid architectural techniques or if Feature 23 is the only example. It is also unknown if there are additional small, rectangular wall-trench structures like Feature 5 and Structure 1 and whether their floors were plastered with yellow clay. Additional excavation is necessary to investigate these possibilities further.

5

Ceramic Traditions

Ceramics are the often the most ubiquitous form of material culture–type at Woodland- and Mississippian-period archaeological sites in the Southeast and Midwest, making them a common source of archaeological inquiry. However, the study of pottery produces more than just large datasets; pottery bridges the gap between the everyday and the ceremonial, elite and commoner, mortuary and domestic. Yet unlike lithic artifacts, whose appearance and purpose are subject to change over time through the nature of reductive production and sharpening processes, ceramic objects embody the production process from paste mixing to firing (Rye 1981). Ceramics are products of human action and represent the cultural choices of the people who made them, imbuing them with social, political, economic, and ideological information (Sinopoli 1991: 69). For these reasons, ceramic analysis in the Middle Mississippian culture area has produced a robust body of data, identifying cultural boundaries (Esarey 2000; Green and Nolan 2000; Harn 1991; Studenmund 2000), determining cross-cultural interactions (Claflin 1991; Conrad 1991; Delaney-Rivera 2004, 2007; Richards 1992; Stoltman 1991; Wilson 2015a), and, perhaps most importantly, developing a reliable ceramic chronology for Cahokia-style ceramics (Holley 1989; Pauketat 1998b; see also Wilson et al. 2018).

Analysis of the Audrey site ceramic artifacts provides evidence regarding the adoption of Cahokian material culture, the degree to which Woodland-era methods of pottery production were maintained, and interactions between Audrey site inhabitants and groups outside the LIRV. The ceramic assemblage from the Mississippian occupation of the Audrey site is broadly similar to Stirling-phase pottery (AD 1100–1150) from Cahokia and the northern American Bottom, and, importantly, lacks the Woodland influence often observed in northern hinterland Mississippian pottery (Delaney-Rivera 2004, 2007; Emerson 1991b; Millhouse 2012; Wilson 2015a; Wilson et al. 2017). Despite stylistic and morphological similarities, there are important implications for differences in social organization between Audrey and Greater Cahokia ceramic assemblages related to vessel class. While Audrey potters produced shell-tempered jars virtually indistinguishable from those found at Cahokia, very few Cahokia-style fineware vessels were recovered. Audrey inhabitants also produced fewer servingware vessels than were common in and around Cahokia. These patterns suggest a less status-laden social organization at Audrey, where inhabitants did not incorporate the same formality that characterized Cahokian foodways (Wilson et al. 2017).

The prominence of Ramey Incised pottery in the northern hinterland complicates this notion. Ramey Incised jars, originally produced at Cahokia, are utilitarian vessels imbued with cosmological imagery. This religiously charged potting tradition seems to have been overemphasized by northern hinterland groups who claimed it for their own, incorporating Woodland-derived motifs and arranging them using local concepts of space (Friberg 2018a; Wilson et al. 2017). Although Audrey inhabitants did not consume Ramey Incised pottery to the same degree as their northern neighbors, LIRV potters did occasionally use local interpretations of design layout, which is a pattern we see in the northern hinterland as well (Friberg 2018a). Finally, a comparative analysis of non-Cahokian exotic pottery at Audrey, the Central Illinois River Valley (CIRV), and Apple River Valley (ARV) shows that these groups were engaged in interactions with multiple outside groups, both in the surrounding area and at distant locales.

The remainder of this chapter outlines these patterns and their significance, in detail. First, I discuss previous research on Audrey site ceramics. I then review regional comparisons of Mississippian pottery assemblages and how they inform the methods of analysis used in the current study. Finally, I present details of the original analysis of the 2016 Audrey site ceramic assemblage, followed by a comparative analysis of Audrey pottery to American Bottom, CIRV, and ARV assemblages.

Previous Research

Previous archaeological research in the LIRV characterized artifact assemblages as an intermixture of Late Woodland, Jersey Bluff phase, and Mississippian material culture (Clafflin 1991; Farnsworth and Emerson 1989; Farnsworth et al. 1991: 83; Studenmund 2000; see also Chapter 2 for more detail). Farnsworth and colleagues (1991; see also Farnsworth and Emerson 1989) argue that Jersey Bluff populations continued to occupy settlements in the LIRV as late as AD 1250. However, these observations are, admittedly

(Farnsworth and Emerson 1989: 27), based primarily on a limited number of radiocarbon dates from small-scale excavations and surface collections from surveys of plowed agricultural fields, and thus lack the appropriate context for definitive conclusions to be drawn about the contemporaneity of Jersey Bluff and early Mississippian settlements. A decade of archaeological excavations (1973–1983) at the Audrey site through the Center for American Archaeology (CAA) were never documented in formal publication, but unpublished reports supported Farnsworth et al.'s model of contemporaneous Jersey Bluff and Mississippian occupations at this LIRV village site (Cook 1981; 1983). Alice Berkson's controlled surface collection of the site identified Archaic, White Hall–phase, Late Woodland–Jersey Bluff-phase, and Stirling-phase Mississippian artifact distribution areas. Dr. Thomas Cook, Director of Research and Education Programs at the CAA, opened a 1400 m^2 area, exposing 2 Late-Woodland (single-post) and 6 Cahokian-style (wall trench) structures, 1 circular sweat lodge, 75 pit features, and possible palisade segments. However, these excavations were not well documented and the materials went largely unanalyzed. Fortunately, a later detailed analysis of pottery from the CAA excavations at the Audrey site begins to amend this narrative (Delaney-Rivera 2000, 2004).

As part of her dissertation research, Colleen Delaney-Rivera (2000) analyzed all pottery from the CAA investigations at the Audrey site, including Berkson's surface collection, but concentrating primarily on materials from Cook's excavations. She analyzed a total of 13,775 (35.54 kg) sherds, identifying 728 diagnostic rim sherds mostly from feature and plow zone contexts (Delaney-Rivera 2000: 182). To assign ceramic phases and assess vessel class, her analysis focused on the temper of both body and rim sherds and a minimum number of vessels (MNV) analysis for diagnostic (rim) sherds. She also collected detailed data on rim types and surface treatment, and she calculated rim protrusion ratios (RPR) for diagnostic rim sherds, publishing the data in her appendixes for future researchers. As this was the first detailed ceramic analysis conducted on the collection, Delaney-Rivera did not separate her analysis by component (that is, Woodland vs. Mississippian features) and considered the entire Late Woodland and Mississippian occupations collectively. This method allowed her to identify 16 hybrid pottery vessels at Audrey, in addition to hybrid vessels at the nearby Schild and Moss site cemeteries (Delaney-Rivera 2000, 2007); hybrid vessels are those that have a combination of both Late Woodland and Mississippian ceramic attributes—such as a jar that is Mississippian in form but tempered with grit, or a shell-tempered early Mississippian jar with Late Woodland–style cordmarking or lip notching. She identified pottery from both the early Late Woodland–White Hall phase (AD 400–600) and the late Late Woodland–Jersey Bluff phase (800–1200?). From the Mississippian-period features at the site, Delaney-Rivera found pottery that was typical of early Stirling-phase (AD 1100–1150), American Bottom assemblages, including Cahokia-style fineware vessels. A small-scale petrographic analysis of sherds from these assemblages revealed nonlocal Mississippian, local Mississippian, and locally produced hybrid pottery (see also Stoltman 1991, 2001).

Due to the nature of the collection, there were some understandable limitations to Delaney-Rivera's analysis. The quantity of ceramic objects and imperfect excavation records left an enormous collection with little contextual data to aid in interpretation. For this reason, Delaney-Rivera used a blind analysis approach, considering all pottery within the site's assemblage collectively, rather than separating analysis by cultural phase. Second, some of the data are summarized, such as body sherd weights, leaving only count data for temper and surface finish. Finally, in providing such a wealth of information, certain details on methods of data collection (such as measurements used for calculation of RPR values) are missing, making it difficult to evaluate whether her data are comparable to other similar ceramic analyses. Overall, Delaney-Rivera's ceramic analysis was invaluable in providing the first empirical insight into the history of the Audrey site, but the resulting data have limited value for comparative analysis.

Through her analysis of the ceramic collection from the CAA's excavations at the Audrey site, Delaney-Rivera (2000) concluded that the LIRV was colonized by nonlocal Mississippians around AD 1050, influencing local Jersey Bluff populations to incorporate aspects of a Cahokian way of life (see also Delaney-Rivera 2004, 2007). She contested Farnsworth's argument that Late Woodland groups persisted in the valley alongside Mississippians into the twelfth century, citing a meager 8 percent of the Audrey ceramic assemblage as belonging to the Jersey Bluff phase (and noting that the majority of these sherds were recovered from plow-zone rather than feature contexts) (Delaney-Rivera 2000: 222–223).

Methods of Analysis

Ceramic sherds from the 2016 excavations were analyzed using standard methods to gather data on weight, count, temper, and surface treatment of all sherds, in addition to vessel class, orifice diameter, and more detailed measurements of rim sherds.

Paste and Surface Treatment

Paste is an attribute through which to examine the retention of Woodland-era practices versus influence from the American Bottom based on the percentage of grit-tempered to shell-tempered pottery; furthermore, Woodland-Mississippian hybrid vessels are often described as having pastes that contain both shell and grit. Surface treatment can also be used to examine the degree of Woodland versus Mississippian influence. While many northern groups continued to produce Woodland-era cordmarked pottery, Stirling-phase vessel assemblages at Cahokia and in the American Bottom are more often characterized by vessels with plain, slipped, or burnished surfaces.

Minimum Number of Vessels (MNV)

An MNV analysis was conducted by refitting pottery rims from adjacent levels within each feature. Once the refitting was complete, rim analysis was conducted, identifying vessel class, measuring rim and lip shape, and recording other important attributes used in comparative analyses (see Friberg 2018b: Table 5.5 for more detailed rim analysis data). An analysis of vessel class (for example, jars, bowls, bottles, beakers, plates, and so on) makes it possible to calculate a serving-to-utilitarian ware ratio; this ratio is important for comparing vessel assemblages to investigate differences in the complexity of social organization through foodways. Orifice diameter was also recorded if a sufficient portion of the rim was present to give an impression of vessel size. An assemblage of mostly small jars might suggest Audrey residents were cooking for small groups; alternatively, an assemblage of primarily large jars might suggest the opposite.

Ceramic Seriation

Both Holley (1989) and Pauketat (1998b) have demonstrated that the lips of Cahokian jars tend to become longer relative to the vessel thickness over time. A measurement of the lip protrusion of a jar, or LP index (also referred to as rim protrusion ratio, or RPR), can be used to seriate Mississippian jar rims by subphase. In this case, Lohmann-phase jar rims have the highest LP indexes (closest to 1), and Sand Prairie–phase LP indices are the lowest; an early Stirling–phase jar rim should have a relatively high LP index. Researchers studying ceramic assemblages from settlements outside the American Bottom have been successful in using this method for relative dating (Bardolph 2014; Friberg and Wilson 2015; Wilson 2015a; Wilson et al. 2018). Rim angles (RA) and rim curvature (RC) of Mississippian jars have also been shown to change over time (Holley 1989; Pauketat 1998b). The angles of Lohmann-phase rims were steep, and rim angles became flatter throughout the Stirling phase. As for rim curvature, early jars tended to have more outflaring rather that in-slanting rims.

LP values from Audrey are used to seriate the site against Lohmann and early and late Stirling–phase pottery from Tract 15A at Cahokia (Pauketat 1998b). For comparative purposes, I use my own rim analysis of the 2016 collection; for the purpose of consistency in data collection, Delaney-Rivera's RPR measures will not be used. The same comparison will be done for Rim Angles[1] (RA). These data are then considered against AMS and radiocarbon dates taken from both Late Woodland and Mississippian features at the Audrey site. Dates were calibrated using OxCal v4.3.2 (Bronk Ramsey 2017) and the IntCal13 atmospheric curve (Reimer et al. 2013).

Comparative Analysis

A comparison of Audrey's pottery to ceramic assemblages from the Greater Cahokia area is useful in assessing the degree to which Audrey inhabitants incorporated aspects of Cahokian lifeways by addressing the following questions: (1) did Audrey site potters use the same methods of pottery production observed in the American Bottom; (2) were Audrey inhabitants' foodways structured by Cahokian hierarchical social organization; and (3) how did Audrey inhabitants incorporate Cahokian ceremonialism into their foodways?

Cahokia ceramic data used in comparative analysis was taken from the ICT II (Holley 1989) and Tract 15A (Pauketat 1998b) excavations, incorporating late Lohmann- and early Stirling–phase data. Recognizing that Cahokia may not be representative of the broader patterns in the Greater Cahokia area, a number of American Bottom and eastern uplands sites are also used for comparison: the Lohmann site, one of the few early Mississippian single-mound centers in the American Bottom (Esarey and Pauketat 1992); two smaller outlying American Bottom Mississippian settlements, Miller Farm (Wilson and Koldehoff 1998) and Robert Scheider (Fortier 1985); the Knoebel site, an early Mississippian village site in the eastern uplands (Alt 2002b); and the Dugan Airfield site, a civic node in the southern American Bottom uplands (Wilson 2018). Additional data from Kunnemann Mound at Cahokia (Pauketat 1993) and other outlying American Bottom sites are also referenced, including Miller Farm (Wilson and Koldehoff 1998), Robert Schneider (Fortier 1985), and Range (Emerson 1997a).

It is also important to compare Audrey's ceramic assemblage to sites outside the American Bottom in order to assess the degree to which Woodland-era methods of pottery production were maintained. In contrast to Greater Cahokia's politically complex settlement pattern, the early Mississippian LIRV consisted of numerous, small Mississippian farmsteads—such as the Eileen Cunningham site (Fishel 2018)—centered on two small villages, including the Audrey site, and associated mortuary complexes at Schild and Moss cemeteries (Delaney-Rivera 2000: 149, 2004; Goldstein 1980: 22–23).

North of the LIRV, there are several well-documented Mississippian sites that demonstrate the maintenance of local Woodland-era traditions (see Chapter 2 for more detail on these patterns). The CIRV follows a 209 km segment of the Illinois River immediately north of the LIRV, from Meredosia northeast to Hennepin, Illinois. At the present time, the early Mississippian settlement pattern in the region is characterized by a mix of nodal ceremonial centers, farmsteads, and mortuary complexes (Conrad 1991; Conrad 1993; Meinkoth 1993; Wilson 2012b: 526), although preliminary investigations are currently under way at a Lohmann-phase mound center in the Peoria area (Wilson et al. 2020). The Lamb site, located in the lower portion of the CIRV near the confluence of the LaMoine and Illinois Rivers, is an early Mississippian farmstead where inhabitants interacted with local Late Woodland peoples (Bardolph 2014; Bardolph and Wilson 2015). Other CIRV farmsteads considered in this study include the Tree Row site (Meinkoth 1993) and the Garren site. The Eveland site is an early Mississippian ceremonial node with Cahokian special-purpose buildings, located in the upper portion of the CIRV near the Spoon River area (Conrad 1991); the site is immediately adjacent to Dickson Mounds, a Mississippian mortuary mound complex (Harn 1975). Finally, Kingston Lake is another mortuary site in the CIRV (Conrad 1993); both Dickson Mounds and Kingston Lake include burials that are closely reminiscent of the headless and handless individuals buried in Mound 72 at Cahokia.

Mississippian settlements in the ARV differ from those in the CIRV in that they include large villages and mound centers (Emerson 1991b; Emerson et al. 2007; Millhouse 2012). Data from two sites in the Apple River Valley (ARV) of northwest Illinois are used for comparison. John Chapman (Millhouse 2012) and Lundy (Emerson et al. 2007) are both early Mississippian villages with patterns of Woodland/Mississippian hybridity. In addition, data from the Fred Edwards site in southwestern Wisconsin are also considered as representing the ARV (Finney 1993). The Fred Edwards site is a large palisaded Mississippian village with a Late Woodland component and overlapping Late Woodland–Mississippian contexts and hybrid pottery.

Analysis

Assemblage Summary, 2016

A total of 8,573 sherds, weighing 18,504.55 g were recovered in the 2016 excavations at Audrey, 85 percent of which came from feature contexts (Table 5.1; see Friberg 2018b: Table 5.1, for more detail). Other sherds were encountered in the excavation of the plow zone above the features. The majority of the ceramic sherds are shell-tempered with plain surfaces; the remaining shell-tempered sherds are either burnished and black, brown-slipped, or red-slipped (Table 5.2). The non–shell-tempered pottery is mostly represented by small sherds with indeterminate tempers. Finally, a small percentage (4 percent by weight) of the sherds recovered in the 2016 excavations was sand- or grit-tempered plain, sand- or grit-tempered cordmarked, and limestone-tempered, mostly dating to the Late Woodland White Hall–phase (AD 400–600). Only 9 sherds had a mixed grit/shell temper, which is often seen as a Woodland-Mississippian hybrid ceramic paste.

A minimum number of 82 vessels was identified in the analysis of the 2016 ceramics. Seventy-two of these (88 percent) were jars. Additionally, eight bowls, one bottle, and one beaker were identified. These vessels will be described in more detail below. When combining these vessel counts with those from Delaney-Rivera's (2000) analysis of existing collections (which contained a higher number of serving vessels), a servingware percentage of 16 percent is calculated.

Pastes

The analysis of pastes comes from sherd weights for the entire 2016 assemblage and from Delaney-Rivera's (2000) entire assemblage summary data. Due to the nature of data collection for Delaney-Rivera's enormous dataset (derived from the CAA excavations), temper was not discussed in terms of counts, and therefore weights are used to be able to combine data for the present analysis. These data highlight the difference between the CAA collection and the UCSB-excavated collections from Mississippian contexts excavated in 2016. Whereas Delaney-Rivera's analysis found a majority of sand-tempered White Hall-phase sherds, shell is the dominant temper of the combined (both CAA and UCSB) existing collections. In the analysis of the UCSB collection, the majority of non–shell-tempered sherds appear to be sand-tempered; the only distinctly grit-tempered sherds were recovered from Feature 28, a Jersey Bluff–phase pit feature truncated by the basin of Feature 5. The remaining non–shell-tempered pottery are limestone- or shell/limestone-tempered sherds (1 percent by weight). There is a negligible percentage (<1 percent) of mixed/hybrid pastes; the limited presence of hybrid pastes is documented better in Delaney-Rivera's analysis of diagnostic rim sherds, but was not considered in her overall ceramic assemblage summary that included body sherds.

Delaney-Rivera's later unpublished ceramic analysis was able to assign phase designations to the majority of features excavated by the CAA at Audrey based on pottery temper (Delaney, personal communication 2017). As demonstrated in Chapter 3, the spatial distribution of features by primary pottery temper identifies sand-tempered pottery primarily in the southwest portion of the site; shell-tempered pottery is predominantly situated to the north and east, and there was only a limited number of features with grit-tempered pottery. Although there is some spatial overlap resulting in admixture of Woodland pottery in Mississippian features, further analysis shows that the two major occupations of the Audrey site represented in the ceramic assemblage are separate and not overlapping. The first is a White Hall–phase occupation in the southern and southwestern portions of the site. This area was the focus of previous excavations and is a large factor in conclusions made regarding Audrey site occupation in the past (Cook 1981, 1983; Farnsworth and Emerson 1989; Farnsworth et al. 1991). The second occupation is that of a Mississippian village, which was documented by Cook (1981, 1983) and Delaney-Rivera (2000). The presence of one possible Jersey Bluff–phase pit (Feature 28) excavated in 2016 complicates Audrey's settlement history, but there does not seem to have been a significant presence at the site during the late Late Woodland period. While Delaney-Rivera's analysis is valuable, especially for understanding site use over time, she considers the entire collection as a whole rather than separating features by component. Isolating the analysis by Mississippian features, however, is necessary to identify the use of grit temper in Mississippian-period pottery as evidence of the maintenance of Woodland potting traditions or interaction with contemporary local Woodland groups. For this reason, I will be

Table 5.1. Sherd temper

	Grit		Sand		Shell		Limestone	
	n	Wt (g)	n	Wt (g)	n	Wt (g)	n	Wt (g)
Delaney-Rivera	1,490	5,846.5	6771	14,981.2	4,473	12,914.8	33	501
Friberg	8	38.74	339	670.12	7,390	17,246.35	34	43.1
TOTAL	1,498	5,885.24	7110	15,651.32	11,863	30,161.15	67	544
Percent	6.70	10.89	31.81	28.96	53.08	55.81	0.30	1.01

	Shell/Limestone		Mixed (grit/shell)		Indeterminate		Total	
	n	Wt (g)	n	Wt (g)	n	Wt (g)	n	Wt (g)
Delaney-Rivera	–	–	–	–	1008	1,293.4	13775	35,537.3
Friberg	13	12.54	9	26.29	780	467.45	8573	18,504.55
TOTAL	13	12.54	9	26.29	1788	1,760.85	22348	54,041.85
Percent	0.06	0.02	0.04	0.05	8	3.26	100	100

Source: Delaney-Rivera (2000), Friberg (2020).
Note: – = 0.

using only the 2016 ceramic data from the Mississippian-period occupation of the site for comparative analyses (see Table 5.1).

Taking a closer look at pastes from 2016 rim sherds to examine shell temper versus fine shell and limestone, it is clear that finely tempered vessels account for less than 10 percent of the vessels identified. Overall, the pastes of the shell-tempered vessels recovered from the 2016 Audrey site excavations are very similar. There is one grit-tempered vessel (rim sherd) in the assemblage, although this likely represents Woodland admixture resulting from the Mississippian occupants of the site excavating into previously existing Woodland features, breaking up and intermixing the pottery with their own refuse. Finally, the paste of one of the jars from the 2016 excavations includes some fine grit. It should be noted that the local clay used by Audrey potters appears to have natural grit and sand inclusions, and it seems that for many of the finer made vessels, a purer clay was chosen before mixing in the crushed mussel shell.

Surface Treatment

Surface treatment analysis incorporated data from the entire 2016 assemblage, including both rim and body sherds. Given the large size of the CAA Audrey ceramic collection, Delaney-Rivera collected data on surface treatment only for the diagnostic rim sherds rather than the entire assemblage; due to the refitting of diagnostic rims whereby the number of sherds per rim was not recorded, weights rather than counts were used to combine data for the two assemblages (see Table 5.2). Where Delaney-Rivera identified some 20 percent of the pottery from Audrey as cordmarked, with the addition of the 2016 excavations, only 9.5 percent of the pottery is cordmarked. These differences are likely due to the fact that the area excavated by the CAA contained a number of Woodland-period pit features, while the 2016 excavations targeted Mississippian houses and features. Isolating analysis to Mississippian features only is essential for determining whether cordmarking was used by Audrey site potters during the Mississippian period. If so, the patterns would have important implications for the maintenance of Woodland-era potting traditions.

Ceramic Seriation

Holley (1989) and Pauketat (1998b) were able to demonstrate diachronic changes in lip shape and rim angle for Mississippian jars that can be used as reliable comparative metrics for relative dating. These methods can be used to determine during which Cahokia ceramic subphase people lived at Audrey. Using boxplots, I compare Audrey site 2016 jar-rim metrics to those from late Lohmann- and Stirling-phase contexts in Cahokia's Tract 15A excavations (Pauketat 1998b). Boxplots, often referred to as box-and-whisker plots, are useful for comparing the spread of values between different datasets. The box represents the middle 50 percent of the data, the whiskers extending from the box show the range, and outliers are represented by asterisks. When the box is notched, the center marks the median, and the notched portion displays the 95 percent confidence interval for the median. If the notches on two boxplots overlap, the medians for those two datasets are significantly similar. If they do not overlap, the opposite is true and the medians for the two datasets are significantly different at the 95 percent confidence interval. I then compare the results to AMS dates from recently excavated features and radiocarbon dates from various studies of CAA excavated features. Based on Delaney-Rivera's (2000, 2004) assessment of the

Table 5.2. Surface treatments of sherds

	Delaney-Rivera Wt(g)	Friberg Wt(g)	Total	%Total
Brushed/Combed/Scraped	33.4	–	33.4	0.12
Burnished	235.5	–	235.5	0.83
Cord-Impressed	85.2	–	85.2	0.3
Cordmarked	2,100.5	616.66	2,717.16	9.53
Dark-Slipped	809.2	1,906.9	2,716.1	9.53
Fabric-Impressed	14.3	–	14.3	0.05
Plain	6,474.6	8,226.31	14,700.91	51.56
Red-Slipped	711.4	7,296.52	8,007.92	28.09
TOTAL	10,464.1	18,046.39	28,510.49	100

Source: Delaney-Rivera (2000); Friberg (2020).

Note: – = Not present.

Audrey site and my own visual analysis, I expect the jar rims to indicate an early Stirling–phase date (AD 1100–1150).

LP Index

Mississippian jar lips tend to become longer (protrude further) respective to their thickness over time (Holley 1989; Pauketat 1998b). If Audrey potters were producing jars during Cahokia's early Stirling phase, as is suspected, the shape of Audrey jar lips should have a greater statistical similarity to early Stirling (S1)–Cahokia jars than those from earlier or later subphases. LP indexes will be compared using boxplots of the 2016 shell-tempered jar rims and late Lohmann-, early and late Stirling–phase assemblages from Cahokia Tract 15A (Pauketat 1998b). Figure 5.1 shows that Audrey's LP indexes overlap significantly with Cahokia's early-Stirling LP indices in addition to having some overlap with Cahokia-late Lohmann–phase LP indices. There is no significant overlap between Audrey and late Stirling LPs. These data show that Audrey's jars are statistically similar in lip shape to Cahokia's jars, and also supports the estimation that the site dates to the early Stirling phase.

Rim Angle (RA)

The angle of Mississippian jar rims becomes flatter over time, with the resulting RA value declining from the Lohmann to the Stirling phase (Holley 1989; Pauketat 1998b). Given the previously described similarities, we would expect the angle of the rims on Audrey's jars to be statistically similar to

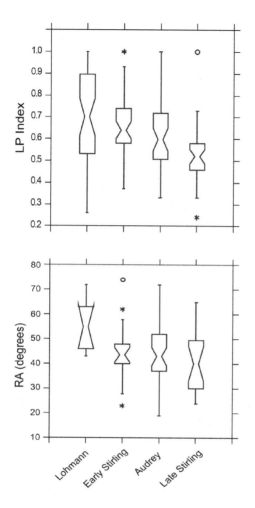

Figure 5.1. Boxplot comparing LP indexes (*top*) and Rim Angles (*bottom*) for Audrey and Lohmann, early and late Stirling–phase jars from Cahokia Tract 15A.

Cahokia's early Stirling–phase jars. Figure 5.1 shows a boxplot of the RAs for jars from Audrey (using the 2016 analysis) and those from Cahokia's Tract 15A late Lohmann, early and late Stirling. Audrey's rim angles, as with the LP indices, overlap significantly with Cahokia's early Stirling phase and to a lesser extent with late Stirling jar rims. However, there is a much broader range of rim angles at Audrey than is represented by the subphases of the Cahokia Tract 15A collection.

Dating the Audrey Site Occupations

The pottery collected during the 2016 excavations at the Audrey site is statistically similar to early Stirling–phase pottery at Cahokia in terms of lip shape and rim angle. These data, in conjunction with AMS dates from the Mississippian features at Audrey, should confirm an early Stirling–phase Mississippian occupation of the site. Four samples for AMS dating were pulled from processed flotation samples. One maize kernel each from Feature 23 zones B and C, and one maize kernel from Feature 5 zone B were submitted for AMS dating to confirm the early Stirling–phase (AD 1100–1150) date and to see whether or not the Feature 5 area of the site dates earlier than the Feature 23 area. An additional sample (a hickory nut fragment) from Feature 28 was submitted for AMS dating. Feature 28 is a storage pit feature into which Feature 5's house basin intrudes; Feature 28's pottery was highly fragmented, but cordmarked and grit-tempered, thus presumably dating to the late Late Woodland–Jersey Bluff phase. It should be noted that the AMS sample (nutshell) from Feature 28 was taken because no maize was recovered from the feature. These samples were sent to the UC Irvine Keck Lab where they were processed for AMS dating (Table 5.3).

In addition to the AMS dates run for this project, previous researchers submitted samples for radiocarbon dates from the 1980s CAA excavations at the Audrey site (see Table 5.3). Studenmund (2000) published three dates from the Audrey site in her chapter on Late Woodland occupations of the LIRV. Her samples were pulled from White Hall–phase features and dated within the expected range, but the samples included unidentified wood, and a combination of wood and nutshell; wood is problematic for dating because of the old-wood problem (long-term use and reuse) and the mixing of stratigraphic contexts. Goldstein (1982: 662) published a date from the beam of a burned Mississippian structure in Block 6 of Cook's excavations; this date was much earlier than expected considering the Stirling-phase pottery present in the feature, likely due to the dating of old wood, and will not be used in the current analysis. The remaining four samples were submitted by Delaney-Rivera for her dissertation work and published in a 2004 journal article. The samples, one of which was dated using AMS (ISGS-A-0029) and the other three using conventional radiocarbon methods, are of unknown material. One of the samples from a mixed context (ISGS-4192) came back with a date 300 years later than expected; this is likely an error and as such this date will not be used in the current analysis.

Although these samples were dated using different methods, if we exclude the two most problematic dates, the remaining dates can be used in conjunction with dates from recent excavations to create a sequence of occupation at the Audrey site. Using OxCal v4.3.2, I calibrated the dates from both excavations to reveal expected, yet significant, patterns (Figure 5.2).

Table 5.3. AMS and radiocarbon dates from the Audrey site

Sample	Feature	14C (0/00)	13C (per mil)	14C age (years BP)	Ceramic Component	Sample Material
ISGS-1,771[a]	F601	–	25.8	1,570 ± 70	White Hall	Unidentified wood
ISGS-1,682[a]	F535	–	25.7	1,420 ± 70	White Hall	65% wood, 35% nutshell
ISGS-1,683[a]	F416	–	-25.8	1,220 ± 70	White Hall	85% wood, 15% nutshell
UCSB- 20,0815[b]	F28 Zone A	-130.4 ± 2.0	–	1,120 ± 20	Jersey Bluff	Hickory nut
ISGS-881[c]	Block 6 Structure	–	–	1,090 ± 70	Early Stirling	Charcoal, house beam
ISGS-A-0029[d]	F310	–	–	1,055 ± 50	Bluff phase	–
ISGS-4,188[d]	F104	–	–	950 ± 70	Mixed	–
UCSB-200813[b]	F23 Zone C	-105.7 ± 2.1	–	900 ± 20	Early Stirling	Maize
UCSB-20,0812[b]	F23 Zone B	-105.6 ± 2.0	–	895 ± 20	Early Stirling	Maize
UCSB-20,0814[b]	F5 Zone B	-105.3 ± 2.0	–	895 ± 20	Early Stirling	Maize
ISGS-4,189[d]	F304	–	–	840 ± 70	Early Stirling	–
ISGS-4,192[d]	F503	–	–	620 ± 70	Mixed	–

Sources: a. Studenmund (2000); b. Friberg (2018b); c. Goldstein (1982): 662; d. Delaney-Rivera (2004).
Notes: – = Not available.

First, the two Mississippian houses excavated in 2016 (Features 5 and 23) are precisely contemporaneous with a date range of cal. AD 1060–1210, and they fall, as expected, within the American Bottom Stirling-phase date range of AD 1100–1200. The range is broad but cannot be refined further due to "irregularities in the atmospheric calibration curve corresponding with the late twelfth and early thirteenth centuries" (Wilson et al. 2018: 12). However, these dates in combination with the ceramic seriation confirm that the primary Mississippian occupation of the Audrey site is contemporary with the early Stirling phase at Cahokia. Perhaps more notable, the hickory nut sample from Feature 28 (directly underneath Feature 5) dates from cal. AD 890–990, supporting the assertion that it is a Jersey Bluff–phase feature. Furthermore, this Jersey Bluff–phase date does not overlap with the Mississippian period dates for the site at 95 percent confidence, confirming that there is no temporal overlap between Woodland and Mississippian occupations of the Audrey site. This point is significant as it differs from Delaney-Rivera's assessment that the Audrey site had mixed Woodland-Mississippian contexts; it is important to note that her analysis is based on Cook's excavations which seem to have produced inconsistent and unreliable data. If the Jersey Bluff inhabitants of the Audrey site were interacting with Mississippians, we would expect to see some evidence, such as hybridized material culture or evidence for maize cultivation in Late Woodland features. However, my analysis of Audrey's ceramic assemblage found no hybrid pastes or ceramic styles to suggest a temporal overlap. Finally, the flotation sample from Feature 28 did not contain any maize (Bardolph, personal communication 2017).

Regarding Studenmund's samples, the earlier two contexts date to the White Hall phase (cal. AD 400–750), and the later date has a range of cal. AD 660–990. This range is likely due to the mixing of material for acquiring an "averaged" feature date; ISGS-1683 was a combination of 85 percent wood and 15 percent nutshell. In this case, in addition to the old-wood problem, combining materials for dating introduces the possibility of combining material from two different temporal contexts (in this case the White Hall phase and Jersey Bluff phase). This method is no longer practiced. Overall, the sequence of AMS and radiocarbon dates, in conjunction with ceramic data from the Audrey site, suggests three separate and nonoverlapping occupations of the site during the Late Woodland–White Hall phase, late Late Woodland–Jersey Bluff phase, and the early Stirling–Mississippian phase.

OxCal v4.3.2 Bronk Ramsey (2017); r:5 IntCal13 atmospheric curve (Reimer et al 2013)

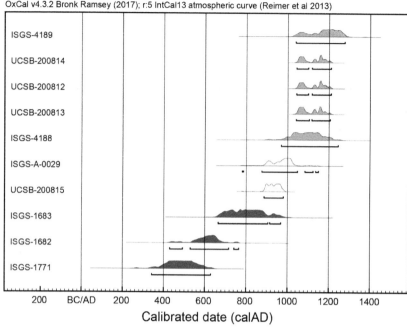

Figure 5.2. AMS and radiocarbon dates from the Audrey site. The curves represent the entire probability distributions for each date; the black bars underneath indicate the range at 95% confidence.

Ceramic Phase

▨ Early Stirling

☐ Jersey Bluff

■ White Hall

Vessels

Jars

A total of 88 percent of the 82 vessels recovered from 2016 excavations at the Audrey site are jars (n=72) (Table 5.4; see Friberg 2018b: Table 5.5 for more detail). The shell-tempered Stirling-phase jars from the Audrey site have plain, burnished, red-slipped, and/or incised surfaces. Many of the jars have the distinct Stirling-phase angular shoulders, which suggests the rim was produced separately from the base and attached before drying, as appears to have been the practice at Cahokia (Pauketat 1998b: 172). The jars are discussed by type below. Emerson has cautioned against using Cahokian typologies for Mississippian sites outside the American Bottom, so as not to overlook locally derived interpretations. However, as will become apparent later, Audrey's pottery is quite stylistically similar to Cahokian pottery, and, given the LIRV's proximity to the American Bottom, I have chosen to conservatively use the Cahokian types Powell Plain and Ramey Incised where applicable.

Sand-Tempered Plain

One sand-tempered jar was identified. This vessel has an extruded and folded lip with decorative impressions and may represent minor admixture from the previous White Hall–phase occupation of the site.

Shell-Tempered Plain Jars

Just over half of the jars are shell-tempered with plain surfaces. The majority of these have rolled lips, half of which have a distinctively flattened shape, likely from resting upside-down during the production process. Griffin (1949: 54) referred to vessels of this type at Cahokia as St. Clair Plain, but there is too much stylistic variability among the plain, shell-tempered jars from the 2016 collection to assign them to such a local American Bottom category. For example, the remaining eight plain jars have extruded, applied, or folded lips, which are not typical of Stirling-phase jars at Cahokia (Figure 5.3).

Handles

The remaining jars are represented by four loop handles. All four handles are attached to plain-surfaced, shell-tempered jar rims, each of which would have had a set of two loop handles. As these rims are modified for the attachment of handles, it is difficult to say for certain what the angle and shape of the rims were, although the lips appear to be rolled (see Figure 5.3). The presence of these handles is worth noting as, although rare, the bifurcated loop handle is a horizon marker of Lohmann- and early Stirling–phase St. Clair Plain pottery at Cahokia (Griffin 1949: 54; Holley 1989: 47; Pauketat 1998b: 172).

Slipped and Burnished Shell-Tempered Jars

Forty percent of the jars are shell-tempered slipped and burnished. Twenty-three of these have sharp-angled shoulders and rolled lips, eight of which are also flattened, like many of the plain shell-tempered jars; these burnished jars are very similar to what Griffin (1949: 50) defined as Powell Plain jars from Cahokia's Stirling phase. Thirteen have red-slipped and burnished exteriors, with the slipping usually extending to the interior of the vessel lip. The remaining 10 Powell Plain-like jars are dark-slipped, which is often

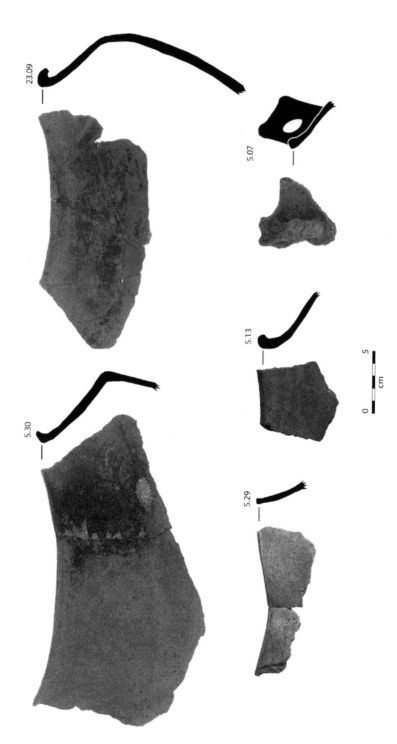

Figure 5.3. Select plain jars from the 2016 excavations at the Audrey site.

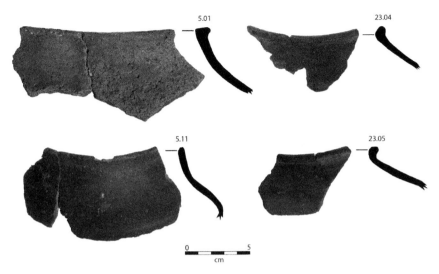

Figure 5.4. Select slipped/burnished and red-slipped jars from the 2016 excavations at the Audrey site.

accomplished by firing red-slipped vessels in a low oxygen environment. In fact, of the three dark-slipped jars that have slipped lips, one's lip (vessel 23.04) is red-slipped—not because of pigment, but instead as a result of an oxidized firing environment where the smoke did not reach the lip (Figure 5.4). These characteristics indicate strong stylistic similarities with Cahokia and the American Bottom, where red-slipped jar lips were commonplace (Griffin 1949: 54; Holley 1989; Wilson 2018).

A subset of five slipped and burnished jars have attributes that are more commonly found in Lohmann-phase jars at Cahokia. For example, some of the vessels have flattened (or extruded) or unmodified rather than rolled lips, and steeply angled, slightly flared rims; this is in contrast to the flatter rims and sharp-angled shoulders characteristic of the Stirling phase (see Figure 5.4, vessels 5.01, 5.11). The presence of these jars in the assemblage suggests that the Mississippian occupation at Audrey dated very early in the Stirling phase.

Ramey Incised

Ramey Incised jars are similar to Powell Plain jars, except their rims are incised with iconographic symbols related to Mississippian cosmographic imagery. Recent research demonstrates that Ramey Incised jars were occasionally used in the preparation of the Black Drink, a ritual decoction

Table 5.4. Ceramic vessels from 2016 excavations at the Audrey site

Feature	Jars			Ramey Incised Jars		Bowls		Beakers	Bottles	Total	Comments
	pl	brs	rs	brs	rs	pl	brs/rs				
F5	24	5	12	–	3	2	3	–	1	50	Fineware bowl
F9	–	1	1	–	–	1	–	–	–	3	Duck head effigy bowl
F16	–	–	–	–	–	–	–	1	–	1	Bright red slip
F17	–	–	–	–	1	–	–	–	–	1	Oversized Ramey
F23	12	5	4	2	–	2	–	–	–	25	– –
House Block	1	1	–	–	–	–	–	–	–	2	– –
Total	37	12	17	2	4	5	3	1	1	82	– –

Source: Compiled by author.
Notes: brs = burnished; pl = plain; rs = red-slipped; – = Not present.

made from the leaves of the yaupon holly (Miller 2015). The sharp-angled shoulders of these jars would have made their decoration highly visible to the individual using and looking down on the pot. The incised designs may have also been visible to others as well, especially on larger examples of these jars. There are six Ramey Incised jars, representing 8.5 percent of the shell-tempered jars in the 2016 Audrey site ceramic assemblage (Figure 5.5; Figure 5.6).

The Ramey pots from Audrey are mostly medium-sized, with the exception of one oversized vessel with an interior orifice diameter of 45 cm. Vessel 17.1 was recovered from the refuse inside a storage pit (Feature 17), at its base, and is represented by a quarter of the vessel's rim and some of the body below the shoulder (Figure 5.6). The vessel body is thin (averaging 5 mm in thickness) and finely made, likely by pressing tempered clay into a mold. The rim is thicker and was made separately using a coiling technique. Before drying, the broad rim was attached to the molded base and, when leather-hard, the rim was incised with a continuous scroll motif of eight nested lines, repeated four times around the vessel. The entire exterior was then slipped, burnished, and fired in an oxygenated environment, giving it a red color (although there are some reduced, blackened areas). There is sooting on the shoulder and rim of 17.1 which suggests that this oversized Ramey Incised jar was used for cooking. There is only one other Ramey vessel (and a similar Powell Plain jar) of this size known to date, found by Gregory

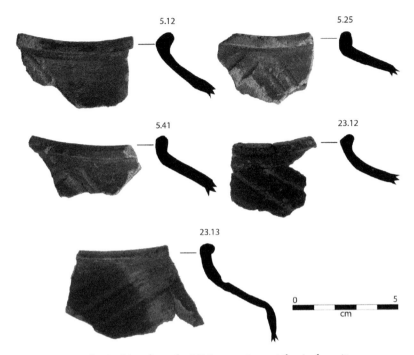

Figure 5.5. Ramey Incised jars from the 2016 excavations at the Audrey site.

Perino in the Ramey Field east of Monks Mound in the 1940s–1950s and currently on display at the Cahokia Mounds Museum (Iseminger 2016, Personal Communication). The oversized Ramey Incised and Powell Plain jars from Cahokia have molded bases with coiled rims and orifice diameters of 46 cm; even the vessel thicknesses and rim widths are comparable to the Audrey vessel. What's more, Cahokia's oversized Ramey jar features the same design as the Audrey example: a continuous scroll motif with eight nested lines. The similarities between these two rare vessels are intriguing, especially when considering interactions between LIRV and American Bottom groups. For example, it is possible that Audrey's oversized Ramey jar was actually produced at Cahokia; the exchange of such a vessel would have been deeply symbolic, particularly if these large jars were used in Cahokia-style feasting rituals. A closer analysis and further testing (that is, chemical sourcing and residue analysis) are necessary to draw definitive conclusions.

As for the remaining Ramey Incised jars, Vessels 5.12, 5.25, and 5.41 are also red-slipped, with red-slipped lips, while Vessels 23.12 and 23.13 are dark-slipped (see Figure 5.5). Most of the Ramey Incised rims are highly fragmented, but chevron designs can be identified on vessels 5.12, 5.41, and

Figure 5.6. Vessel 17.1, oversized Ramey Incised jar.

23.13. All Ramey Incised jars are tempered with shell, although two have a finer shell paste.

Jar Orifice Diameter

Regarding orifice diameter of shell-tempered jars at Audrey, there seems to be a range of vessel sizes from 8 to 49 cm in diameter. With the exception of an oversized Ramey jar and three other large jars, most of the vessels fall in the medium-sized range, between 16 and 31 cm.

As mentioned below, there seems to be a correlation between orifice diameter and surface finish, where plain jars are smaller on average than slipped and burnished jars. This difference in size would suggest that slipped and burnished jars served different purposes than plain jars. For example, plain jars were used more frequently for cooking, as 34 percent of them have sooted exteriors, while only 18 percent of burnished jars exhibit sooting. It is unusual that burnished vessels would be used for cooking since exposure to heat would alter the original color achieved in firing (Wilson 2018: 129). Perhaps the large burnished jars at Cahokia were used for serving large groups and occasionally preparing food for public events (as may have been the case with vessel 17.1, the oversized Ramey Incised jar).

Bowls

Eight bowls were identified in the ceramic assemblage (Figure 5.7). Five of these vessels were recovered from Feature 5, two of which were finely made. Vessel 5.18 is tempered with fine shell and limestone, and dark-slipped and burnished on the interior and exterior; this finely made bowl also appears to have unfired yellow clay on the interior, possibly from being deposited on top of the yellow clay floor of Feature 5. Vessel 5.51 is tempered with fine shell and grog, and has red slipping on the interior and exterior. Two bowls were recovered from Feature 23, one of which (Vessel 23.15) features a rim tab. Finally, a duck head effigy bowl (Vessel 9.4) was recovered from Feature 9.

Delaney-Rivera (2000) identified 13 shell-tempered bowls in her assemblage, with a mixture of plain and slipped-surface treatments. At least one

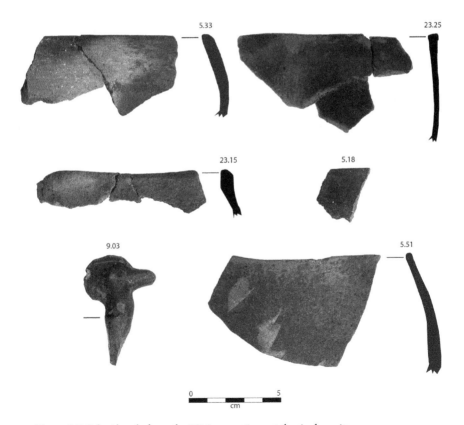

Figure 5.7. Select bowls from the 2016 excavations at the Audrey site.

of these bowls had a rim tab; Delaney-Rivera (2000: 209–211) identified various fragmented lip lugs and rim tabs. She also identified two bird head effigies that would have been attached to bowl rims (Delaney-Rivera 2000: 211). Lip tabs or lugs and bird effigy bowl attachments are also found in the Greater Cahokia area (Esarey and Pauketat 1992: 91; Holley 1989: 134–135; Pauketat 1998b: 195; Wilson 2018: 133). The presence of bowls in Audrey's assemblage is important because these serving vessels represent a departure from Woodland-era assemblages north of the American Bottom, where they are scarce or absent (Esarey 2000; Farnsworth et al. 1991; Green and Nolan 2000); Audrey's bowls are likely the result of contact with Cahokian groups (Wilson et al. 2017).

Bottles

Fragments of one bottle were discovered in the excavation of Feature 5 (small Mississippian house). Although the neck and lip of the bottle are not intact, the component sherds reveal the curvature of the bottle's shoulder and the constriction of the neck (Figure 5.8). The bottle was tempered with fine shell, dark-slipped and burnished on the exterior, and plain on the interior. Delaney-Rivera (2000) counted four Cahokia-style bottles (including water bottles and hooded water bottles) in her analysis of Audrey material from the Cook CAA excavations and Denny Vetter's private collection, although it is unclear whether Delaney-Rivera identifies the bottles as fineware. The presence of even a few hooded and long-neck water bottles at Audrey is significant as these vessel classes are relatively rare in the American Bottom (Wilson 1999) and even scarcer in northern hinterland assemblages (Wilson et al. 2017).

Beakers

Beakers are thin-walled, mug-like vessels classified as fineware in American Bottom assemblages. In addition to being finely made, a recent chemical analysis shows that Cahokian beakers were occasionally used for the ritual serving of the Black Drink (Crown et al. 2012). One fragment of a Stirling-phase beaker was recovered from Feature 16 (a storage pit feature). This thin-walled vessel was tempered with crushed shell and slipped a bright red (see Figure 5.8). The lip is not present on the sherd, making its orientation and an estimation of orifice diameter impossible. Additionally, the small sherd does not appear to have engraved lines, the presence of which is a common feature of Stirling-phase, Cahokian fineware beakers. Delaney-Rivera counted four beakers in her analysis, one of which was grog-tempered,

5.06   16.01

0   5
cm

Figure 5.8. Bottle and beaker from the 2016 excavations at the Audrey site.

slipped, and burnished with engraved lines; it represents a likely example of Cahokia fineware (Wilson 1999; see also Wilson et al. 2017: 114).

Ceramic Disks

Two perforated ceramic disks (weighing 17.89 g) were recovered from the 2016 excavations, one from Feature 17, and the other from Feature 9. Both disks appear to be formed from recycled pottery sherds. Although the function of ceramic disks is often debated, the perforations in these examples from Audrey suggests that they were used as spindle whorls to spin fibers for textile production (Pauketat 1998b: 227).

Exotic Vessels

The current analysis has not identified any exotic pottery from the Mississippian occupation at Audrey, although, as Stoltman (2001) demonstrates, it is possible some of the finely made vessels from Audrey were produced at Cahokia. Stoltman's petrographic analysis of pottery from the Audrey site (among other hinterland sites) demonstrates the presence of nonlocally produced pottery and suggests that the pastes of certain vessels are similar to Cahokian pastes, and are thus examples of pots imported to the Illinois Valley from the American Bottom (Stoltman 2001; see also Delaney-Rivera 2000). For example, locally made vessels have pastes with a high amount of sand in the clay and more clay than temper, while the pastes of the presumed American Bottom pots have less sand in the clay and a high percentage of temper relative to clay (Delaney-Rivera 2000: 214).

In addition to these possible Cahokian imports, Delaney identifies examples of exotic Woodland-period pottery. One of these is a Late Woodland,

Maples Mills (Mossville-phase) jar from the Spoon River area of the CIRV. A Maples Mills jar outside of its region of origin is significant, considering that leading up to the Mississippian period in the CIRV, there is little evidence for interactions between groups within the Illinois River Valley (Green and Nolan 2000: 369). Delaney-Rivera (2000: 221) suggests the Maples Mills, Mossville-phase jar at Audrey could represent a late Lohmann interaction with CIRV groups. The vessel was recovered from plow-zone contexts above an excavation block containing a Mississippian wall-trench structure, but without a specific provenience, it is impossible to say when exactly this interregional interaction took place. Regardless, this Maples Mills jar at Audrey is an indication of either Late Woodland- or early Mississippian–period interaction between LIRV and CIRV groups.

Previous excavations at Audrey also uncovered a Holly Fine Engraved vessel, found near a Mississippian wall-trench structure. While these stylistically Caddoan vessels may have been emulated in Cahokian fineware, the vessel's identification as Caddoan was confirmed by Timothy Perttula, an expert in the field (Delaney-Rivera 2000: 225). Furthermore, an instrumental neutron activation analysis (INAA) of the vessel from Audrey indicates that it was produced (as would be expected) in northeastern Texas and imported to the LIRV from the Caddoan region (Delaney-Rivera 2000: 225; Perttula 2002: 97). The presence of this exotic vessel suggests inhabitants of the Audrey site had access to extraregional exchange networks involving Caddoan groups; it is a possibility that interaction or affiliation with Cahokia helped to broker these interactions.

Comparative Analysis

To assess the significance of the analysis presented above, it is important to evaluate Audrey's ceramic assemblage[2] within a broader regional context. Comparative analyses of pottery production (considering temper and surface finish) and pottery consumption (discussing vessel class, orifice diameter, and Ramey Incised jars) will allow me to address the degree to which Cahokian practices were adopted and Woodland-era traditions were maintained at the Audrey site. In the production of well-emulated Mississippian pottery, northern hinterland potters in the CIRV and ARV often used hybrid pastes, surface and lip treatments, and other techniques consistent with Woodland potting practices (Bardolph 2014: 76; Delaney-Rivera 2000: 205–208, 2004; Emerson 1991b: 177; Millhouse 2012: 140; Richards 1992: 297; Wilson 2015a; Wilson et al. 2017; Zych 2013: 27). Furthermore, while Greater

Cahokia groups structured their foodways based on complex hierarchical social organization—as represented by a suite of specialized utilitarian, serving, and fineware vessels—hinterland groups produced mainly jars, indicating a less complex organization of foodways (Wilson et al. 2017). Given the Audrey site's proximity to Cahokia, and likely frequent interactions with Greater Cahokia groups, it is expected that Audrey's ceramic attributes and practices of pottery production and consumption would be more similar to sites in the American Bottom than to sites in the northern hinterland, where Woodland-Mississippian ceramic hybridity has been observed. Finally, a discussion of nonlocal pottery in these regions sheds light on interregional interactions in the Mississippian world.

Mississippian Pottery Production

If Audrey inhabitants were engaging in regular interactions with Greater Cahokia groups, we would expect their methods of pottery production to be more similar to those used at Cahokia and the American Bottom than those in northern hinterland regions, where the maintenance of Woodland-era potting traditions has been documented (Wilson et al. 2017). Pottery production is explored quantitatively through an intersite comparison of temper and surface finish, and qualitatively through a discussion of vessel form.

Temper

The maintenance of Woodland-era traditions has been observed at northern hinterland Mississippian sites, including the continued use of grit and hybrid pottery tempers (Bardolph 2014; Wilson et al. 2017; Wilson and VanDerwarker 2015). We would expect groups with closer ties to Cahokia to incorporate more shell and less grit in their pastes, resulting in a higher percentage of shell-tempered pottery compared with more Woodland-influenced assemblages. Intersite comparisons of pottery temper are complicated for multiple reasons. First, variable methods of analysis produce discordant datasets; where one analyst may have published counts and weights for all pottery sherds by temper, others only published weights or (perhaps dealing with unscreened collections) analyzed only rim sherds. Second, the American Bottom tradition of limestone tempering of bowls and other special-purpose vessels (rare north of the Greater Cahokia area) skews those datasets when all vessels are considered. For these reasons, the current comparison uses data from jar rims recovered from early Mississippian features: (1) at Cahokia Tract 15A (Pauketat 1998b) and the Lohmann site (Esarey and

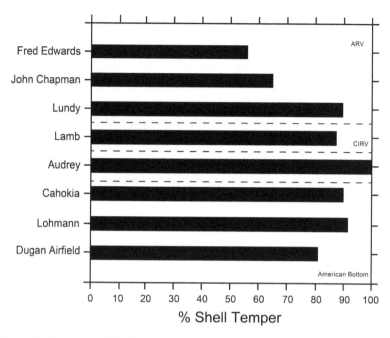

Figure 5.9. Percentage of shell-tempered sherds within each site's ceramic assemblage, with dashed lines separating regions.

Pauketat 1992) in the American Bottom; (2) at the Dugan Airfield site in the uplands (Wilson 2018); (3) at the Audrey site 2016 excavations; (4) at the Lamb site in the CIRV (Wilson 2015a); and (5) at the Lundy site (Emerson et al. 2007), the John Chapman site (Millhouse 2012), and the Fred Edwards sites in the ARV (Finney 1993). The Eileen Cunningham site in the LIRV is excluded due to its small sample size.

The chart in Figure 5.9 shows the percentages of shell tempering within each site's jar assemblage. One hundred percent of jars from Audrey's Mississippian features were shell-tempered, more than at any other site. The pattern is similar for Eileen Cunningham's Mississippian jars, with the exception of one jar with a mixed chert and shell-tempered paste; Fishel (2018: 53) suggests the chert is a natural clay inclusion and not intentionally added as temper. Potters in the Greater Cahokia area produced mostly shell-tempered jars, although some jars were tempered with limestone, grog, or mixed pastes. The Lamb site in the CIRV and the Lundy site in the ARV are both comparable to Greater Cahokia jar assemblages in terms of their use of shell temper; other jars were tempered with grit or a mixture of grit and shell. However, both the John Chapman and Fred Edwards sites in the ARV have relatively low percentages of shell-tempered jars compared with regions to its south. Twenty-seven percent of jars from John Chapman were tempered with a mixture of grit and shell, representing a Woodland-Mississippian hybrid temper, whereas only 2 percent of jars from Fred Edwards are considered hybrid vessels (Finney 1993). Forty-two percent of jars from the Mississippian occupation of the Fred Edwards site are local and exotic Woodland-style, grit-tempered jars. In terms of temper of jars, Audrey's potters seem to have been more influenced by Cahokian potting practices than their northern neighbors, who continued to incorporate a degree of Woodland-era tradition in their pottery production.

Surface Treatment

An examination of surface treatment in a Mississippian ceramic assemblage can provide information regarding the degree of Woodland influence that still existed in these early Stirling–phase communities. Cordmarking and cord impression were common surface treatments used during the Late Woodland period in the regions discussed here (Esarey 2000; Green and Nolan 2000; Studenmund 2000). In the Lohmann-phase American Bottom, however, potters traded in their cord-wrapped paddles for smooth ones and often slipped and burnished the surfaces of their pots. The presence of cord-marked pottery at Mississippian sites indicates a continuity of Woodland potting traditions. If potters from the Audrey site were more influenced by Woodland traditions than Mississippian potting practices, we would expect the percentage of cordmarked pottery to be higher than in the American Bottom and similar to sites in the northern hinterland. If Audrey potters were more influenced by Mississippian potting practices, we would expect the opposite to be true and for the percentage of cordmarked pottery at Audrey to be similar to American Bottom ceramic assemblages and lower than northern hinterland assemblages. As with temper, this comparison is complicated, but as cordmarking can be found on various types of vessels, I chose to compare percentages of all vessels with cordmarked exteriors.

To investigate Woodland influence in pottery production, I graphed the percentage of cordmarked vessels from early Mississippian occupations at, as listed above, Cahokia Tract 15A (Pauketat 1998b), Dugan Airfield (Wilson 2018), Lohmann (Esarey and Pauketat 1992), Audrey, Lamb (Wilson 2015a), John Chapman (Millhouse 2012), Lundy (Emerson et al. 2007), and Fred Edwards (Finney 1993). Data from the Eileen Cunningham site were excluded due to its small sample size. Figure 5.10 shows low percentages of

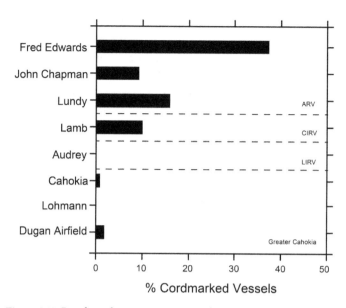

Figure 5.10. Bar chart showing percentage of cordmarked vessels by region.

cordmarked vessels in the American Bottom, and higher percentages in the northern hinterland regions. Audrey's ceramic assemblage included zero cordmarked *rim* sherds, which shows a similar pattern to the fewer than 2 percent of cordmarked vessels encountered in the Greater Cahokia area. It should be noted, however, that a number of fragmented cordmarked *body* sherds were recovered from the 2016 excavations at Audrey; 65 percent of these were recovered from Feature 5, a small Mississippian house built on top of, and intruding into, a Jersey Bluff–phase (late Late Woodland) pit feature (Feature 28). The presence of cordmarked sherds in the Mississippian features at Audrey is likely due to admixture in the Mississippian feature fill. As corroborated by AMS dates discussed above, these eroded cordmarked sherds mostly date to a period hundreds of years before the Mississippian occupation of the site. In fact, very few local late Late Woodland, Jersey Bluff–phase sherds were found at Audrey, as identified by Delaney-Rivera in her analysis of the CAA collection; what's more, the one dated Jersey Bluff feature (Feature 28) is not contemporaneous with the Stirling-phase Mississippian occupation of the site.

All sites north of the LIRV seem to have more Woodland influence than Audrey, as demonstrated in the higher percentages of cordmarked vessels in the CIRV and ARV; indeed, both John Chapman and Lundy have several

Woodland-Mississippian hybrid vessels, although most of the cordmarked pots from Lamb represent Woodland vessels from interactions with local Bauer Branch groups (Wilson 2015a). The Fred Edwards site in southern Wisconsin has the highest percentage of cordmarked and cord-impressed vessels, which suggests that the site's inhabitants may not have had regular interactions with American Bottom groups, but they seem to have had connections with multiple Woodland groups in adjacent regions.

Vessel Form

In terms of pottery attributes, the lack of grit/hybrid tempers or cordmarking in Audrey's ceramic assemblage shows that it is quite similar to Greater Cahokia Mississippian sites at this basic level. In addition to choosing similar tempers and surface treatments, transitional Mississippian potters also made decisions regarding vessel form. The shape of a Mississippian globular jar may seem easy to emulate, but similarities in the shape of the rim and lip can only come with direct influence on pottery techniques. For example, Mississippian potters in the LIRV (Delaney-Rivera 2000: 139; Schild and Moss Cemeteries) and ARV (Emerson 1991b: 173) occasionally notched the lips of their otherwise Cahokia-style jars, a practice that seems to have been carried over from local Woodland potting traditions (Esarey 2000; Studenmund 2000). The same pattern is not found at Audrey. In fact, as demonstrated above, the Audrey site potters produced jars with lips and rims stylistically similar to those produced by contemporary Cahokia potters.

Pottery Consumption and Practice

At the same time they were adopting Cahokian practices, however, Audrey inhabitants were renegotiating social identities through alterations to ingrained daily practices, such as food processing and storage, and the social interactions determined by community organization. Such organizational changes would have meant a shift away from identities structured by communally oriented, Woodland-era traditions and toward those negotiated through a more privatized, hierarchically organized Cahokian way of life. For this reason, it is also important to evaluate how pottery was consumed. Ceramic vessels were used in the processing, cooking, and serving of food, which are domestic practices that were structured by the types of social interactions Woodland and Cahokian individuals enacted on a daily basis (Bardolph 2014: 84). Woodland groups were communally oriented, and thus processed and stored food in public, sharing spaces with little fanfare

(Bardolph 2014; Wilson and VanDerwarker 2015) whereas Cahokians, negotiating hierarchical social relations, privatized their domestic activities (Kelly 1990) and introduced a level of hierarchy into their foodways (Wilson et al. 2017).

Interactions with American Bottom groups may have influenced the accurate emulation of the vessel attributes and production techniques of Mississippian-period, Cahokia-style pottery, but did Audrey inhabitants also adopt the hierarchical social organization of their neighbors to the south? Furthermore, to what degree did Audrey inhabitants incorporate the ceremonial use of pottery? While a functional analysis of pottery vessels was not conducted due to high fragmentation of the collection, we can evaluate how pottery was used at Audrey by comparing the types of vessels produced, the sizes of jars in the assemblage, and variation in the production and use of Ramey Incised jars in the American Bottom and its northern hinterland.

Vessel Classes

Mississippians in the American Bottom organized their foodways to accommodate an emerging hierarchical social organization. This meant that in addition to jars, Greater Cahokia potters also produced fineware vessels and serving vessels such as bowls, plates, bottles, and beakers. Wilson et al. (2017) demonstrate a scarcity of servingware in northern hinterland settlements, suggesting a continuity of Woodland-era concepts of community-centered social organization. As for the LIRV, we tend to see less-localized ceramic styles. Indeed, the jars from the Audrey site ceramic assemblage are nearly indistinguishable from those of Cahokia; similarly, the jars that constitute the small vessel assemblage from the Eileen Cunningham site closely resemble Powell Plain and Ramey Incised jars from Cahokia (Fishel 2018: 53). Furthermore, although only three examples have been found at Audrey to date—a Caddoan Holly Fine Engraved bottle, a grog-tempered engraved beaker, and a grog/shell-tempered fineware bowl—the presence of fineware at the site sits in contrast to a lack of these specialty vessels at northern hinterland sites (Wilson et al. 2017). However, a minimum number of vessels (MNV) analysis of the Audrey ceramics reveals an overall scarcity of serving vessels. To see how this pattern compares to other Mississippian vessel assemblages, I calculated the Audrey's servingware ratio and combined these data with Wilson et al.'s (2017) recent analysis of pottery from Cahokia and the northern hinterland.

Figure 5.11 illustrates that, similar to early Mississippian sites in the CIRV and ARV, the Audrey site has a lower servingware ratio than is common for

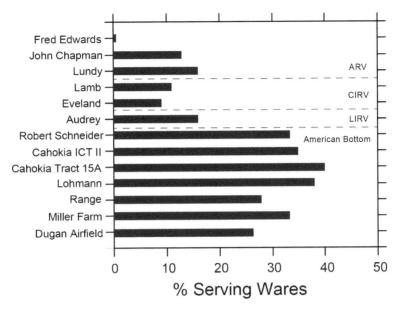

Figure 5.11. Bar chart of servingware percentages for American Bottom, LIRV, CIRV, and ARV.

American Bottom groups; all of the vessels recovered from the four Mississippian features at Eileen Cunningham were jars (Fishel 2018: 53). This pattern suggests that LIRV and hinterland Mississippians placed less of an emphasis on the ceremonialism of foodways than did their American Bottom counterparts. In addition to a low servingware percentage, the Audrey assemblage included only one pan and lacks any funnels or stumpware, utilitarian vessel types often found in early Stirling American Bottom assemblages (see Delaney-Rivera 2000). Funnels and stumpware seem to be part of the local, utilitarian American Bottom material culture and are rarely, if ever, found outside of the region. Thus, the scarcity of funnels or stumpware at Audrey is not surprising, but supports the idea that the residents of the Audrey site had their own local cooking technologies that did not involve these rare ceramic types.

Orifice Diameter

If foodways were organized in line with hierarchical social organization in the Greater Cahokia area, in addition to incorporating fineware and servingware vessels, specialized commensal events may have also accommodated large groups of people. In this case, we would expect American

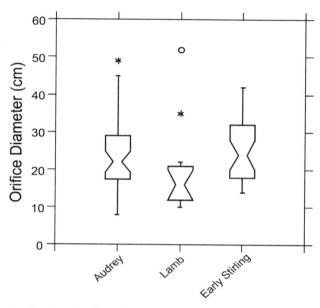

Figure 5.12. Boxplot of early Stirling–phase jar orifice diameters from Audrey, Lamb, and Cahokia Tract 15A.

Bottom vessels to be larger on average than vessels from LIRV and northern hinterland sites. I compare orifice diameters as a proxy for size of jars from Cahokia Tract 15A (Pauketat 1998b) and the Lohmann site (Esarey and Pauketat 1992) in the American Bottom, the Lamb site in the CIRV (Wilson 2015a), and the Lundy (Emerson et al. 2007) and John Chapman sites (Millhouse 2012) in the ARV, with orifice diameters of the jars from Audrey's 2016 excavations. As expected, Cahokia has the largest jars on average. Audrey's orifice diameters match more the patterns of larger jars at Cahokia and the American Bottom, while sites farther north, such as Lamb and John Chapman, tend to have smaller jars or a scarcity of larger vessels in general, such as at the Lundy site. Limited data on orifice diameter for the Eileen Cunningham site in the LIRV suggest a broad range of jar sizes, although the majority of jars exhibit orifice diameters of 18 cm or less (Fishel 2018: 51); however, with such a small sample size (n=13 shell-tempered jars), it is difficult to draw any meaningful conclusions from the assemblage at Eileen Cunningham.

Including available vessel data from Cahokia's Tract 15A (Pauketat 1998b) and the Lamb site (Wilson 2015a), a boxplot (Figure 5.12) shows the similarity between Audrey and Cahokian jar-orifice diameters, and that the assemblage from the Lamb site (CIRV) has significantly smaller jars. This pattern of large jars at Audrey could be associated with the preparation of food for larger groups of people, perhaps in a public context (although Audrey lacks the serving vessels to support this). Either way, the Lamb site jars have significantly smaller orifice diameters, setting them apart from those at Cahokia and Audrey. This disparity is unsurprising as the Lamb site has been demonstrated to be a settlement of local Woodland peoples who selectively adopted certain Cahokian practices while maintaining Woodland-era patterns of food preparation and storage (Bardolph 2014; Wilson 2015a; Wilson and VanDerwarker 2015); it is also possible that, since the Lamb site was a small farmstead and not a large village like Audrey, the small size of jars from the site is more representative of a small number of people preparing and consuming food. The fact that Audrey is more similar to Cahokia than to Lamb with regard to vessel size suggests Audrey inhabitants adopted Mississippian practices to a higher degree than local peoples to the north; this adoption may have been the result of Audrey's proximity to the American Bottom and more frequent interactions between Cahokians and LIRV inhabitants.

Ramey Incised Jar Consumption

The overall ceramic patterns suggest that Audrey inhabitants did not incorporate ceremonialism into their foodways to the same degree as Greater Cahokia Mississippians. I argue that the one large exception to this pattern is the oversized Ramey Incised jar from Feature 17 at Audrey. In addition to the emergence of sociopolitical hierarchy, another important facet of the Mississippian phenomenon was the spread of Cahokian religious ideology. Interactions between Mississippian groups had strong socioreligious implications (Brown and Kelly 2000; Conrad 1991; Emerson 1989; Emerson 1991a, 1997b; Emerson and Lewis 1991; Fowler et al. 1999; Hall 1991; Kelly 1991b; Knight et al. 2001; Pauketat 1997a, 2004; Wilson 2011). Certainly, a number of the practices adopted by hinterland groups had religious underpinnings. In addition to temple and mound construction and the curation of Cahokian religious paraphernalia, Mississippian peoples not only collected, but also locally produced Ramey Incised jars (Hall 1991: 21; Harn 1991: 142–143; Pauketat and Emerson 1991; Stoltman 1991: 115).

Ramey Incised pots are not classified as fineware and often served utilitarian purposes such as cooking (rather than serving). However, these jars, recovered from both mortuary and domestic contexts, are often finely made and incorporate incised motifs of political and religious significance. As with other Mississippian cosmographic objects, Ramey iconography was often organized in a quadripartitioned manner, directly referencing the composition and motion of the cosmos in addition to cosmological narratives and themes (Pauketat and Emerson 1991). These domestic cosmograms were sometimes used for ritual drink preparation (Miller 2015). Indeed, the oversized Ramey Incised jar recovered from the Audrey site—with an orifice diameter of 45 cm and a scroll design nearly identical to the only other vessel of its kind, from Cahokia—exhibits exterior sooting, which suggests it was used for direct cooking over a fire (Hally 1986: 275). This ceremonial use of Ramey Incised jars likely bundled cosmic relationships and understandings for Mississippians. With this is mind, and considering the large size of the Ramey jar from Feature 17, this pot stands out as a ceremonial vessel likely used for food preparation and serving of large groups at public events.

While *oversized* Ramey Incised jars have yet to be found at northern hinterland sites, hinterland regions seem to have placed a major emphasis on the production of these iconic pots. Wilson et al. (2017) compare vessel classes from American Bottom sites with those from the LIRV, CIRV, and ARV to show that hinterland sites have higher percentages of Ramey Incised jars in their vessel assemblages. Updating Wilson et al.'s (2017: Figure 4.8) graph with the current Audrey ceramic analysis, Figure 5.13 clearly shows higher percentages of Ramey Incised at CIRV and ARV sites, but that Audrey's percentage is more in line with American Bottom sites (with the exception of Tract 15A at Cahokia). The overall pattern suggests Audrey site potters seem to have placed less of an emphasis on the Ramey Incised pottery tradition than did their northern counterparts, although this pattern may not be consistent with farmstead sites in the LIRV.

Northern hinterland potters may have engaged in the consumption of Ramey Incised vessels to a higher degree than in the American Bottom, but researchers have observed stylistic differences between northern hinterland Ramey pots and those found in the Greater Cahokia area. Northern Ramey pastes were sometimes of mixed temper, the surfaces are often plain and sometimes cordmarked (rather than burnished), and the pots frequently featured handles and lip notching (Conrad 1991; Delaney-Rivera 2000: 130, 139; Emerson 1991a, 1991b: 173; Esarey 2000; Mollerud 2005). Differences in the production of these religiously charged vessels elicit questions regarding the incorporation of Cahokian religious practices within local contexts. If Cahokians did use Ramey Incised jars as a type of cosmogram, as Pauketat and Emerson (1991) have suggested (see also Alt and Pauketat 2007), an interregional analysis of the selection and spatial arrangement of

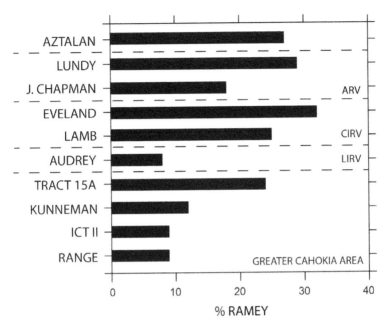

Figure 5.13. Percentage of Ramey Incised jars within shell-tempered vessel assemblages.

Mississippian iconographic motifs on Ramey Incised jars would highlight whether variation also exists in the ways in which Mississippians interpreted and interacted with the cosmos.

Elsewhere, I have published my research on Ramey Incised motifs and design layouts from the American Bottom, LIRV, CIRV, ARV, and the Aztalan site in southeastern Wisconsin (see Friberg 2018a for a detailed discussion of this topic). Local hinterland and LIRV potters tended to favor Woodland-derived motifs (Figure 5.14), such as the chevron, over less-familiar motifs, such as the trapezoid, spiral, and circle. Northern potters also organized Ramey design fields using presumably local concepts of space. Deviating from the quadripartite, cosmographic design layout favored in the American Bottom, Aztalan and ARV Ramey pots used mostly continuous design layouts, connecting motifs rather than leaving space between them; this practice may represent the influence of fabric impressions and cordmarked designs from local Woodland-era pots, which often featured continuous chevron designs (see Figure 5.14; Benn 1995; Esarey 2000; Sampson 1988). In the central and lower Illinois River valleys (the sample includes Audrey in addition to Moss and Schild cemeteries) the majority of intact vessels reveal a tripartite layout consisting of six motifs, rather than the typical

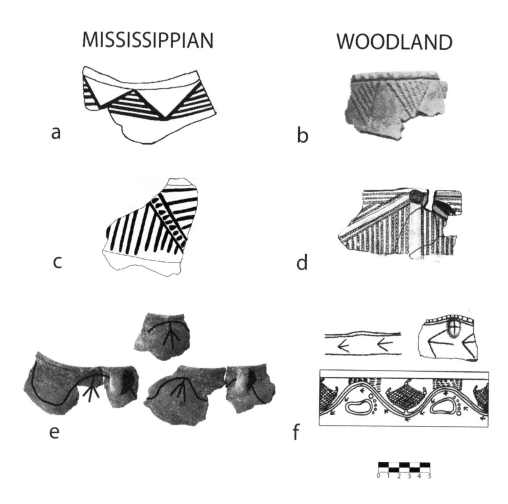

MISSISSIPPIAN   WOODLAND

a   b

c   d

e   f

0 1 2 3 4 5

Figure 5.14. Mississippian Ramey Incised Woodland pottery motifs: (*a*) Barred-triangle motif from Aztalan (Richards 1992); (*b*) Madison Cord Impressed from Iowa (Benn 1995: Figure 2), image courtesy of the Iowa Office of this State Archaeologist; (*c*) barred-triangle from the John Chapman site in the ARV (Mollerud 2005); (*d*) Maples Mills Cord-Impressed from the Audrey site in the LIRV (image courtesy of Colleen Delaney); (*e*) bisected angle and undulating line motif from CW Cooper site in the CIRV; (*f*) Maples Mills Cord-Impressed motifs (not to scale) (Sampson 1988: Figure 11b, c), image courtesy of the Wisconsin Archaeological Society.

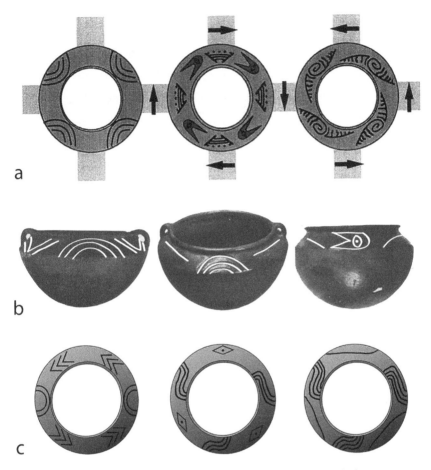

Figure 5.15. Ramey Incised design layouts: (*a*) American Bottom vessels showing quadripartite design layout (Pauketat and Emerson 1991: Figure 7); (*b*) tripartite design layouts from the LIRV (adapted from Perino 1971) with permission from the Illinois Archaeological Society; (*c*) tripartite design layouts from the CIRV.

four or eight found on American Bottom Ramey (Figure 5.15). Only one of the Ramey vessels recovered from Audrey was large enough to permit an examination of the design layout—the vessel (17.1) has a quadripartitioned continuous scroll design, identical to its twin at Cahokia. These patterns of variation in Ramey Incised motifs and design layout suggest that northern groups incorporated the religiously charged potting tradition in a way that was meaningful within local contexts.

As for the Audrey site specifically, the sample size is too small to make any broad conclusions regarding the production and consumption of Ramey

Incised jars. Two of the jars have chevron designs, and the remaining three include a feathered scroll, plain scroll, and trapezoid and scroll–combination design, all popular in the American Bottom. The best case to be made for parity with the American Bottom is the oversized Ramey jar; as previously stated, the possibility that this vessel was manufactured at Cahokia is still under investigation. However, at the Schild and Moss cemeteries, where Audrey inhabitants may have interred their dead (Delaney-Rivera 2004: 52), tripartite design layouts suggest these interpretations of Ramey were influenced by local worldviews. The Ramey Incised jars at Audrey and in the broader LIRV both suggest close sociopolitical ties with Greater Cahokia and highlight the complex negotiations of local groups incorporating aspects of Cahokian religion.

Increased Interaction: Pottery Exchange

With only two examples of exotic pottery from the Audrey site, there is not good evidence for the exchange of pottery. Nevertheless, an evaluation of the presence of exotic pottery at Late Woodland and early Mississippian northern hinterland sites suggests an increase in interaction through the process of Mississippianization. Not only were hinterland settlements interacting with Greater Cahokia groups, they seem to have also engaged with neighboring communities with whom they may have previously been in conflict (see VanDerwarker and Wilson 2016, and Wilson 2012b for a discussion of the history of warfare in the Illinois Valley). Indeed, leading up to the Mississippian period in the CIRV, there is little evidence for interactions between groups within the region (Green and Nolan 2000: 369). Late Woodland ceramic assemblages in the northern portion of the CIRV consist of Maples Mills pottery, while groups near the LaMoine River to the south produced Bauer Branch pottery; these two Late Woodland, CIRV pottery types are rarely, if ever, found at the same site, "suggesting mutual avoidance and perhaps antagonistic relations" (Green and Nolan 2000: 369). In this case, if the Maples Mills Mossville–phase jar from Audrey does represent a late Lohmann–phase interaction with CIRV Woodland groups, as Delaney-Rivera suggests (2000: 221), these interactions may have implications for repaired regional intergroup relationships within the broader Illinois Valley.

Green and Nolan (2000: 372) posit that group interaction was increasing during the Late Woodland period in west-central Illinois, although this was happening more intensively at the same time in the American Bottom. Indeed, Esarey (2000) suggests late Late Woodland Mossville–phase pottery from the CIRV shows evidence of Lohmann-phase Cahokian influence. A famous example of Late Woodland and American Bottom Mississippian interaction was documented by Claflin (1991) at the Shire site in the Sangamon River drainage of the central Illinois prairie. The site is described as a Late Woodland village later cohabited by immigrants from the American Bottom, resulting in a pattern of intermixed Late Woodland, Mississippian, and hybrid material culture recovered from Mississippian houses (Clafin 1991: 166).

Claflin suggests that Shire, and the broader Sangamon River drainage, became a center for interaction long before the introduction of American Bottom groups. Indeed, Woodland ceramic types found in the Sangamon River drainage include Maples Mills and Bauer Branch pottery from the CIRV, various Bluff wares from the LIRV, Starved Rock Collared wares from northern Illinois and southern Wisconsin, and Albee cordmarked pottery from the lower Wabash River Valley of east-central Indiana (Claflin 1991: 170). The Late Woodland village and mortuary center at Shire, located at a confluence of waterways, may have acted as a political center for various Late Woodland groups (Claflin 1991: 171). Green and Nolan's (2000: 370) research in the CIRV also supports extensive interaction between Late Woodland communities, further suggesting that large, river valley mound groups may have served as "multigroup ritual and ceremonial centers." The ceramic assemblage at the Rench site in the CIRV is a testament to increased interaction in the region during the Late Woodland/Mississippian transition. Rench is a farming hamlet with a late Late Woodland/Mississippian component, identified by the presence of both locally produced late Late Woodland pottery and Cahokia-style pottery in shared contexts. Also present are a minimum of three Starved Rock Collared jars from northern Illinois, suggesting the local Late Woodland inhabitants of the Rench site interacted with both Cahokians to the south and groups to the north (McConaughy 1991: 120; McConaughy et al. 1993: 91–92).

Farther north in the ARV, interactions were also intensifying between Mississippian hinterland groups and contemporary local Woodland populations. For example, in addition to Mississippian-style, local Late Woodland Grant series, and hybrid pottery, Misssissippian-period features excavated at the Fred Edwards site in the ARV included a number of nonlocal Late Woodland ceramic wares, including Aztalan Collared vessels from southwest Wisconsin and Hartley wares produced near the Hartley Fort site in northeast Iowa, among others (Finney 1993: 120–125; Finney and Stoltman 1991: 243). Not only were the inhabitants of the Fred Edwards site actively engaged in interactions with Cahokian groups, but they also had ties with local peoples to the west and north, similar to the Shire site. While there is only one sherd at Audrey that may support interactions with CIRV Woodland groups, the presence of a Holly Fine Engraved Caddoan vessel from northeast Texas suggests Audrey inhabitants may have engaged in far-flung interactions well outside the Illinois Valley.

In his synthesis of the Mississippianization of Cahokia's northern hinterland, Emerson (1991a: 232) suggests that trade and interaction were integral to the spread of Mississippian lifeways, emphasizing the connection between northern groups rather than focusing on engagements with Cahokia. The above examples of pottery exchange outside of the American Bottom support Emerson's suspicions. The exchange of pottery throughout the northern hinterland (and possibly the immediate periphery), suggests northern groups did not solely engage in one-way Mississippianizing interactions with Cahokian groups. Northerners also negotiated new identities through interactions with their neighbors, connected by their mutual interest in Cahokian religion and the Mississippian way of life.

Conclusion

The pottery assemblage from the Audrey site mostly comprises locally produced Stirling-phase, Cahokia-style jars, many of which are finely made. The rim shape of these jars is stylistically comparable to those produced contemporaneously at Cahokia, and radiometric dates confirm the Stirling-phase assignment of the Audrey site. Differences between Audrey and American Bottom ceramic assemblages, however, point to important organizational differences related to social hierarchy and ceremonialism.

Through the process of Mississippianization, Audrey inhabitants renegotiated social identities, altering ingrained daily practices and the social interactions determined by community organization. I hypothesized that such organizational changes would have resulted in a shift away from identities structured by communally oriented Woodland-era traditions, and toward those negotiated through a more privatized, hierarchically organized Cahokian way of life. Yet, an interregional comparative analysis of pottery consumption suggests that Audrey inhabitants, like their northern neighbors, had few of the many formal servingwares found in American Bottom assemblages, where hierarchical social organization involved a level of ceremonialism in the preparation and serving of food; but while northern hinterland groups practiced their foodways with less "fanfare" than was the tradition in Greater Cahokia, they placed more emphasis on the production and consumption of the religiously charged Ramey Incised jar (Wilson et al. 2017). At the same time, hinterland potters produced Ramey pots with reference to existing worldviews, favoring Woodland-derived motifs and local concepts of space. The same can be said of Ramey Incised jars in the LIRV, although the frequency of these vessels at the Audrey site is similar to sites in the American Bottom. While Audrey inhabitants did not overemphasize the production of these pots, the oversized Ramey jar should not be overlooked with regard to commensal ceremonialism. With the distinctive Cahokian religious iconography easily visible on its insloping rim, and sooting on the exterior of the vessel, this grand domestic cosmogram was almost certainly used in community-oriented public events involving the ritual consumption of its contents. Also, I propose that the striking similarities between Vessel 17.1 and the only other known oversized Ramey jar from Cahokia provide evidence for close sociopolitical ties between Audrey and Cahokia.

The ceramic analysis presented here suggests that Mississippian peoples north of the American Bottom did not exhibit the same level of hierarchical social organization that developed in the Greater Cahokia area, and seemed to place an emphasis on the religious aspects of Cahokian lifeways. Nevertheless, the Audrey site ceramic assemblage stands out from northern hinterland sites as more closely resembling American Bottom assemblages. Scarce evidence for ceramic hybridity and statistical similarities in jar lip shape and rim angle suggest Audrey's potters were directly influenced by contact with Cahokia. Wilson et al. (2017) suggest that patterns of emulation emphasizing religious aspects of Cahokian lifeways—in combination with the maintenance of Woodland-era ceramic traditions in the LIRV, CIRV, and ARV—point to a model of Mississippianization through Cahokian missionaries. I argue that the recent analysis of the Audrey site ceramic assemblage supports this hypothesis, the LIRV having engaged in more frequent contact with American Bottom groups than with more northern groups as a result of their closer proximity to the region.

Finally, evidence for pottery exchange throughout the northern Midwest highlights the complexity of interactions stimulating the panregional Mississippian phenomenon. Leading up to the Mississippian period, there is little evidence for peaceful interaction between Late Woodland populations (Green and Nolan 2000), and strong evidence for violent encounters (Perino 1971; VanDerwarker and Wilson 2016; Wilson 2012b). Cahokian interactions may have helped to broker relationships between northern groups that were avoided or contentious in the Late Woodland period. At the Fred Edwards site in the ARV, Finney and Stoltman (1991: 231) suggest that interactions with distant Woodland groups represent a "far-flung exchange system that almost certainly had Cahokia as its moving force." The evidence certainly supports this assertion for not only Fred Edwards, but for Audrey and all northern hinterland sites. Indeed, the increased interactions in the north beginning in the late Late Woodland period seems to be in line with the burgeoning of Greater Cahokia. As such, perhaps the foundation of the Mississippian phenomenon is not simply a shared material culture. Before we see Cahokian emulation in the northern hinterland, we witness a renewed spirit of interaction and political alliance boiling over from the American Bottom, perhaps fueling a need for a shared, Mississippian identity.

6

Lithic Tool Industries

Lithic assemblages in the Mississippian Midwest and Midsouth have traditionally been overlooked in pursuit of more robust ceramic datasets (Koldehoff 1987; Koldehoff and Brennan 2010). In some cases, lithic analysis is limited to basic tool identification and general patterns. More recently, Mississippian researchers have focused on detailed analyses of specific lithic craft industries and their implications for political economic activities in and around the American Bottom (Brown et al. 1990; Cobb 1989; Koldehoff and Wilson 2010; Pauketat and Alt 2004; Yerkes 1989). These studies have had a significant impact on American Bottom archaeology; fortunately, detailed lithic data have been published in dozens of reports by the Illinois State Archaeological Survey. These data can be used in comparative analyses to discuss variation in the organization of lithic tool industries and to test the degree of involvement of other settlements in vital Cahokian craft production and exchange activities.

As outlined in Chapter 1, to understand the nature of the relationship between Lower Illinois River Valley (LIRV) and American Bottom groups, it is necessary to examine the types of interactions occurring among them. I hypothesize that the LIRV's proximity to Cahokia may have enabled certain social, political, and economic interactions with American Bottom groups that did not transpire with more distant groups. The lithic assemblage at Audrey is essential to addressing this hypothesis, particularly with regard to the fundamental economic interactions occurring in the American Bottom that involved the production and/or exchange of basalt celts, Mill Creek chert hoes, and marine shell beads. As will be demonstrated below, analysis of the lithic assemblage from Audrey suggests that this hypothesis is partly correct, and that the proximity of the LIRV to Greater Cahokia did result in closer economic ties with the polity. Indeed, a morphological analysis of basalt celts from Audrey reveals that they closely resemble celts produced and distributed in the American Bottom as part of Cahokia's basalt celt industry.

A lack of evidence for celt production at Audrey further suggests that their celts may have arrived at the site through exchange with Greater Cahokia groups. Nevertheless, there is presently no evidence that Audrey inhabitants were tied into other Cahokian craft exchange networks. While a cache of 120 marine shell beads was recovered in the 1980s at the Audrey site, current analysis failed to recover any microlithic drills like those used in the production of marine shell beads at Cahokia and select American Bottom sites (Trubitt 2000: 676; Yerkes 1989: 102). Audrey villagers also do not seem to have been directly involved in the Mill Creek hoe exchange network. A comparative analysis of the percentage of Mill Creek objects in chert assemblages from Greater Cahokia, the Audrey site, the Central Illinois River Valley (CIRV), and the Apple River Valley (ARV) suggest that Mississippian settlements north of the American Bottom did not have access to this network, regardless of distance from the Mill Creek quarries. Overall, while Cahokia had direct control over these craft exchange networks within the American Bottom, northern groups (including in the LIRV) were not engaged in important aspects of Cahokia's centralized political economy.

An analysis of Audrey's lithic assemblage also helps characterize the lithic tool industry at the site, the types of activities taking place at the village, and important organizational differences between northern hinterland and Greater Cahokia systems of lithic procurement, production, and circulation. Audrey's lithic assemblage is indicative of a Mississippian expedient flake tool industry, a common pattern at Mississippian sites throughout the midcontinent (Koldehoff 1987). Cahokia organized their lithic industry to exploit Crescent Hills Burlington chert and maintain centralized production of bifaces at the source (Kelly 1984; Koldehoff 1987: 178); in contrast, Audrey inhabitants engaged in all levels of lithic production locally, meaning they did not organize their lithic economic activities with the same level of hierarchical complexity as was the practice at Cahokia. Audrey inhabitants did, however, engage in other important economic activities. Evidence for the production of adzes and other large chert bifaces suggests Audrey villagers practiced woodworking, which would have been essential for building the numerous wooden structures comprising this large village. Additionally, a comparatively high number of projectile points and end scrapers at Audrey suggests a higher degree of deer hunting and hide processing than is observed in the Greater Cahokia area.

Finally, a comparison of exotic cherts from the Audrey site and within the American Bottom and northern hinterland area provides interesting routes for future research into the types of interactions taking place throughout the Mississippian world. The current study finds that exotic northern lithic materials, including quartzite, Knife River Chalcedony, Hixton silicified sediment, and galena were circulated throughout the northern hinterland, LIRV, and Greater Cahokia area. Furthermore, an analysis of Hixton in Mississippian chert assemblages suggests that Cahokia did not have direct economic control over these northern exchange networks.

This chapter presents the data that support these patterns and provides the context for discussing their significance in detail. First, I discuss previous research on Mississippian lithic raw materials and tool industries. I then outline the analytical methods used in the current study, particularly as they relate to evaluating political and economic interaction. Finally, I present details of original analysis of the 2016 Audrey-site lithic assemblage, followed by a comparative analysis of Audrey lithics to American Bottom, CIRV, and ARV assemblages.

Background and Previous Research

Raw Materials

Cherts

The most common type of lithic raw material in the Mississippian-period American Bottom and lower and central Illinois River valleys is chert from the Burlington Formation (Kelly 1984: 44; Meyers 1970: 12). This chert-rich limestone formation runs through Illinois and much of Missouri, with chert deposits often exposed in the limestone bluffs of river valleys (Kelly 1984; Koldehoff 1995: 45). The Crescent Hills variety of Burlington chert, from the quarries in the eastern portion of the Missouri Ozarks, is a high-quality chert heavily utilized by Cahokians and others in the American Bottom (Figure 6.1). There is also a source of Burlington located close to the Audrey site in the LIRV, in modern-day Grafton and Alton, Illinois (Kodlehoff 2006: 370). Generic Burlington chert (not Crescent Hills) is often a poor-to-moderate–quality fossiliferous chert that is white to light gray in color. Burlington develops a pinkish color and luster when heat-treated, and when burned or charred, acquires a smoky hue (with the interior remaining white) (Koldehoff 2006: 369). Low-quality, Valmeyer Burlington chert from Monroe County, Illinois (south of Cahokia), is highly fossiliferous and coarse in texture, occasionally with calcite inclusions (Koldehoff 2006: 369). Cahokians may have opted for the Crescent Hills Burlington over this poor-quality Valmeyer variety. At the Audrey site, inhabitants relied mainly on a local source of Burlington; yet similar to the Valmeyer variety, much of the local LIRV Burlington chert is also highly fossiliferous, with only thin bands of good-quality, smooth chert within each cobble (Meyers 1970: 12). The Burlington Limestone Formation is extensively exposed in the LIRV, providing easy access for local flintknappers; in fact, the Illinois River flows directly through the Burlington Formation in this location, forming the bluffline cliffs along both the eastern and western margins of the valley (Meyers 1970: 12). Also present in American Bottom lithic assemblages, St. Genevieve chert comes from south of Cahokia in nearby Randolph and western Monroe counties, Illinois.

There are also a number of nonlocal cherts common at Cahokia and sometimes found in regions to the north (see Figure 6.1). The presence of these exotic materials at Audrey could mean close connections with Cahokia, or extraregional interactions aided by political affiliation with Cahokia. Three of these exotic cherts come from southern Illinois. Kaolin chert is a residuum from Iron Mountain in Union County, Illinois. The material is of moderate to high quality and varies in color and texture, but is known for its translucent appearance (Koldehoff 1995: 46; 2002: 137). Cobden chert, from the St. Louis Formation in Union County, Illinois, is a high-quality, nodular chert that is dark in color and often banded (Koldehoff 1995: 46; 2002: 136). Finally, Mill Creek chert is the residuum from the Ullin Limestone Formation in Union County, Illinois, that occurs in long, flat nodules ideal for large biface production. The chert is light gray to tan/brown in color and its grainy texture provides great strength and durability (Koldehoff 2002: 138). Recent experiments suggest that bifacial hoes made from durable Mill Creek chert would have been able to withstand heavy use in the effort to intensify agricultural production, particularly in the clay soils of the American Bottom and eastern uplands (Hammerstedt and Hughes 2015; Milner et al. 2010).

Two additional knappable materials from northern regions need to be discussed as well. The first is Hixton silicified sediment, a striking white, granular stone from a single, far-northern source at Silver Mound in west-central Wisconsin (see Figure 6.1). Hixton is found in lithic assemblages in and around Cahokia, 850 km south of the source. Flakes and points made from the material are also found at sites in the LIRV, CIRV, and ARV. Finally, Knife River Chalcedony is a finely and uniformly textured, nonporous lithic material from Dunn County in western North Dakota (Frison 1978). The translucent brown to dark brown chert features white fossil inclusions which distinguish it from other similar cherts. This high-quality material is rare but present at certain Mississippian sites north of the American Bottom.

Igneous/Metamorphic

In the American Bottom, the only available local igneous material is glacial till from within a 5–10 km radius of a given site for local procurement. Other types are brought in through exchange (Koldehoff 1995: 53). A famous example is the basalt mined from quarries in the St. Francois Mountains of the Missouri Ozarks (see Figure 6.1). This material was broken off in large spalls and transported (likely via canoe) to Cahokia and other American Bottom settlements for the production of stone axe-heads, or celts (Koldehoff and Wilson 2010). These items were important for use in woodworking, especially for cutting down trees for use in house construction and clearing agricultural fields. Glacial till is also available in the LIRV and CIRV where it is used for a variety of groundstone tools. Any nondistinct igneous material (as in not deriving from the St. Francois Mountains) is presumed to be

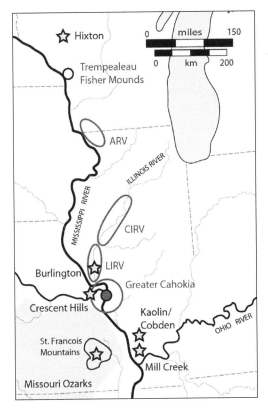

Figure 6.1. Map of lithic raw material sources.

local glacial till which occurs in small cobbles in riverbeds and streams. At the current time, chemical sourcing (such as Portable X-Ray Fluorescence Spectrometry, or pXRF) has proven to be unreliable in characterizing these heterogeneous materials (Butler 2014). The materials can also vary within a source, making it difficult to discern the difference between types of igneous material with the naked eye. Microscopic visual analysis by experts familiar with local and nonlocal lithic materials is generally accepted as a reliable means of identifying the material source.

Cahokian Craft Industries and Political Economy

Settlements in the American Bottom and its eastern uplands are considered to be within Cahokia's inner sphere of influence (Pauketat 1998a: 50), as they show direct evidence of political and economic ties with the paramount center of Cahokia through the production and exchange of certain Cahokian crafts (Alt 2002a; Emerson and Jackson 1984; Hanenberger 2003; Kelly 1991a, 1991b; Milner 1984; Pauketat 1994: 73–80, 1997b, 2003, 2004: 96–97; Pauketat et al. 2012; Wilson et al. 2006). Lithic craft industries included an extensive Mill Creek hoe-exchange network, the production and distribution of St. Francois basalt celts, and microlithic chert drills for the production of marine shell beads; these craft industries were probably integral to Cahokia's rise to power (Cobb 2000; Emerson 1989, 1997a, 1997b; Kelly 2008; Koldehoff and Kearns 1993; Muller 1997; Pauketat 1994, 1997a; Pauketat and Alt 2004; Wilson 2001; Yerkes 1983, 1989). Mill Creek hoes are named for the chert quarries in the Mill Creek locality in far southern Illinois (Koldehoff 1985; Koldehoff 2002), where the hoes were manufactured and later exchanged in finished form (Cobb 1989, 1996, 2000). Mill Creek hoes were economically significant to Cahokians as they facilitated the intensification of agriculture (Brown et al. 1990; Hammerstedt and Hughes 2015; Koldehoff 1985).

Cahokians also produced stone celts (axes). These hafted woodworking tools were often made of basalt from the St. Francois Mountains (Kelly 2008; Koldehoff and Wilson 2010; Pauketat 1997a: 6). Although groundstone tools could have been made using igneous rock scavenged from local glacial till, large slabs of St. Francois Mountain basalt were transported back to Cahokia for the production of celts, the largest of which were as long as 25 cm (Koldehoff and Wilson 2010: 234). It has also been suggested that the Missouri Ozarks, and the region's raw materials (basalt, galena, flint clay, and possibly cedar trees), may have held a spiritual significance for

Cahokians (Emerson and Hughes 2000; Kelly and Brown 2012). An uneven distribution of celt production debitage at Cahokia and associated sites has been interpreted as evidence that this industry was under some level of elite control. Caches of these celts have been found at 10 sites in the American Bottom and eastern uplands, ranging in size from 2 to over 100 celts per cache (Butler 2014: 3–4; Pauketat and Alt 2004: 782). Access to these implements would have greatly facilitated the clearing of agricultural fields and the collection of building materials.

The production of shell beads using microlithic chert drills was restricted primarily to a subset of the residential groups at Cahokia, likely linked to elites (Holley 1995; Mason and Perino 1961; Pauketat 1997a; Trubitt 2000; Yerkes 1983, 1989). Some other American Bottom settlements also engaged in bead production, but most did not. The economic significance of marine shell beads remains unclear, but their political significance in the Cahokian sphere is demonstrated in the famous beaded burial in Cahokia's Mound 72, where a high-status male was buried atop a bed of approximately 20,000 marine shell beads (Fowler 1991, 1997; Fowler et al. 1999).

While the inhabitants of the greater American Bottom region were heavily involved in Cahokian craft industries and exchange networks, the same cannot be said for hinterland groups. There is abundant evidence for the use of Mill Creek hoes at Richland Complex sites in the eastern uplands of the American Bottom, thought to be related to the contribution of agricultural surplus to the Cahokia polity (Pauketat 1994, 1998a, 2003). However, there are very few Mill Creek hoes found in the CIRV and other northern hinterland regions. Evidence for production and caches of St. Francois basalt celts and marine shell beads have been identified at American Bottom and Richland Complex sites (Pauketat and Alt 2004). In contrast, archaeological research at hinterland sites north of Cahokia has revealed little evidence for the production of these basalt celts or beads (Emerson et al. 2007; Wilson 2011).

Mississippian Expedient Flake Tool Industry

Formal lithic artifacts, such as Cahokia-style projectile points, microlithic drills, Ramey Knives, Mill Creek hoes, basalt celts, and discoidals are easily recognizable markers of Cahokian material culture. These artifacts, however, do not characterize the majority of lithic tools produced and used in the Mississippian-period American Bottom. Through his analysis of a number of lithic assemblages in southern Illinois, Brad Koldehoff (1987) identifies what he calls the Cahokia flake tool industry. Flake tools, produced by detaching flakes "from unprepared cores" are the most common tool type in the Mississippian American Bottom (Koldehoff 1987: 152; 1995: 61). With an abundant source of high-quality Burlington chert nearby, American Bottom Mississippians acquired the material from the Crescent Hills area in large cores, and sometimes stored it in caches (Fortier 1985, Koldehoff 1995: 58; Milner 1983). It should be noted that expedient flake tool industries were also used in the Late Woodland period, a time during which people in the American Bottom region were transitioning to more intensified agricultural practices and sedentary lifestyles. Koldehoff (1987: 175) suggests that formal lithic tools became less practical for people with reduced settlement mobility, and daily tasks could be performed more effectively using simple flakes. If subsistence practices and sedentism are reasons for this informal tool industry, this pattern is likely present throughout the Middle Mississippian world writ large.

Methods of Analysis

There are several methods of analysis that have produced data that can be used to address this project's research questions.

Basic Analytical Methods

Material Type

Identification of different types of cherts is important for understanding LIRV interactions with groups outside of the region. While the Audrey lithic assemblage is overwhelmingly comprised of local Burlington chert, a close examination of each flake and piece of groundstone is necessary to identify any exotic materials acquired through exchange with distant groups. Of particular interest here is Mill Creek chert and St. Francois Mountain basalt.

Usewear Analysis

In addition to identifying formal tools, each flake of chert was examined for usewear using a hand lens or magnifying headset to look for chipping, striations, and polish. This is because so few formal tools were identified in this dense lithic assemblage. Audrey residents were clearly producing and using chert tools, but perhaps they relied more on flake tools than formal tools. Since the Mississippian expedient flake tool industry is found to be the common pattern for Mississippian lithic assemblages in the American

Bottom, we would expect to find a large quantity of expedient flake tools in the Audrey assemblage as well.

Size Analysis

Size analysis (or count-to-weight ratio) of the lithic assemblage can be used to evaluate the different stages of lithic production that occurred at a site. Due to Audrey's proximity to a local source of Burlington chert, we would expect more large pieces from primary-stage production and reduction of large cores. Koldehoff has used a measure of mean weight to examine this at Cahokia (Koldehoff 1995: 54). At many Mississippian sites, the raw material comes from a distance, and thus primary stages of production, reducing large cobbles, occurs at the source, before it is transported back to residential sites for later-stage production. This seemingly logical strategy may also be indicative of political economic complexity. Indeed, with multiple sources of nearby chert, Cahokians organized their lithic industry to specifically exploit the Crescent Hills Burlington quarries; in this scenario, the majority of primary production occurred at the source, and finished tools and raw materials were distributed throughout much of the region (Kelly 1984; Koldehoff 1987: 178). This pattern contrasts with the Audrey site's lithic industry which seems to have focused on extraction of local chert and household-based production at the residential site.

Evaluation of Political and Economic Interaction

For the region's inhabitants, the proximity of the LIRV to Cahokia may have facilitated engagement in the production and/or exchange of economically and politically important Cahokian craft items. Evidence of these Cahokian craft industries is generally found at settlements within a 100 km range of Cahokia, demonstrating direct economic ties with the polity (Pauketat 1998a: 50). As discussed in Chapter 2, there is little evidence of these items outside of Cahokia's "inner sphere" of influence, as in the northern hinterland regions. At 100 km from Cahokia, the Audrey site falls just outside the prescribed range of Cahokian economic control, in the immediate periphery.

Mill Creek Hoes

Did the Audrey site residents have ready access to the economically valuable Mill Creek hoe industry? Cahokia was a major consumer and redistributor of Mill Creek hoes, and the prevalence of these tools in lithic assemblages generally decreases with distance from Cahokia (Cobb 2000; Brown et al. 1990; Pauketat 1998a: 68). If the LIRV's proximity to Cahokia enabled economic relationships with American Bottom groups, a calculation of the percentage of Mill Creek chert within the Audrey site chert assemblage should show a value closer to those of the American Bottom and its eastern uplands than to hinterland sites. Furthermore, if Audrey inhabitants had direct economic ties with American Bottom groups and access to the Mill Creek chert exchange network, we would expect their consumption of Mill Creek chert to be similar. Mill Creek hoes were circulated and used extensively in American Bottom and upland farming, and unused hoes were stored in caches for later distribution (Alt 2002a: 113; Daniels 2007: 745; Hammerstedt and Hughes 2015: 151; Pauketat 2003: 55; 2004: 103). At the same time, northern hinterland groups had access to only a limited number of these valuable tools, and often recycled the material. Indeed, Mill Creek hoes are occasionally found in the ARV, but often times the chert was reworked into other tools, such as projectile points or end scrapers (Finney 1993: 158; Millhouse 2012: 302). If Audrey inhabitants had greater access to Mill Creek hoes than did hinterland groups, they would have practiced less curation and recycling of Mill Creek chert. An evaluation of the average size of Mill Creek chert artifacts will shed light on the consumption of Mill Creek chert at different sites in the Mississippian sphere.

Basalt Celts

Audrey residents may have also had access to St. Francois basalt for celt production. The celts, made from varieties of basalt, are occasionally found in caches at American Bottom and Richland Complex sites, yet are relatively absent in areas outside of Cahokia's inner sphere of influence in the northern hinterland (Pauketat 1998a: 66). Northern hinterland celts are usually made of igneous/metamorphic glacial till. Identification of finished basalt celts in the lithic assemblage will suggest Audrey inhabitants may have had access to the Cahokian celt exchange system. In this case, celts would have been brought into the LIRV through exchange. Groups who participated directly in Cahokia's basalt celt industry may have been subsidized with unworked blocks of basalt for celt production (Pauketat 1997a: 10; Pauketat and Alt 2004: 793). If Audrey inhabitants were participating in the production and exchange of celts within this network, we would expect the presence of basalt debitage, celt preforms, and spherical chert hammerstones.

Another difference between northern hinterland and American Bottom celts is the size and shape. Northern hinterland celts tend to be smaller and narrower (more similar to Woodland-era celts), and less formally designed than Mississippian celts from the American Bottom (Wilson and Koldehoff 2009). The large size of American Bottom celts would have facilitated the intensification of woodworking activities necessary for constructing houses, temples, special-purpose buildings, and palisades of the region's highly nucleated settlements, and, perhaps most importantly, the clearing of fields for agricultural production. If Audrey site inhabitants participated in the basalt celt exchange network, we would expect the celts from Audrey to be more similar in size and shape to American Bottom celts than to northern hinterland or Woodland-era celts.

Marine Shell Beads

Direct political ties among Cahokian elites and LIRV groups may have provided Audrey residents with access to marine shell (from the Gulf of Mexico) for bead production. The production of shell beads occurred mostly at large Mississippian mound centers and was less common at smaller settlements in the American Bottom, where production was restricted to certain households (Trubitt 2000: 676; Yerkes 1989: 102). The restriction of this craft industry is thought to be related to elite control of production and consumption of shell beads, and likely also the distribution of marine shell raw material in and around Cahokia (Pauketat 1997a: 5). Bead-producing communities in regions outside the American Bottom (such as the Richland Complex), with access to marine shell, were likely very closely connected with Cahokia.

Although finished beads are found at northern hinterland sites, evidence for bead production is scarce (Emerson et al. 2007; Wilson 2011). A cache of 120 shell beads was found at Audrey in the 1980s, but was never fully analyzed (Cook 1983). If Audrey inhabitants had close political and economic ties with Cahokia, we would expect to find more evidence of bead production than is present at northern hinterland sites. Bead detritus would be a clear identifier of production, but shell often does not preserve well. In this case, we would expect to see lithic evidence in the form of microlithic drills (and cores) (Koldehoff and Kearns 1993; Trubitt 2000; Yerkes 1983, 1989).

Analysis

A total of 14,439 lithic artifacts, weighing 71 kg, was recovered from the 2016 excavations at the Audrey-North site. These include chert artifacts and debitage, 98 percent of which are primarily made from a local source of

Burlington chert; groundstone tools; and limestone, sandstone, basalt, and other groundstone materials and minerals. Overall, the lithic assemblage at Audrey resembles a typical Mississippian flaked tool industry, consisting primarily of expedient Burlington chert flake tools with a small number of formal tools. There is a scarcity of formal groundstone tools, but Audrey inhabitants used limestone heavily, likely for food production and cooking purposes.

Groundstone Artifacts

A total of 3,070 groundstone artifacts, weighing 39.41 kg, were recovered at Audrey. These include both formal (such as celts and pitted anvils) and informal tools (such as sandstone abraders and hammerstones) (Table 6.1), in addition to unmodified material, such as limestone, sandstone, basalt, and various minerals (n=3047; 36.71 kg; Table 6.1; see Friberg 2018b: Table 6.2, Table 6.3 for more detail). The predominant material within the groundstone collected is limestone, in the form of poorly preserved cobbles and pebbles.

Celts

A total of two broken basalt celts were recovered from the excavations, one from Feature 5 and one from Feature 23 (Figure 6.2; see Table 6.1). It is difficult to determine the source of the basalt without chemical or petrographic analysis, but the material is distinct from other igneous glacial till found on the site. The fact that Audrey's celts were made of basalt (rather than local glacial till) is significant, as much of the basalt used to produce celts at Cahokia and in the American Bottom was also nonlocal, and can be sourced to quarries in the St. Francois Mountains (70 km to the southwest) (Kelly 2008; Koldehoff and Wilson 2010; Pauketat 1997a: 6). It is also noteworthy that the site's landowner has 13 Mississippian basalt celts in his private collection (recovered during plowing). Of these, eight are intact and range from 8.5 to 18 cm in length and from 4.5 to 9 cm in width. Weights and thicknesses of these items were not recorded. There is not strong evidence for celt production at Audrey; analysis identified no unfinished celts, spherical hammerstones for celt pecking, or basalt debitage. This evidence suggests that Audrey's Mississippian inhabitants did not have arrangements with American Bottom groups to provide raw material for celt production. However, Audrey's celts are made of basalt, which suggests the celts were acquired through trade with American Bottom groups. In contrast,

Feature 23

bits

Feature 5

0 _____ 5
cm

Figure 6.2. Celts recovered from Feature 5 and Feature 23.

Mississippian sites in the CIRV offer evidence for local production of celts made from a variety of glacial till materials, suggesting that CIRV inhabitants may not have participated in the American Bottom basalt celt exchange network (Wilson and Koldehoff 2009).

Basalt Cobble

One large cobble of basalt was found on the floor of a rectangular wall-trench structure (Feature 23). The cobble measures 23.28 cm in length and 13.77 cm in width (weight >2 kg). The large basalt cobble has been fire-affected and has several cracks, with many (n=102) small bits of basalt crumbling off the core. Considering this heat alteration and the lack of evidence of other modification, along with a general lack of evidence for celt production at the Audrey site, this basalt cobble was probably not intended for celt manufacture. It was more likely placed in a fire and used for cooking, then later discarded at the bottom of the Feature 23 house basin.

Hammerstones

Two hammerstones were recovered from Feature 5. These direct percussion tools were identified by evidence of pitting usewear on their surfaces. The larger of the two is made of basalt and is round in shape with pecking and pitting on much of its surface. The smaller hammerstone is an angular cobble of igneous/metamorphic glacial till probably used for flint knapping. Both hammerstones were found in Feature 5, where there is abundant evidence for refuse related to chipped-stone-tool production and use.

Pitted Anvil

One pitted anvil was recovered in the machine scraping of the House Block area. This large tool, sometimes referred to as a "nutting stone," is a round cobble of igneous/metamorphic glacial till that shows evidence of pitting, or percussion usewear, on one side. Pitted anvils are thought to have been used as processing platforms for breaking open nuts with another rock.

Sandstone Abraders

A total of 18 sandstone abraders were recovered: 1 from the plow-zone backhoe scrape of the House Block, 4 from Feature 23, and 13 from Feature 5 (Figure 6.3). These tools were identified as larger pieces of sandstone (ranging from 9.01 g to 503.01 g, in contrast to the smaller sandstone pebbles), with either smooth, flattened surfaces or linear abrasions. As most of the local sandstone at Audrey is quite friable, these artifacts may be fragmented. Abraders may have served a number of purposes. For example, the abraders with linear grooves (n=10), sometimes referred to as slot abraders, were likely used for shaping or sharpening bone tools or wooden shafts (Jackson and Emerson 1984: 109–110). Abraders with smooth surfaces (n=5) were used for grinding activities. Finally, three of the sandstone abraders appear to have both grooves and smoothed surfaces, meaning the tools had multiple purposes. An interesting example is a slot abrader found at the bottom of Feature 23 basin fill; this tool features a U-shaped groove (likely for shaft straightening), but its rounded and elongated shape, and abrasions on the reverse side, suggest the sandstone object may have originally been used as a mano, pestle, or some type of percussion tool.

Unmodified Lithic Cobbles

Three large cobbles of unidentified lithic material with an average weight of 94.5 g were recovered. The objects had not been modified or fire-affected.

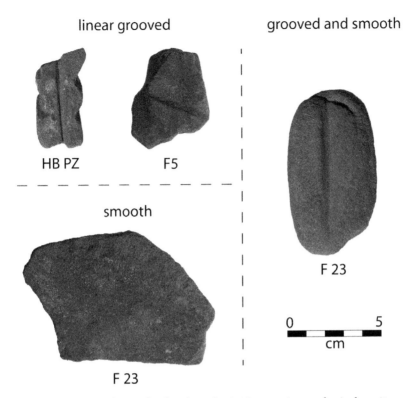

linear grooved

grooved and smooth

HB PZ   F5

smooth

F 23

F 23

0 —————— 5
cm

Figure 6.3. Select sandstone abraders from the 2016 excavations at the Audrey site.

Sandstone

In addition to sandstone abraders, 179 (2.01 kg) pieces of unworked sandstone were recovered. These items ranged in size from large cobbles to small pebbles, with a mean weight of 11.25 g. The smaller pieces, usually rounded and eroded, are likely the result of the crumbling of larger, friable cobbles. Some of these items appear to be fire-affected and may have been used in cooking features, although no evidence of hearths or in situ burning was encountered during the 2016 excavations.

Limestone

A total of 2,324 pieces of limestone were recovered. The Mississippian inhabitants of Audrey Village heavily exploited limestone resources from the nearby Burlington Formation for cooking and food processing, but in ways that differed from their Woodland predecessors. These items ranged in size from large cobbles to small pebbles with an average weight of 12.83 g. Most

Table 6.1. Groundstone tools and materials

Feature	Pebble		Abraders		Hammerstones		Celts		Pitted Anvil		Limestone		Basalt		Comments
	n	Wt (g)	n	Wt (g)	n	Wt (g)	n	Wt (g)	n	Wt (g)	n	Wt (g)	n	Wt (g)	
F5 PZ	–	–	–	–	–	–	–	–	–	–	37	233.68	3	150.28	
F5	–	–	13	646.4	2	628.35	1	219.42	–	–	588	233.68	1	150.71	Basalt hammerstone, celt broken
F9	–	–	–	–	–	–	–	–	–	–	40	9,567.74	1	0.17	
F14	–	–	–	–	–	–	–	–	–	–	14	339.18	–	–	
F16	–	–	–	–	–	–	–	–	–	–	11	53.13	–	–	
F17	–	–	–	–	–	–	–	–	–	–	195	42.9	–	–	
F20	–	–	–	–	–	–	–	–	–	–	65	945.6	–	–	
F22	–	–	–	–	–	–	–	–	–	–	75	1,451.04	–	–	
F23	1	23.2	4	256.06	–	–	1	246	–	–	1,251	14,436	102	2,000	Quartzite pebble possible polishing stone; basalt cobble
F27	–	–	–	–	–	–	–	–	–	–	3	8.25	–	–	
F28	–	–	–	–	–	–	–	–	–	–	42	935.19	1	174.81	
HB	–	–	1	24.59	–	–	–	–	1	675.41	3	351.65	9	139.86	
Total	1	23.2	18	927.05	2	628.35	2	465.42	1	675.41	2,324	28,598	117	2,615.83	

Source: Compiled by author.
Notes: PZ = plow zone; HB = House Block; – = Not present.

of the limestone recovered from Audrey features was eroded and crumbling, and much of it had been burned or heated in an oxidizing environment, changing the material's color from white to shades of pink, red, and orange. Some pit features were filled with concentrations of burned limestone (along with other forms of domestic refuse), although no evidence for in situ burning was evident. It appears limestone at Audrey was not used for direct cooking, such as in Woodland-era earth ovens. Cook (1983) documented circular features he described as containing limestone, although these features were not dated; the landowner has observed these as well in his deep plowing episodes, describing them as burned, red circles. These may be the remains of Woodland-era earth ovens heated with hot limestone, scorching the earth around them.

Fire-Cracked Rock

In addition to burnt limestone and sandstone, a total of 93 pieces (1.96 kg) of nonchert, fire-cracked rock were recovered. Material type was impossible to determine. These objects averaged 21.05 g in weight and may have been used in cooking or heating features.

Minerals

Minerals are another lithic resource, often collected and used for pigments. Lab analysis identified glauconite, limonite, ochre, and galena in the lithic assemblage (Table 6.1). Glauconite is an iron potassium phyllosilicate mineral that develops in sand or impure limestone formations and is identified by its bright green color (https://www.mindat.org/min-1710.html). Eighteen fragments of glauconite (18.32 g, possibly crumbled from 1 or 2 larger pieces) were recovered from Feature 5, Zone B. Only 1 piece (0.62 g) of limonite, a form of iron ore with a yellow-to-brown color, was recovered from Feature 23. Red ochre was found in both houses, with 3 pieces in Feature 5 (0.66 g) and 7 pieces in Feature 23 (15.48 g). Finally, 13 cubes of galena were recovered from Feature 5. Galena, or lead ore, is a material that was used by Mississippians primarily for the production of an iridescent pigment (Milner 1990: 22; Walthall 1981).

Chipped Stone

The 2016 excavations at the Audrey site recovered a total of 11,369 chert artifacts, weighing 31.61 kg. The majority of the chipped-stone material is local Burlington chert, although also present in the assemblage is Cobden,

Kaolin, and Mill Creek cherts from Union County, southern Illinois; Hixton silicified sediment from western Wisconsin; Knife River Chalcedony from North Dakota; quartzite; and unknown types of cherts. Most of the chipped-stone material came from the two houses, Feature 5 and Feature 23. Feature 5 dominates the assemblage, containing 81 percent of all chert by count and 64.2 percent by weight, compared to the considerably larger Feature 23, which only represents 13 percent of chert by count, and 23.93 percent by weight.

The chipped-stone artifacts fall into two general categories: formal (bifacial) tools and production failures, and expedient tools and debitage. This assemblage consists of 99.5 percent flake tools, cores, and debitage by count. With a majority of expedient tools and few formal chipped-stone tools, the Audrey lithic assemblage fits the description of a Mississippian expedient flake tool industry; this will be discussed in more detail below.

Formal Bifacial Tools and Biface Production Refuse

In contrast to the expedient tools described above, the formal chipped-stone tools from the Audrey site represent bifacially worked objects whose production was planned and either executed or failed. I also include resharpening flakes because they represent the remains of efforts to maintain or repurpose formal tools. These bifaces include projectile points, adzes and woodworking tools, one Mill Creek hoe and hoe-resharpening flakes, and other unidentifiable bifaces (see Friberg 2018b: Table 6.5 for more detail).

Projectile Points

A total of 27 projectile points and 6 projectile-point production failures were recovered from the Audrey site excavations (Table 6.2; see Friberg 2018b: Table 6.4 for detailed projectile point data), including 18 Mississippian style points (Figure 6.4), 2 Late Woodland points, 4 Middle Woodland points, and 3 unidentifiable projectiles (Figure 6.5). All projectile points are produced from local Burlington chert and the majority were heat-treated to strengthen the stone and improve knappability.

Thirteen of the Mississippian points fit the description of the typical triangular notched Cahokia point, although none of the points feature a third, bottom notch (like those in the famous beaded burial from Mound 72 at Cahokia). Only four of the points are entirely intact, while the others have broken tips and bases. Of the seven with intact bases, three of the bases are completely flat while the other four have a distal curvature to the base. Interestingly, the blade of Point N features protrusions that may be

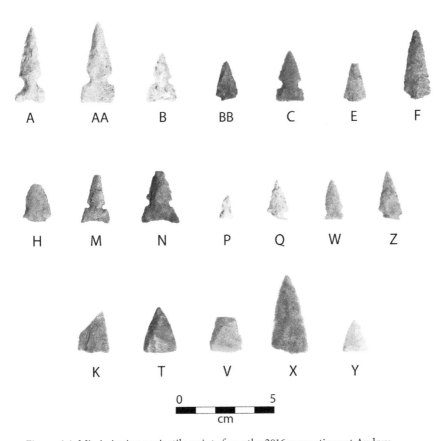

Figure 6.4. Mississippian projectile points from the 2016 excavations at Audrey.

remnants of an additional set of notches; a similar point was recovered from the Lamb site in the CIRV (Wilson 2015b). Eight of the notched points were heat-treated.

Four of the Mississippian points are Madison points, triangular in shape with no formal base. Three of the points were heat-treated. The remaining Mississippian projectile point represents the tip of a point (Point P), which, given its narrow shape, was likely from a triangular notched variety.

Both Late Woodland points are identified as the Mund variety (Figure 6.5). Mund points are long and narrow with a tapered and slightly flared base. Point G was found as a surface collection, churned up by the plow, while Point U (intact) was found in Zone B of Feature 5. While this could have been curated by Mississippians living at Audrey, it is also possible the

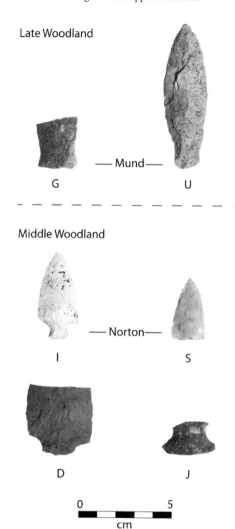

Figure 6.5. Woodland-period diagnostic projectiles from the 2016 excavations at the Audrey site.

point came from intermixing with the Late Woodland pit (Feature 28) below the floor of Feature 5.

Four Middle Woodland points were found, two of which are possible examples of Norton points, with the base of Point S broken off. The types for the other two characteristically Middle Woodland points could not be determined due to both being broken, and Point D being reworked. All of the Middle Woodland points were heat-treated. The remaining three points were unable to be sorted in any reliable category or time period due to breakage or reworking; these three are heat-treated as well.

It should be noted that, aside from the 4 points that were recovered from plow-zone contexts, most of the points came from the basal levels of feature excavations. In other words, the points either sank down through the house basin and pit feature fill or they were placed in these features before being filled. Seven of the 8 points from Feature 23, 10 of the 12 points from Feature 5, and both points from Feature 17 were recovered in the basal strata. During excavation, we noticed a higher concentration of projectiles as excavation reached the floors of the house, but time restrictions prevented us from collecting detailed provenience data as to whether or not these points were deposited on the floor.

Projectile Point Production Rejects

Six artifacts recovered represent failures of the projectile-point production process due to breakage or other unintended reduction errors. The clearest example is Artifact K, which represents a Madison point production failure (see Figure 6.4). Two of the other production failures were meant to be Mississippian projectile points. The remaining three are Woodland period projectile preforms (Brad Koldehoff, personal communication 2018); as these were found in and around Feature 5, it is possible that they were included in admixture from subfloor and surrounding Woodland features.

Adzes

Adzes are large, somewhat rectangular bifaces with broad working edges or bits. Another identifying attribute is usewear; adzes, used in woodworking, feature a dull polish on their bits in contrast to the mirror-like gloss sand leaves on agricultural chert hoes. The remains of six adzes, one adze preform, and one adze resharpening flake, were recovered at Audrey (Table 6.2). Four of the adzes are made from local Burlington chert (Figure 6.6) and the remaining two were reworked from Mill Creek hoes (Figure 6.7). With all of the informal and expedient chipped-stone tools in the Audrey lithic assemblage, these adzes stand out because they indicate that woodworking activities took place at Audrey.

A1 is a heat-treated Burlington chert biface with a high degree of gloss from use. This surface find appears to be the bit of an adze, whose use as a woodworking tool left a glossy finish on its surface. A2 is broken, but appears to be the butt of a well-formed large biface, perhaps a hoe or an adze. Broken along its wide axis, the intact edges of this heat-treated biface do not show signs of usewear. A3's working edges are broken but the tapered shape of this formally knapped, heat-treated tool suggests it was used as either a

Table 6.2. Bifacial tools

Feature	Projectile Point*		Adze*		Blade		Large Biface		Production Reject		Repurposed Projectile		UID Biface		Comments
	n	Wt (g)	n	Wt (g)	n	Wt (g)	n	Wt (g)	n	Wt (g)	n	Wt (g)	n	Wt (g)	
F5 PZ	6	19.68	1	12.37	–	–	–	–	1	29.85	–	–	2	3.15	
F5	14	112.3	5	221.68	2	9.72	6	158.44	–	–	3	16.92	4	61.46	Two adzes are reworked MCHs
F9	1	3.23	–	–	–	–	–	–	–	–	–	–	–	–	
F16	–	–	–	–	–	–	–	–	–	–	–	–	1	1.45	
F17	2	2.52	–	–	–	–	–	–	–	–	–	–	–	–	
F22	–	–	–	–	–	–	–	–	1	15.27	–	–	–	–	
F23	8	22.08	–	–	–	–	–	–	1	5.2	–	–	–	–	
HB	1	15.09	–	–	1	4.03	–	–	–	–	–	–	–	–	
SC	1	5.6	1	27.68	–	–	–	–	–	–	–	–	–	–	
Total	33	180.5	7	261.73	3	13.75	6	158.44	3	50.32	3	16.92	7	66.06	

Source: Compiled by author.

Notes: *Values include production rejects; PZ = plow zone; HB = House Block; SC = surface collection; MCH = Mill Creek hoe; – = Not present.

Figure 6.6. Burlington chert adzes, adze preform, and adze resharpening flake from the 2016 excavations at the Audrey site.

hoe or an adze; it is difficult to tell whether the shiny surface of the biface in places is due to heat treating or usewear from woodworking. At first glance, A4 appears to be an Archaic-period Turkey Tail projectile. However, the broken edge has been bifacially worked into an adze bit; glossy usewear near the working edge supports A4's use for woodworking.

The last two adzes are made of Mill Creek chert. The shape, size, and form of A5 and A6 (both recovered from Feature 5) suggests they were produced as adzes or woodworking tools with wide, bifacially worked bits (see Figure 6.7). A close inspection of these adzes shows hoe polish on the unretouched surfaces, meaning the tools were recycled from spent Mill Creek hoes.

hoe polish

A5

A6

0   5
cm

Figure 6.7. Adzes reworked from Mill Creek hoes, recovered from Feature 5.

The lithic assemblage also shows evidence that adze production took place at Audrey. For example, one adze preform (A7) was recovered. The large flake of heat-treated Burlington chert was shaped into an adze and worked on the dorsal side, but few modifications were made to the ventral side, and a formal adze bit was never formed; it is possible this adze preform was never completed due to a flaw in the chert encountered during knapping. A7 is also much smaller than the intact adzes in the assemblage. Additionally, one Burlington chert–adze resharpening flake was found in the early stages of Feature 5 excavation. The resharpening flake was identified by the polish on its dorsal side.

Mill Creek Chert Hoes

One Mill Creek hoe was found during excavations in the 1980s, but recent excavations mostly recovered polished hoe-resharpening flakes (n=81, 64.85 g) in addition to two adzes made from Mill Creek chert (discussed above). In the process of maintaining these Mill Creek hoes and reworking two of them into adzes, a significant number of flakes was produced. A high degree of polish on many of the flakes indicates that the objects they were struck from were used as hoes (see Milner et al. 2010). While one Mill Creek hoe-resharpening flake each was found in Features 22 and 23, and two in the plow zone of the House Block area, the remainder came from Feature 5 basin fill. This makes sense, as the two reworked Mill Creek adzes were also recovered from Feature 5. These objects and their significance at the Audrey site will be discussed in further detail below.

Other Bifaces

In addition to projectile points and adzes/large bifacial woodworking tools, a total of 19 bifacial tools and 3 bifacial production rejects were also re-covered (see Table 6.2; Figure 6.8). These objects, made of local Burling-ton chert, cannot be confidently placed in the other formal chipped-stone tool categories. With the exception of 1 biface each from Feature 16 and the House Block plow zone, the remaining 17 bifaces were all recovered from Feature 5 or hand-excavated plow-zone levels above Feature 5.

Six of these tools, all of which were recovered from Feature 5, are large bifaces, often uneven in shape due to their reduction from sharpening over time (see Figure 6.8: B4, B5, B6). Three of these other bifaces are blades. This type of formal tool is uncommon in the Audrey Mississippian lithic as-semblage, and two of the three appear to be heat-treated, Woodland-period blades (see Figure 6.8: B8). The presence of these blades in Feature 5 may be related to admixture from Feature 28, the Late Woodland pit feature below the house. The only other blade-like biface was found on the other side of the site, in the House Block plow zone.

Three of the bifaces resemble projectile points, but seem to have been put to different uses. B11, for example, resembles a carefully knapped, heat-treated Madison point, but it has a broken tip and its edges are more ser-rated than would be expected for a Madison point (see Figure 6.8). In ad-dition, the semisteep angle of one of the edges would have made this tool good for scraping. The remaining seven bifaces could not be categorized. Six of the bifaces were broken in a manner that obscures usewear or other attributes that could aid in tool-type identification.

Bifacial Production Rejects

As additional evidence of biface production at Audrey, three of the lithic artifacts recovered are categorized as bifacial production rejects (see Table

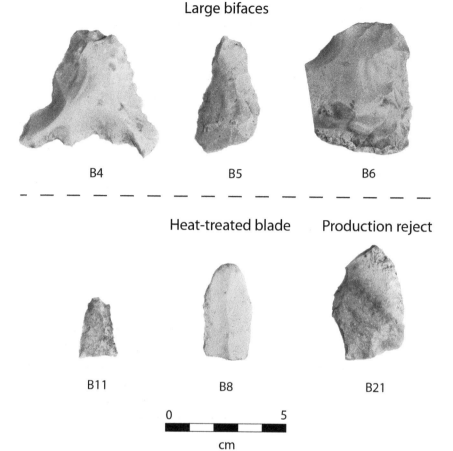

Figure 6.8. Select other bifacial tools from the 2016 excavations at Audrey.

6.2). These items were all in the process of being manufactured into tools, but were discarded prior to completion and do not show signs of use (see Figure 6.8: B21). It is unclear what the Audrey flintknappers' intentions were. These bifacial production rejects are found across the site.

Expedient Tools and Debitage

This category comprises not only chipped-stone debitage, but also expedient lithic cores, retouched and utilized flakes, end scrapers, chert hammerstones, and one chert abrader (see Friberg 2018b: Table 6.6 for more detail). The 2016 excavations yielded a massive quantity of lithic material: 11,317 pieces of expedient chert tools and debitage. The mean size of Burlington chert chipped-stone artifacts (calculated by dividing the total weight of Burlington chert expedient tools and debitage by the total count) is 2.66 g.

Cores

Audrey's lithic assemblage includes a total of 85 Burlington chert cores with an average weight of 55.71 g. Most interestingly, none of the cores is a prepared, prismatic core. Prepared cores are used for producing blades that can be worked bifacially or further knapped into drills; this action is repeatable, working in one direction around the core to knock off blades, and is the most efficient use of a core. I specifically note the lack of microlithic cores, which are used to produce microdrills for making shell beads. The Audrey cores, on the other hand, are all informal, multidirectional cores. These Burlington chert artifacts, four of which were heat-treated, were used expediently to produce flakes that could be retouched or used in a quick task. This type of core is common in Mississippian expedient flake tool industries (Koldehoff 1987: 152, 1995: 61).

Flake Tools

Flake tools are flakes detached from a core that were used expediently or that were retouched and used as tools. Flake tools would have served as everyday cutting-and-scraping tools for a variety of domestic tasks for which formalized tools were unnecessarily complicated. All of the flake tools from Audrey (n=224) are made from local Burlington chert. Two hundred and ten of these expedient tools are utilized flakes. Utilized flakes were identified during analysis by the presence of usewear on one or more of the flake's sharp edges. About a third of the utilized flakes were detached from heat-treated cores.

Retouched flakes were also among the flake tool assemblage at Audrey. However, it seems Audrey residents did not see an advantage in retouching expedient flake tools, as only 14 retouched flakes were recovered from recent excavations. Four of these tools were detached from heat-treated cores.

End Scrapers

End scrapers are a more specialized form of flake tool. They are made from flakes with steep-angled edges that are then shaped and retouched to strengthen and sharpen them, primarily for use in scraping deer hides. Five end scrapers were found at Audrey (two of which were heat-treated) (Figure 6.9). These small, expedient special-purpose tools were found across the site: two from Feature 5 basin fill, one from Feature 23, one from Feature 22

0   5

cm

Figure 6.9. End scrapers from the 2016 excavations at the Audrey site.

(a processing pit just outside Feature 23), and one from Feature 14 (a storage pit 4 m south of Feature 23). This spatial distribution of end scrapers suggested that hide processing was taking place across the site.

Other Chert Tools

In addition to two igneous/metamorphic hammerstones, two chert hammerstones were also found. Both from Feature 5, these heavy and battered cortex-covered cobbles are similar in size and weight to their nonchert counterparts (also found in Feature 5). There was also a small chert abrader found in Feature 23. With an abundance of sandstone available to Audrey villagers, a chert abrader seems an odd choice, but perhaps the use of an otherwise unusable piece of local chert as an abrader was in the interests of Mississippian expediency.

Debitage

The remaining 10,909 chert objects (23.32 kg) are classified as debitage (see Friberg 2018b: Table 6.7). This category includes flakes (intentionally percussed), flake shatter (broken flakes), and angular shatter (accidentally removed material). Distinguishing between these types of debitage has been useful in some detailed studies of lithic technology, but given the immense size of the collection, this level of analysis was not feasible.

The vast majority of the debitage (99.5 percent by count and 95.87 percent by weight) is from local Burlington chert, 20.36 percent of which (44.42 percent by weight) is heat-treated. The mean weight of Burlington chert debitage is 2.06 g overall, although the heat-treated flakes tend to be larger (mean = 3.75 g) than non–heat-treated debitage (mean = 1.72 g).

In addition to Burlington chert, the debitage also includes quartz (n=4; 8.09 g) and quartzite (n=4; 229.21 g), Cobden (n=4; 2.86 g) and Kaolin (n=4; 4.87) cherts from southern Illinois, Knife River Chalcedony (n=8; 16.85 g) from North Dakota, Hixton silicified sediment (n=6; 2.53 g) from west-central Wisconsin, and unidentifiable non-Burlington cherts (n=20; 263.51). There were also 81 flakes of Mill Creek chert, which are reported in the section on formal tools.

Comparative Analysis

The Audrey site Mississippian lithic assemblage is comprised of both expedient flake tools and more formal lithic tools. A number of formal chipped-stone tools were produced and used at Audrey, including projectile points for hunting and adzes for woodworking. Nevertheless, the majority of the tools used by the village's inhabitants were expedient in nature, such as multidirectional cores, flake tools, end scrapers, and sandstone abraders. This pattern, common in the American Bottom, has also been documented at multiple sites in the CIRV, ARV, and probably the entire middle Mississippian culture area (Koldehoff 1987, 1995). For example, investigations at Lundy yielded a high volume and density of lithic material (also likely due to Lundy's close proximity to an abundant source of chert), and the assemblage lacked formal core reduction techniques (Emerson et al. 2007: 74). Similarly, the Lamb site in the CIRV lacked formal tools (with the exception of projectile points and Mill Creek hoe flakes), instead consisting primarily of expedient flake tools, informal cobble tools, and abraders (Wilson 2015b: 213). Despite the similarities in the use of expedient flake tools at various Mississippian sites, there is important interregional variation in the production and use of lithic tools.

Comparative analyses are presented below to address the implications of these differences in lithic assemblages among the Audrey site, northern hinterland regions, and the Greater Cahokia area. I first address the organization of Mississippian lithic procurement, production, and distribution as they relate to sociopolitical complexity. Second, I discuss the implications of differences in lithic assemblages for variation in local practices, such as the hunting and processing of deer. I then discuss the circulation of northern exotic lithic materials within the American Bottom, its immediate periphery, and its northern hinterland, and the implications for complex interregional interaction. Finally, I present an in-depth interregional analysis of the shell bead, basalt celt, and Mill Creek hoe industries to address how Mississippian economic interactions and exchange relationships shaped the Mississippian world.

Organization of Mississippian Lithic Industries

Perhaps the most fundamental difference between Mississippian lithic assemblages has to do with the organization of lithic industries. For example, inhabitants of the Lamb site in the CIRV focused mainly on the production of expedient tools, and they seem to have organized their lithic industry with a focus on the local procurement of lithic raw materials (Wilson 2015b: 213). The same is true of the Audrey site, where excavations recovered a number of large primary-stage reduction flakes, suggesting that large cobbles of nearby local Burlington chert were brought back to the site for reduction. In contrast to the Illinois Valley Mississippian pattern of localized chert procurement and production, Cahokia's lithic industry was centered around a distant source of chert, and evidence suggests that formal chipped-stone tools (such as large bifaces) were not produced by inhabitants of American Bottom settlements (Koldehoff 1987: 178; Koldehoff and Brennan 2010: 139).

Koldehoff (1995: 54) posits that at sites where the raw material is obtained from farther away (such as Cahokia), primary-stage reduction tends to occur at the source prior to transporting the material back to the site. This system of centralized quarry production is indicative of more than just transportation logistics. Cahokians chose to concentrate their lithic industry on the extraction of chert specifically from the Crescent Hills quarries (~50 km away), rather than exploiting nearby resources. Finished tools, blanks, and raw materials were then distributed throughout the American Bottom. The organization of this lithic industry would have required support from complex regional and centrally articulated networks of production and circulation (Kelly 1984; Koldehoff 1987: 178; Koldehoff and Brennan 2010: 147).

While a discussion of the mean size of chert debitage would be useful for demonstrating the degree of primary-stage lithic production occurring at the Audrey site or American Bottom sites, material from many American Bottom excavations was not screened, and thus not all the available data are reliable for quantitative comparison. A full comparison of density-of-chert debitage is also not possible. However, the volume of local Burlington chert recovered from excavations, along with the observation of primary-stage reduction flakes and the proximity to a source of Burlington chert, suggests that all stages of lithic production were occurring at Audrey. In contrast to the American Bottom, Audrey inhabitants seem to have had a simpler and more localized system of chert extraction and distribution, which was framed in part by the accessibility of Burlington chert in the LIRV. Audrey's lithic industry was likely also structured by a less complex, less centralized political economy than existed in the American Bottom.

Local Practices: Deer Hunting and Processing

Through analysis of lithic and faunal material from the American Bottom and CIRV, Wilson and Kuehn (2011) demonstrate that deer-hunting and -processing practices varied between the two regions. They found that American Bottom Mississippians consumed fewer deer than CIRV groups, and focused on the high utility portions of the deer due to logistical complexities related to deer resource depletion from hunting pressure (see also Kelly 1979: 16, 20). Without comparative faunal data from Audrey, two lines of evidence are explored here related to the practice of hunting and processing deer: projectile points for hunting and end scrapers for processing hides.

An abundance of end scrapers and projectile points within a site's lithic assemblage (in addition to hematite and red ochre) has been associated with an economic focus on large mammal hunting and hide processing (Struever 1968); red ocher may have acted as a preservative for the hides (Keeley 1980). Such a pattern is observed to a notable degree at the Fred Edwards site in the ARV, where a tremendous number of end scrapers (n=246) and projectile points (n=438) was recovered from a relatively small, 1.2 ha portion of the site (Finney 1993: 172–173). Finney (1993: 173) argues that hide processing at the Fred Edwards site likely represents "an economic undertaking at a scale not previously known" in the Midwest, claiming that end scrapers are not characteristic of either Late Woodland or Middle Mississippian lithic assemblages and are rare at American Bottom sites (Finney 1993: 176). If the LIRV's proximity to the American Bottom allowed for frequent interaction, we might expect the focus of economic activities in the two regions to be similar, and for LIRV economic activities to vary from those in the northern hinterland; in this case, Audrey inhabitants may not have engaged in hide processing to the degree that northern hinterland groups did. However, as deer-resource depletion seems to be a main cause of the declines in deer hunting and processing observed in the American Bottom, Audrey inhabitants, 100 km to the north, may have taken advantage of a healthy deer population and exploited this resource similarly to their neighbors to the north.

Projectile Points

Projectile points tend to be uncommon in Stirling-phase assemblages in the American Bottom, which is likely related to the previously mentioned depletion of the region's deer population (Kelly 1979: 16; Wilson and Kuehn 2011). At the same time, Cahokia-style projectile points (such as Madison and Mississippian notched points) are found in the CIRV and ARV in more abundant quantities. Wilson and Kuehn (2011) used a standardized projectile point–abundance index (calculated by dividing the total number of points by the total count of all chipped-stone material for each site) to show that point abundance corresponds to deer hunting, and that inhabitants of the CIRV hunted more deer and produced more projectile points than did American Bottom groups. With varying recovery methods (that is, screened versus unscreened excavations) and such a high density of chert debitage at the Audrey site, chert counts may not be the most reliable measure for comparative analysis. For this reason, I calculate point abundance as a ratio of projectile points to jar rims: (n projectile points/n jar rims) *100. As jars are the most consistently ubiquitous type of diagnostic material culture at Mississippian sites, using jar-rim counts in comparison to point counts should produce a relatively standardized ratio. Point abundance indexes were calculated using projectile-point counts from Wilson and Kuehn (2011) and jar-rim counts from Stirling-phase contexts at the Sponemann (Jackson 1992 et al.) and Dugan Airfield (Skousen 2018; Wilson 2018) sites in the American Bottom, Lohmann- and Stirling-phase contexts at Cahokia Tract 15A (Pauketat 1998b), the Lamb site in the CIRV (Wilson 2015b), and the Lundy site in the ARV (Emerson et al. 2007).

There is no reason to suspect that the inhabitants of the LIRV had a major impact on the deer population (as occurred in the American Bottom) or that deer resources would have been difficult to access at that time (see VanDerwarker and Wilson 2016 for a discussion of food insecurity in the thirteenth-century CIRV). Therefore, we would expect Audrey villagers to have engaged in deer hunting to a similar degree as their northern neighbors. If Audrey inhabitants were engaging in a high degree of deer hunting, Audrey's point abundance should be more similar to Lamb and Lundy's than to sites in the American Bottom. Figure 6.10 shows that Audrey's point abundance falls between American Bottom and northern hinterland

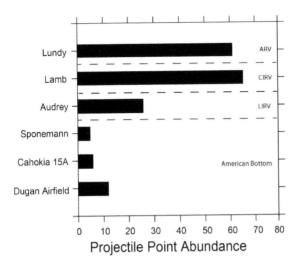

Figure 6.10. Point abundance indices for early Mississippian sites, calculated as a ratio of jar rim to projectile point counts.

groups. This suggests Audrey inhabitants hunted deer more regularly than did dwellers of the American Bottom, but to a lesser degree than CIRV and ARV groups. Indeed, a preliminary report of faunal remains from the Audrey site indicates that "entire field-dressed deer were regularly brought back to the site for processing," a pattern that differs from the American Bottom (Kuehn 2017). More work is necessary to integrate Audrey's faunal data with Wilson and Kuehn's (2011) study of American Bottom and northern hinterland deer exploitation to fully understand patterns of deer hunting, transportation, consumption, and processing in the LIRV. However, the current lithic analysis suggests that the LIRV may not have had the same restrictions on large mammal resources that existed in the American Bottom. Also, Audrey inhabitants did not exploit large mammal resources to the same degree as did their northern neighbors.

End Scrapers

End scrapers are often expedient tools whose steep-angled edges are ideal for the scraping and processing of deer hides. Eight end scrapers were recovered from the Lamb site in the CIRV (Wilson 2015b) and 42 from the Lundy site in the ARV (Emerson et al. 2007). However, end scrapers tend to be rare in the American Bottom (Hall 1967: 177; Wilson 2015b); a review of reports of early Mississippian American Bottom sites yielded scarcely a mention of end scrapers (as opposed to other types of scraping tools) (Emerson and Jackson 1984; Esarey and Pauketat 1992; Finney 1985; Fortier 1985; Jackson et al. 1992; Jackson and Hanenberger, eds. 1990; Kelly et al. 1990; McElrath et al. 1987; Milner 1984; Pauketat 1998b; Skousen 2018); one exception is the BBB motor site, where 5 end scrapers were recovered (Emerson 1984: 246).

In combination with the abundance of deer and projectile points, the frequency of end scrapers in the CIRV and ARV suggests that northern hinterland Mississippians frequently engaged in deer hunting and hide working (Keeley 1980; Struever 1968). In contrast, the same activities do not seem to have taken place to the same degree in the American Bottom. Five end scrapers were found at Audrey along with 19 projectile points and preliminary evidence for unrestricted access to deer resources; this evidence suggests Audrey residents also engaged in hide working on a similar level to, although possibly to a lesser degree than, their northern neighbors. Perhaps this difference suggests that deer populations in the LIRV were somewhat impacted by the large populations immediately to the south. Indeed, the scarcity of evidence for deer-hide working in the American Bottom is likely related to the overhunting of deer due to the regional consolidation and major settlement nucleation occurring in the American Bottom at that time. The fact that these activities were still happening up north suggests that settlement patterns (density of population and settlements) did not have an impact on the deer population. It is also possible LIRV groups, in the immediate periphery of the American Bottom, engaged in economic interactions with both Greater Cahokia and northern hinterland groups, resulting in a diversification of economic strategies and only a partial participation in the northern deer hide–exchange network. Perhaps deer hides, the availability of which was likely limited for most American Bottom inhabitants, could have been a valuable commodity provided by northern groups in exchange for exotic materials and tools commonly circulating within the American Bottom (Bardolph and Wilson 2015: 145; Finney 1993: 16; Goldstein 1980).

Exotic Materials

While the vast majority of chipped stone from Audrey is locally sourced Burlington chert, it is important to consider the presence of exotic lithic materials as evidence of long-distance interaction and exchange. That said, all of the exotic chipped stone (other than the reworked Mill Creek hoes) is in the form of small flakes, and it is possible that these items represent admixture from previous Woodland-era occupations on the site. Four flakes each of Cobden and Kaolin cherts from southern Illinois were present at Audrey and likely date to the Mississippian occupation of the site; their presence is unsurprising given the LIRV's proximity to the American Bottom where these cherts were frequently circulated during the Mississippian period (Koldehoff 1987: 163; Koldehoff and Brennan 2010). Mill Creek chert is also present but, due to the economic significance of the Mill Creek hoe industry, these items are excluded from the discussion of exotic cherts and discussed in more detail below.

The other exotic chipped stone present at Audrey comes from northern sources. Quartzite can be sourced to northern Wisconsin glacial till (Millhouse 2012: 303); quartzite is the primary chipped-stone raw material used at the Aztalan site, a Mississippian mound complex in southeast Wisconsin (Barrett 1933: 267). Knife River Chalcedony is a rare material from North Dakota that was more commonly traded throughout the Eastern Plains in the Middle and Late Woodland periods, but is not found at Cahokia; the Fred Edwards site in the ARV is the only other site in this study with Knife River Chalcedony (n=2) in its assemblage (Finney 1993: 156). Finally, Hixton silicified sediment comes from Silver Mound in west-central Wisconsin and is found in small quantities at a number of Mississippian sites throughout the Midwest; the distribution of Hixton is discussed further below. Even though there are only a few flakes of these northern cherts, and it is possible they were brought to the Audrey site during the Middle Woodland period, it is worth considering how Mississippian inhabitants of the Audrey Village may have gained access to them.

Millhouse explores this issue at the John Chapman site in the ARV. Burlington chert is an exotic material there, and a lack of cherts from southeast Iowa—where the closest Burlington outcrop is located—suggests Apple River Mississippians obtained their Burlington from other Mississippian groups to the south, perhaps even the LIRV (Millhouse 2012: 300). In general, the Mississippian-period occupation of the ARV (including the Fred Edwards site) saw an increase in exotic cherts from the south, such as Burlington, Mill Creek, and Cobden (Millhouse 2012: 305). It is also possible that Mill Creek chert hoes and Kaolin chert were brought into the region along with Burlington chert from the Crescent Hills quarries just north of the American Bottom (Millhouse 2012: 302). I suggest Apple River groups could have had geographically closer contacts with whom to exchange Burlington chert, such as LIRV Mississippians rather than Cahokian groups. An increase in interactions with nearby neighbors from the Late Woodland to

Mississippian period is certainly observed at the Fred Edwards site, where a number of exotic Woodland-style ceramic vessels were found (Finney 1993); it is possible the Hixton and Knife River chert at Fred Edwards also came to the site through these interactions with surrounding groups. The Lamb site in the CIRV yielded very little exotic lithic material (<0.1 percent) (Wilson 2015b), which may be a product of small sample size; alternatively, Lamb's paucity of exotic chert may be because it is a small and relatively isolated early Mississippian site and its inhabitants may not have engaged in frequent interactions with outside groups.

If the presence of exotic cherts at Mississippian sites represents interactions with outside groups, how do these interactions compare across regions? In addition to Mill Creek chert, there seems to be an exchange of other exotic cherts in the American Bottom (represented by the Sponemann site [Jackson et al. 1992]) and the eastern uplands (represented by Knoebel [Alt 2002b]), with exotic cherts ranging between 1.9 percent and 3.7 percent of lithic assemblages. These higher percentages of exotic cherts are not surprising given the common circulation of cherts from Union County, Illinois (not including Mill Creek chert), within the American Bottom. Cahokia's ICT II Stirling-phase lithic assemblage contains only 1.2 percent exotic chert by count; although, in addition to Kaolin and Cobden, Cahokia's exotic chipped-stone materials also include 30 pieces of Hixton silicified sediment from west-central Wisconsin (Holley 1989). Despite its low percentage of exotic cherts, Cahokia (and affiliations with the settlement) likely played a role in exchange interactions that resulted in higher concentrations of exotic cherts at other American Bottom and upland sites. Indeed, it has been suggested that Cahokia controlled the distribution of a number of craft items and exotic goods within the Greater Cahokia area (Pauketat 1997a, 1998a). The network of interaction and relationships resulting from these political-economic activities may have facilitated other exchange networks, such as the circulation of exotic cherts.

In the north, both the Fred Edwards and Lundy sites in the ARV have comparably high percentages of exotic chipped stone, between 2.2 percent and 2.7 percent; Burlington chert is considered an exotic material in the ARV. Notably, in addition to the Kaolin and Cobden cherts from southern Illinois seen at American Bottom and uplands sites, ARV groups also had access to exotic northern materials such as Hixton silicified sandstone, quartzite from northern Wisconsin, and a small amount of Knife River Chalcedony from North Dakota (Fred Edwards n=2). As mentioned earlier, the reasons for this may have been twofold: (1) interactions with Cahokia and American Bottom groups; and/or (2) increased interactions with nearby Mississippian groups (that is, Illinois Valley Mississippians) and surrounding Woodland groups. Again, Lamb has a low percentage of exotic cherts, which is likely due to the small sample size from the site.

Audrey's percentage of exotic chert is surprisingly low (0.3 percent) considering the wealth of evidence for interaction with American Bottom groups. This low percentage may again be due to the high density of Burlington chert at the Audrey side. Nevertheless, the presence of exotic cherts in Audrey's lithic assemblage, and assemblages in the ARV, indicates some level of long-distance exchange. As discussed in Chapter 5, exchange with outside groups was uncommon during the Late Woodland period in the CIRV and LIRV (Green and Nolan 2000: 369), and increased from the Late Woodland to Mississippian period in the ARV (Finney 1993). While interaction with Cahokia might explain the presence of Union County cherts in the LIRV and northern hinterland regions, it is unclear whether the same can be said of exotic northern cherts in these regions. The question remains: what types of relationships, exchange networks, or affiliations facilitated the circulation of exotic cherts north of the Greater Cahokia area? This question is explored in the following section through a discussion of Hixton silicified sediment.

Hixton Silicified Sediment

How did Hixton silicified sediment come to reach Audrey and ARV sites? Sourced to Silver Mound in west-central Wisconsin, Hixton is found in lithic assemblages in and around Cahokia, 850 km south. At the Trempealeau and Fisher Mounds site complexes (only ~100 km south of the source), Hixton makes up almost 7 percent of chipped-stone artifacts and debitage by count. Arrow points made from Hixton have been found mostly in Lohmann-phase contexts at Cahokia and tend to be less common in subsequent phases (Green and Rodell 1994: 353). If the material were only found at Trempealeau and sites in the Greater Cahokia area, this might suggest a direct exchange system between Cahokians and their outpost in the north, resulting in the distribution of Hixton (in addition to other raw materials from western Wisconsin) in the American Bottom, as some have posited (Green and Rodell 1994: 353; Millhouse 2012: 303). However, the material is also present at Audrey and hinterland Mississippian sites much closer to the source: Fred Edwards, Lundy, and John Chapman in the ARV. Given

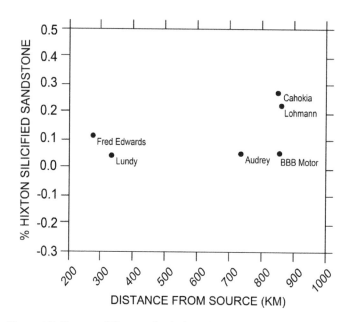

Figure 6.11. Percent of Hixton silicified sandstone versus distance from the source.

the widespread distribution of Hixton, it seems unlikely that Cahokia controlled the distribution of the material, particularly to groups living relatively close to the source.

To better understand this pattern, I calculated the percentages of Hixton silicified sandstone by count in early Stirling chipped-stone assemblages when present in the American Bottom (Esarey and Pauketat 1992; Emerson 1984; Pauketat 1998b), LIRV, and ARV (Emerson et al. 2007; Finney 1993), and plotted them against each site's distance from the raw-material source (calculated using Google Earth). If Cahokia controlled the distribution of Hixton silicified sediment through its outpost at Trempealeau, we would expect sites in the Greater Cahokia area to have higher percentages of Hixton than in the LIRV and ARV. If the distribution of Hixton were not restricted by leaders at Cahokia, we would expect to see higher percentages of the material in the ARV, closer to the source. At first, the resulting scatterplot (Figure 6.11) simply shows that none of these settlements had very much Hixton overall (all less than 0.3 percent); with the exception of Trempealeau (which was removed as an outlier in this graph), even the sites closest to the source do not have a considerable amount. While Cahokia and the Lohmann site have slightly higher percentages of Hixton than other sites, with all sites ranging between 0.04 percent and 0.27 percent of Hixton, this graph does not support the claim that Cahokia controlled the distribution of this rare exotic material. It is more likely that Hixton silicified sandstone was exchanged in small amounts among all of these Mississippian groups. Indeed, Hixton was a common exchange item in the northern Midwest during the Woodland period. Perhaps this pattern hints at the possibility of continued or renewed interactions among northern groups that existed prior to the twelfth century.

Galena

Although not part of chipped-stone lithic assemblages, galena is another exotic lithic resource that has important implications for understanding regional interaction. Thirteen cubes of galena (lead ore's natural form) were recovered from Feature 5 at Audrey. Interestingly, galena would have been an exotic material to Audrey residents. Some have posited that galena at Cahokia may have come from the Missouri Ozarks (Emerson 1991a; Kelly and Brown 2012; Milner 1990), although there are multiple sources of lead ore in the Midwest (Millhouse 2012; Walthall 1981). For example, the galena from John Chapman comes from a fairly local source along the Apple River. In fact, Walthall's (1981: 55) sourcing study of galena suggests that while Cahokia's galena likely came from Missouri, galena found in the CIRV seems to have originated from the Upper Mississippi Valley. If this is true, it supports the notion of Apple River and CIRV groups engaging in exchange relations independent of Cahokia (Millhouse 2012: 316). The source of the galena recovered from Audrey site excavations remains unknown at this time.

Mississippian Economic Interactions

The hypothesis presented at the beginning of the chapter is that the LIRV's proximity to the American Bottom may have facilitated regular interaction and direct economic ties between the inhabitants of both regions. As a result, LIRV groups may have been able to engage in the production and/or exchange of economically and politically important Cahokian craft items such as Mill Creek hoes, St. Francois basalt celts, and marine shell beads. While evidence of these Cahokian craft industries is found at settlements in the Greater Cahokia area (Pauketat 1998a: 50), there is little evidence of these items in northern hinterland regions. An interregional comparative analysis of these craft industries should show that Audrey site inhabitants were engaged in Cahokian exchange networks to a greater degree than were northern hinterland groups.

Shell Beads

Direct political ties among Cahokian elites and LIRV groups may have provided Audrey residents with access to marine shell for bead production. During the 1980s excavations of the Audrey site, a cache of 120 finished, marine shell disk beads was recovered from a suspected elite household (Cook 1983). Additionally, recent UCSB excavations recovered one marine shell disk bead. However, there is currently no evidence for the production of these beads at the Audrey site. No marine shell detritus was encountered during excavation, and lithic analysis failed to identify any microdrills or microlithic cores. The presence of marine shell beads at Audrey and their association with an elite household (Delaney-Rivera 2000: 228) suggest the beads were acquired through interactions with elite groups who controlled the production of shell beads at Cahokia or elsewhere in the American Bottom.

Basalt Celt Industry

Frequent interaction with Greater Cahokia populations may have enabled Audrey inhabitants' involvement in the American Bottom basalt celt industry. These robust stone axe-heads would have facilitated the intensification of woodworking activities necessary for building the houses, temples, special-purpose buildings, and (later) palisades of highly nucleated Mississippian settlements. If Audrey site inhabitants participated in this basalt celt exchange network, we would expect the celts from Audrey to be made of basalt and to be more similar in size and shape to American Bottom celts than to northern hinterland or Woodland-era celts.

The celts recovered from recent excavations and documented in the private collection at the Audrey site appear to be made of basalt. This finding is significant because, other than occasional glacial till, there is no local source of basalt in the LIRV. Based on close visual examination, American Bottom celts appear to be made almost exclusively of basalt from the St. Francois Mountains[1] (Pauketat and Alt 2004: 783). Koldehoff and Wilson's (2010) visual analysis of basaltic and igneous materials is accepted and reliable. Although there are multiple recognizable varieties of St. Francois Mountain basalt (Pauketat and Alt 2004: 783), ranging in color from yellowish green to light and dark gray depending on the freshness of breaks, there is a fairly clear difference between the fine-grained St. Francois diabase flecks with distinct white phenocrysts and local igneous/metamorphic glacial tills (Koldehoff and Wilson 2010: 17). If the Audrey celts are in fact made from basalt, it is likely that the material comes from the St. Francois Mountains. Furthermore, as there is a lack of evidence for celt production at Audrey (no spherical hammerstones and a scant amount of basalt debitage), it is likely that the celts were brought to Audrey via exchange relationships.

Woodland-era celts tend to be small and narrow compared to the more robust celts produced, cached, and circulated within the Mississippian American Bottom (Koldehoff and Wilson 2010: 237–238; Wilson and Koldehoff 2009). In their study of Mississippian celt manufacture, Wilson and Koldehoff (2009) address whether celts produced in the CIRV are more similar to American Bottom Woodland-era or Mississippian celts by comparing lengths and widths between these regions and general time periods. They gathered data on Mississippian celts from eight American Bottom sites, including Cahokia (Pauketat 1998b: 269), Julien (Milner 1984: 89), East St. Louis (Daniels 2007: 725; Pauketat 2005: 240), Primas (Pauketat and Woods 1986), Scott Airforce Base (Holley et al. 2001), Washausen (Betzenhauser 2008), Determann BP (Jackson 1984), and Hawkins Hollow (Jackson 2014), as well as three CIRV sites: Roskamp, Norris Farms, and the Fiedler site (Morse et al. 1953). The Mississippian celts were compared with LW and TLW celts from eight American Bottom sites including Dugan Airfield, Range, Sprague, Woodland Ridge, Scott Airforce Base, Kane Village, George Reeves, and the BBB Motor site. The study found that CIRV celts are smaller and less formally designed than Cahokian and American Bottom celts, and are normally produced from a variety of local glacial till rather than basalt. These qualities align CIRV celts more with Late Woodland celts from the American Bottom than later, Mississippian period ones, and this pattern suggests a local retention of certain Woodland-era traditions in the CIRV (Wilson and Koldehoff 2009).

Where does Audrey fall within this spectrum? The LIRV's proximity to Cahokia may have enabled closer connections with American Bottom groups and their trade networks than was possible in the CIRV; the difference in celt raw material between the CIRV (igneous glacial till) and the LIRV (basalt) already supports this hypothesis. Because Audrey's celts are made of basalt (like Cahokian celts), yet there is no evidence for local manufacture, it is possible that Audrey's celts came to the region through trade with American Bottom groups. If this is the case, we would expect the Audrey celts to be more similar in size to American Bottom Mississippian celts than those from the CIRV. Adding to Wilson and Koldehoff's (2009) data, I gathered measurements from photos of intact celts from the Audrey site landowner's private collection (representing the LIRV) to compare celt length and width between regions and time periods. In the interests of observing general trends, I collapsed all Late Woodland (LW) and Terminal Late Woodland (TLW) data into a single category, and did the same for early- and late Mississippian–period data.

A scatterplot graphing the length of each celt against its width creates a cursory visual comparison of celt size. Figure 6.12 shows that Woodland-era celts are generally smaller than the Mississippian celts, with the American Bottom Mississippian celts standing out as both longer and wider. The CIRV celts do overlap with the American Bottom LW and TLW celts with a few examples that are longer and wider. As for the LIRV, the Audrey celts vary in size, but also overlap with the larger LW and TLW celts, the average-sized Mississippian celts, and even the largest Mississippian celts.

It is important to test whether these differences are statistically significant. The boxplot is a valuable method for evaluating and comparing range, median, and outliers in a dataset simultaneously. The notches in a boxplot represent the 95 percent confidence interval for the dataset. When comparing boxplots, the notches become important. Some overlap of the boxed area means there is overlap in the range of data between two datasets, but if the notched areas of two datasets (confidence intervals) do not overlap, there is strong evidence that the medians differ.

Figure 6.13a is a boxplot of the celt lengths by region and time period. We can clearly see that the Mississippian celts are significantly larger than their Woodland counterparts. The Audrey celts do overlap with the Cahokia Mississippian celts, although they are smaller on average. The CIRV celts are smaller, and overlap with the LIRV celts, but they are significantly different from the American Bottom Mississippian celts.

A boxplot of celt widths shows a very different pattern (Figure 6.13b). While the LIRV celts are only slightly narrower than the large, broad American Bottom–Mississippian celts, they do overlap. However, the CIRV celts are statistically more slender than American Bottom and LIRV celts, and they are most similar to Woodland-era American Bottom celts.

Finally, we address the question of variation within each sample. How much does celt size vary by region and period? If celt production were centralized at Cahokia, we would expect Cahokia's Mississippian-period celts to be more similar in size than those produced in the LW and TLW periods. If Audrey's celts were also a product of Cahokian centralized production, they should also be relatively similar in size. To assess this issue, I ran

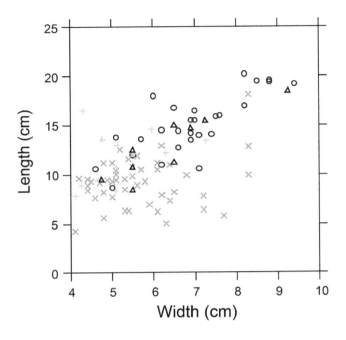

Figure 6.12. Celt length versus width. The LIRV is represented by the Audrey site.

○ American Bottom Mississippian

✕ American Bottom Woodland

＋ CIRV Mississippian

△ LIRV Mississippian

basic statistics, including coefficients of variation (CoV) on the celt lengths and widths (Table 6.3 and Table 6.4). While standard deviation (SD) can be used to examine variation within a sample, SD is specific to the mean value for that sample (that is, a larger sample is likely to have a higher SD than a smaller sample) and thus is inappropriate for comparing variability between datasets. The CoV is a measure of relative variability (independent of the sample mean) and is calculated by dividing the standard deviation of a dataset by its mean. These values are compared between similar datasets to show which dataset has the smallest amount of variation from the mean. In the current study, the CoV is used to evaluate which group of celts varies the least in size (or is more standardized).

In terms of both length and width, the American Bottom Mississippian celts have the lowest CoVs, and the Woodland celts the highest. This means that Mississippian celts vary the least in size compared with the LIRV, CIRV,

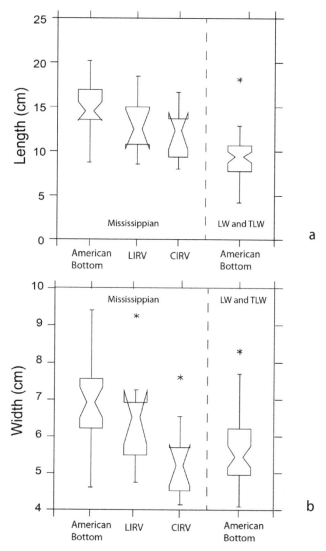

Figure 6.13. (a) Boxplot of celt lengths; (b) boxplot of celt widths. The LIRV is represented by the Audrey site.

and their Woodland counterparts. The pattern further suggests a uniformity of celt production in the Mississippian American Bottom, supporting what some have claimed as controlled production of these items by a select few at Cahokia (Pauketat 1997; Pauketat and Alt 2004).

A comparative analysis of raw material and size of groundstone celts has provided two lines of evidence regarding the LIRV's interactions with

Table 6.3. Basic statistics on celt length

	American Bottom Mississippian	LIRV	CIRV	American Bottom LW and TLW
N Celts	27	9	11	48
Minimum	8.7	8.5	7.822	4.2
Maximum	20.2	18.5	16.5	18.1
Arithmetic mean	15.067	12.917	11.672	9.267
Standard deviation	3.061	3.248	2.831	2.458
Coefficient of variation	0.203	0.251	0.243	0.265

Source: Compiled by author.

Table 6.4. Basic statistics on celt width

	American Bottom Mississippian	LIRV	CIRV	American Bottom LW and TLW
N Celts	27	9	11	48
Minimum	4.6	4.75	4.115	4.1
Maximum	9.4	9.25	7.267	8.3
Arithmetic mean	6.937	6.406	5.178	5.667
Standard deviation	1.213	1.335	0.971	1.063
Variance	1.471	1.783	0.943	1.131
Coefficient of variation	0.175	0.208	0.188	0.188

Source: Compiled by author.

American Bottom groups and how those relationships differed from groups farther north. In terms of material, although CIRV celts are not made of St. Francois Mountain basalt, those from the Audrey collection closely resemble basalt, suggesting the celts were exchanged through interactions with American Bottom groups. Regarding size, the LIRV celts are statistically similar to American Bottom Mississippian celts, which is further evidence that the Audrey celts themselves may have been made in the American Bottom; there is currently no evidence for celt manufacture at Audrey. The slightly smaller length of LIRV celts may be because the items were not from caches of unused celts like many of their American Bottom counterparts and became smaller over time through use and resharpening. In contrast to the LIRV, evidence suggests that inhabitants of the CIRV did not engage in the American Bottom basalt celt exchange network, and that the small size of the region's celts may represent a local style of celt making, which likely stems from earlier production techniques in the region.

Finally, the significance of LIRV celts likely deriving from the American Bottom transcends an involvement in basalt celt exchange. The production and caching of celts at Cahokia and in the American Bottom and uplands suggests an intensification of woodworking. Indeed, these large tools served an important function as increased populations created a need for more houses and the wooden posts that support them. American Bottom Mississippians also needed wood for building temples and other ceremonial structures in addition to large central posts and, by the end of the Stirling phase, palisades. And on a smaller, but more extensive scale, as agriculture intensified, celts were vital for clearing fields. These intensive woodworking activities required the use of large groundstone axe-heads. The presence of the same tools at Audrey suggests that the village's inhabitants were engaging in similar types of activities. Evidence for large biface production at Audrey, in addition to six adzes, an adze preform, and an adze-resharpening flake from the site, further support the presence of woodworking activities at Audrey. Interestingly, while woodworking was certainly an important activity at Cahokia, there is little evidence for large biface production in the American Bottom; Koldehoff (1987: 178) suggests these more specialized tools were likely produced by experienced flintworkers at or nearby the Crescent Hills quarries.

Mill Creek Hoe Exchange

There is abundant evidence for the use of Mill Creek hoes at American Bottom and eastern uplands sites, thought to be related to the intensification of maize and starchy seed production (Brown et al. 1990; Hammerstedt and Hughes 2015; Koldehoff 1985; Pauketat 1994, 1997a, 1998a, 2003). Although it has been demonstrated that Cahokia did not control the raw material source (Koldehoff and Brennan 2010: 152), some researchers argue that Cahokia did restrict the distribution of Mill Creek hoes to groups with whom they had economic ties (Brown et al. 1990; Pauketat 1998a, 2003). This arrangement would have benefited both the farmers in outlying settlements and the central-power holders at Cahokia by providing powerful tools used in the clearing and preparing of fields to facilitate the intensification of agriculture. Of course, Mississippian groups intensified food production for a variety of reasons. However, access to the Cahokian-sponsored Mill Creek hoe exchange network was likely linked with expectations for reciprocal provisions in the form of agricultural surplus; surplus maize could be used by Cahokia elites for sponsoring work projects or craft specialists.

Some suggest this level of Cahokian economic control decreased outside the Greater Cahokia area with distance from the center (Brown et al. 1990: 271, 274; Muller 1997; Pauketat 1998a). In their 1990 publication, Brown and colleagues investigate the general trends in the distribution of Mill Creek hoes both north and south of the raw material source. This was done on a county-wide scale, comparing a value they call "hoe distance," a measure calculated by multiplying the number of intact Mill Creek hoe blades for each county in question by the river distance of the county center from the Mill Creek quarries. They also use a fall-off curve model to evaluate the influence of population and transportation routes on hoe trade with a mathematical formulation of "standardized gravity scores." They conclude that the density of Mill Creek hoes decreased with distance from the source, with the exception that densities appear greater in counties with larger settlements. The pattern suggests that large population centers close to major river systems (Cahokia being the most influential of these) controlled the trade of hoes to outlying sites within a small surrounding zone (Brown et al. 1990: 269–271).

In his study of Mississippian political economy, Muller (1997) reevaluates Brown et al.'s data by calculating the correlation between the natural logarithm of distance from the source to the number of Mill Creek hoes in each county. Muller also considers the influence of Cahokia on hoe distribution outside of the American Bottom and, based on his calculations, concludes that Cahokia did not significantly influence the distribution of Mill Creek hoes; he further concludes that large populations and extensive excavation are responsible for this outlier (Muller 1997: 370).

Brown and colleagues' work makes a valuable contribution to the understanding of Mississippian political economy. They also acknowledge several limitations of their study. First, the available data from museum collections include only intact hoe blades from uncontrolled contexts, and second, while population and transportation were taken into consideration, these measures are often estimated and difficult to standardize. Muller (1997: 368) adds that peaks in fall-off curves can be overinterpreted, and stresses the need to examine other possible explanations for the patterns we find. Given the restrictions of previous research, and the importance of the Mill Creek industry to the development of Greater Cahokia, it is useful to revisit Brown et al.'s study, adjusting several parameters and taking a closer look at domestic consumption of Mill Creek chert at Cahokia, the immediate periphery, and the northern hinterland.

In my analysis of Mill Creek chert, I make three important adjustments to Brown et al.'s approach. First I compare the quantities of Mill Creek chert to other chipped-stone materials (rather than estimated population size) to provide a more realistic evaluation of Mill Creek hoe exchange. Second, I look at entire chert assemblages, which account for not only intact Mill Creek hoes, but also resharpening debitage, repurposed hoe blades, and other tools made from Mill Creek chert. Finally, I utilize data from professionally excavated contexts at individual sites to provide accurate and detailed information on the consumption of this valuable raw material from various Mississippian settlements.

Along with new data from the Audrey site, I compiled available data from published reports, articles, and dissertations on chert assemblages from 18 early Stirling–phase sites. These sites include: refuse contexts from the Linn site 10 km from the Mill Creek source (Cobb 1991: Figure 7); the Wickliffe site just 50 km south of the source (Koldehoff and Brennan 2010: Table 5); Cahokia and 11 sites in the Greater Cahokia area (Alt 2002b; Emerson and Jackson 1984: 240, Table 69; Esarey and Pauketat 1992: 113, Table 9.6; Hanenberger 1990: 477, Table 10, 2003: 300, Table 12.2; Holley et al. 2001; Jackson 1990: 172, Table 7; McCullough et al. 2017; Milner 1984: Table 7; Pauketat 1998b, 2005: 231–240; Skousen 2018); the Lamb site in the CIRV (Wilson 2015b); the Fred Edwards site in the ARV (Finney 1993); and the Trempealeau and Fisher Mound site complexes (a known Cahokia outpost in western Wisconsin) (Pauketat et al. 2015: Table 2).

To create a new fall-off curve, I calculated the percentage of Mill Creek chert by count (including hoes, repurposed tools, and debitage) within each site's total chert assemblage. I restrict my analysis to counts because several of the site reports did not include weight data. I then calculated each site's distance from the Mill Creek quarries using Google Earth's ruler function, following main river routes and historic overland trade routes (Duane Esarey, personal communication 2017). Distance from the Mill Creek source is used rather than distance from Cahokia to minimize bias.

A comparison of percentage of Mill Creek chert to distance from the source is useful to evaluate the distribution of Mill Creek throughout the broader Middle Mississippian region. If Cahokia did control the distribution of Mill Creek hoes in both the American Bottom and northern hinterland, then we would expect Cahokia's level of control to decrease with distance from Cahokia; in this scenario, sites in the Greater Cahokia area would have similarly high percentages of Mill Creek, and Mill Creek percentages would decrease relative to distance from the source. If Cahokia only controlled the distribution of Mill Creek hoes within a small surrounding zone, as Brown et al. (1990) suggest, Mill Creek percentages at Greater Cahokia sites would be similarly high and LIRV and northern hinterland regions would have similarly low percentages of Mill Creek in their chert assemblages. Finally, if Muller's (1997) assertion is correct and Cahokia had little influence on the distribution of Mill Creek hoes, we would expect the percentage of Mill Creek chert at each site to be related to the site's distance from the raw material source; in this scenario, southern American Bottom sites (closer to the source) should have more Mill Creek chert than northern American Bottom sites.

Figure 6.14 is a scatterplot of Mill Creek chert percentages versus distance from the raw material source. First, it is clear that there is not a linear relationship between the percentage of Mill Creek chert and the distance from the source. The graph shows high densities near the source and a cluster of sites in the Greater Cahokia area with similar, relatively high, Mill Creek values. During analysis of the lithic assemblage from the Audrey-North site, the high number of recovered Mill Creek chert artifacts seemed striking in comparison with my observations of excavations of the CIRV, seeming to support the hypothesis that Mississippians in the immediate periphery had closer economic ties with Cahokia than groups farther north.

However, with the exception of only a slightly higher Mill Creek percentage at Audrey and Trempealeau/Fisher Mounds (a Cahokian outpost) than in the CIRV and ARV hinterland regions, in general, it seems that people north of the Greater Cahokia area had negligible amounts of Mill Creek chert (less than 1 percent of chert by count) compared to their southern neighbors. This pattern demonstrates that the density of Mill Creek chert plummets outside of the American Bottom. These findings support both Brown et al.'s (1990) assertion that Cahokia controlled the distribution of these exotic tools and their suspicion that Cahokia's control was limited to a small area, in this case, the American Bottom and eastern uplands. Furthermore, the sharp decline in Mill Creek chert north of the American Bottom not only demonstrates that distance was a factor in Cahokia's economic control, but that groups in the immediate periphery and northern hinterland were not directly involved in Cahokia's Mill Creek hoe exchange network. Muller (1997: 370), with the available data at the time, claimed that

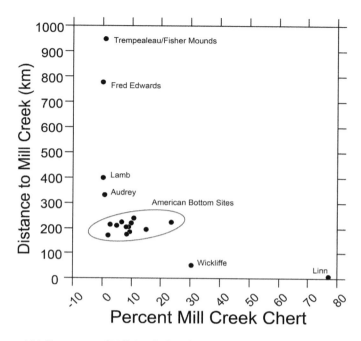

Figure 6.14. Percentage of Mill Creek chert by weight versus distance from the source.

the density of Mill Creek hoes north of the American Bottom was more related to the distance of those settlements from the raw-material source than
from Cahokia. I tested Muller's distance hypothesis for American Bottom
sites by plotting standardized counts of Mill Creek chert versus distance
from the Mill Creek source; these values were calculated by dividing the
number of Mill Creek artifacts by total weight (g) of all chert for each site
(Figure 6.15). Taking a closer look at the American Bottom, we can say for
certain that quantities of Mill Creek chert within the region do not correlate
to distance from the raw material source. In fact, these standardized counts
appear to be more related to settlement type, with less Mill Creek chert at
mound centers and more at smaller outlying settlements (with the exception of BBB Motor); this observation illustrates the presence of a centralized
economy at Cahokia, dovetailing with Pauketat's (2003: 53) argument that
Cahokian elites distributed Mill Creek hoes to rural farmers whom they relied on for agricultural production. As for the northern hinterland, I suggest
that as all of the northern sites included in this study—spanning 700 km of
Mississippi River tributary valleys—have similar percentages of Mill Creek
chert, it is more likely that these Cahokia-emulating groups acquired their

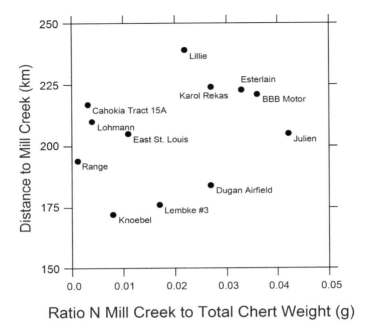

Figure 6.15. Standardized counts of Mill Creek chert versus distance for American Bottom sites.

Mill Creek chert from contact with Cahokia and not with Union County Mississippian groups.

The Consumption of Mill Creek Chert

An examination of Mill Creek chert consumption can help us better understand the ways in which people participated in this important Cahokian exchange system. Due to a lack of screened material from American Bottom excavations, a quantitative comparison of Mill Creek consumption was not possible. However, an analysis of the types of Mill Creek artifacts encountered in different regions suggests that there were a greater number of intact Mill Creek hoes in the American Bottom and a high degree of recycling of a small number of hoes in the lower and central Illinois River valleys and ARV.

Mill Creek hoes were used as agricultural implements in the American Bottom and eastern uplands, demonstrated by the presence of hoes and resharpening flakes with a high degree of polish from use[2] (Alt 2002b: 113; Hammerstedt and Hughes 2015: 151; Pauketat 2003: 55). These valuable hoes were sometimes set aside for exchange within Cahokia's inner sphere. A famous example is the cache of ~70 Mill Creek hoes found at the East St. Louis site by Charles Rau in 1869. The hoes showed no signs of usewear and were carefully and neatly arranged to fill the circular pit feature, perhaps stowed away for later distribution (Daniels 2007: 745; Pauketat 2004: 103).

While the occasional Mill Creek hoe is found at Stirling-phase sites north of the American Bottom, the material was often recycled and used for other tools. For example, the polished hoe-resharpening flakes and the two Mill Creek adzes provide evidence for Mill Creek recycling at Audrey. Overall, the Mill Creek chert from the Audrey assemblage may have derived from just three original hoes, and Audrey inhabitants seem to be curating the material compared with their use of Burlington chert. Audrey is immediately adjacent to (less than 10 km from) an abundant source of Burlington chert, which was mined in large cobbles and brought back by Audrey villagers to produce all manner of expedient chipped-stone tools; Burlington chert is also a perfectly good material for making hoes. Indeed, Mill Creek chert is occasionally found as hoes, reworked hoes, or resharpening flakes in the ARV, but only in early Mississippian–period occupations; the pattern seems to drop off quickly and the Woodland-era tradition of using mussel shell hoes was revitalized (Millhouse 2012: 302). Mill Creek Chert was also recycled at the Fred Edwards site in the ARV, where excavations recovered a projectile point and an end scraper made from the remains of a Mill Creek hoe (Finney 1993: 158).

With a wealth of raw material available to them, Audrey inhabitants (and other groups) did not rely on Mill Creek hoes from Cahokia, yet they prized the little Mill Creek chert they had. Koldehoff and Brennan (2010: 152) have suggested that with no technological reason for the procurement of nonlocal cherts, the presence of exotic chert may represent politically motivated symbolic exchanges. While this is a possibility, in this case, Mill Creek chert has been demonstrated to be a particularly strong material that was easy to knap and could withstand intensive use (Hammerstedt and Hughes 2015). These qualities would make a rare Mill Creek hoe worth resharpening and recycling for people who did not have ready access to the material.

Conclusions

Analysis of the lithic assemblage at the Audrey site and an examination of interactions between LIRV and American Bottom Mississippians reveals interesting patterns that help characterize the nature of the relationship between these two groups. My hypothesis that the LIRV's proximity to

Cahokia enabled certain social, political, and economic interactions with American Bottom groups that did not transpire with more distant groups is only partly supported by these lithic data. The material type and large size of Audrey's celts suggest the site's inhabitants seem to have been tied to Cahokia's basalt celt industry, whereas northern hinterland groups were less so. Yet, like the northern hinterland, LIRV inhabitants were not producing marine shell beads at Audrey, nor were they involved in the Mill Creek hoe exchange network so vital to political and economic development in the American Bottom.

The data presented here support the assertion that there were limits to Cahokia's economic control. While some have suggested that Cahokia had economic arrangements with American Bottom and uplands settlements involving the provision of Mill Creek hoes in exchange for agricultural surplus (Pauketat 2003), or marine shell for the production of shell beads (Pauketat 1997a), the scarcity of Mill Creek hoes and lack of evidence for marine shell bead production north of the American Bottom indicate that these activities did not extend beyond the Greater Cahokia area. From this line of evidence, it seems that, despite the suite of Cahokian practices emulated in the LIRV and northern hinterland, these outlying groups were not in Cahokia's direct sphere of economic control. From a different perspective, Mississippians north of the American Bottom may not have been able to (or possibly chose not to) participate in certain Cahokian exchange networks.

Addressing the issue of Cahokian interaction in the LIRV and northern hinterland goes beyond the craft industries fueling economic interaction throughout the American Bottom. The interactions that lead to the Woodland-Mississippian transition in the LIRV ultimately impacted the regional lithic tool industry and the types of activities taking place at Audrey Village. Indeed, the most significant impacts of Cahokian interaction in the LIRV were less economic in nature and more organizational. For example, the prevalence of flake tools and the lack of formal tools at Audrey are indicative of the Mississippian expedient flake tool industry observed throughout much of the Mississippian world. A shift to sedentism and the focus on agricultural activities that came with a Mississippian way of life reduced the need for formal tools when expedient tools were effective and easy to make, and there was no need to worry about accumulating or transporting excess lithic material (Koldehoff 1987). Audrey inhabitants were also engaging in intensified woodworking activities, a pattern seen in the American Bottom. In addition to clearing fields, Audrey's basalt celts would have been essential for felling trees used for the construction of houses, temples, ceremonial buildings, and perhaps palisades. Although the celts were not produced at Audrey (possibly acquired by trade with American Bottom groups), large bifaces, including adzes, were produced and also used in woodworking. The highly nucleated Mississippian settlement pattern at Audrey Village would have required a lot of material for building, and connections with Cahokia may have provided them with some of the best tools for the job.

In addition to these Mississippian-influenced activities, Audrey residents also engaged in activities less frequently practiced in the American Bottom. The high number of projectile points, in combination with the presence of end scrapers, suggests that Audrey inhabitants were not only hunting deer with more frequency than American Bottom groups, but that they were processing the hides to a greater degree. Hide working is also practiced at northern hinterland sites, but there is less evidence for this activity in the American Bottom. As some have suggested (Bardolph and Wilson 2015: 145; Finney 1993: 16; Goldstein 1980), deer hides may have been a craft item that LIRV and other northern groups could have used in exchanges with groups to the south.

Finally, a comparison of exotic cherts from the Audrey site and within the American Bottom and northern hinterland area provides interesting routes for future research into the types of interactions taking place throughout the Mississippian world. Although the physical evidence of exotic cherts (other than Mill Creek chert) is minimal, especially given the density of local Burlington chert at the Audrey site, it is important to consider the implications of the presence of these exotic materials for long-distance interactions. Cobden and Kaolin cherts were likely acquired through interactions with American Bottom groups, who, considering their involvement in the Mill Creek chert industry, likely circulated these additional Union County materials throughout the region. However, the circulation of exotic northern cherts—whose distribution likely was not controlled by Cahokia—at sites in all study regions suggests a less centralized network of Mississippian interaction. Indeed, it is possible that Audrey inhabitants acquired galena in addition to northern chipped-stone material through interactions with groups in the ARV. In addition to Mississippian interaction, ARV exchange relationships may have been subject to outside political and social forces, including non-Mississippianized Woodland peoples to the north and the emerging Oneota populations nearby (Millhouse 2012: 307). Meanwhile, in the CIRV, there is virtually no evidence of exotic lithic material. These variations in lithic exchange patterns highlight the complex nature of interaction throughout the Mississippian world.

The overall patterns of lithic tool production, consumption, and exchange in the LIRV, CIRV, and ARV begin to paint a picture of a Mississippian interaction sphere occurring beyond Cahokia. It is clear that while Cahokia may have exercised leverage over the means of production in the American Bottom and eastern uplands, those types of relationships did not exist with northern settlements. The significance of these findings is not simply in the demonstration of the limits to Cahokia's economic control, but in the implications this has for the nature of interactions between and within the immediate periphery and northern hinterland. If it was not reliance on or participation in Cahokia's political economy that fueled the Mississippianization of northern groups, we must consider the power of the social and political ties between these groups as a catalyst for the broad-reaching Mississippian cultural phenomenon. Furthermore, without the economic benefits and elite power brokerage that fueled the Mississippian transition in the American Bottom, we must question exactly why more distant groups adopted Mississippian lifeways and signaled Mississippian identities.

7

Making Mississippian

Cahokia was the largest and most influential pre-Columbian city north of Mexico, and its late eleventh century–coalescence in the American Bottom floodplain had lasting impacts on peoples throughout the Midwest and Midsouth. The Mississippian phenomenon has been a topic of archaeological inquiry for decades, with an effort to investigate both the nature of Cahokian interaction in distant regions, and how and why local groups participated in them. Political economic approaches contributed a great deal to our understanding of the expansion of Cahokia's power and influence through the establishment of a complex network of settlements comprising Greater Cahokia (Brown et al. 1990; Emerson 1997c; Kelly 1991b; Pauketat 1994, 1997a, 1998a). Further research characterized Mississippianization as a complex historical process involving the movement of things, people, and ideas across the landscape, demonstrating that economic, political, and religious movements in, around, and outside of Cahokia were simultaneous and codependent (Alt 2006a; Baltus and Baires 2012; Betzenhauser 2017; Emerson 1997a; Emerson et al. 2008; Pauketat 2003; Pauketat 2013; Pauketat and Emerson 1997; Wilson et al. 2017).

Research on the spread of Cahokia's influence to the northern hinterland regions has made great strides in documenting the ways in which northern groups selectively adopted aspects of Mississippian lifeways while maintaining certain local traditions (Bardolph 2014; Bardolph and Wilson 2015; Friberg 2018a; Wilson et al. 2017; Wilson and VanDerwarker 2015). The most recent scholarship on Mississippianization engages with the concepts of migration, pilgrimage, and diaspora to explore how diverse groups of immigrants came to Cahokia to participate in the historical events (often religious in nature) unfolding there (Baltus and Baires 2017; Pauketat et al. 2017; Skousen 2016; Wilson et al. 2017; Wilson et al. 2018b). Some of these immigrants would have eventually returned to their distant homelands with altered identities along with knowledge of Cahokian practices to share with their kin. Even as our knowledge and understanding of the Mississippian phenomenon continues to develop, these studies leave lingering questions about how and why the process of Mississippianization unfolded outside the American Bottom.

The Lower Illinois River Valley (LIRV), a geographical zone separating the northern hinterland and Greater Cahokia, presents an opportunity to investigate these questions. The Mississippian occupation of the LIRV has received less attention, possibly because early archaeological surveys suggested the region was primarily inhabited by Woodland people of the Jersey Bluff culture through the duration of the Mississippian period (Farnsworth and Emerson 1989; Farnsworth et al. 1991). Excavations (and subsequent analysis) at the Audrey site in the 1980s and early 2000s revealed a substantial nucleated Mississippian settlement with a number of wall-trench buildings, a sweat lodge, Cahokia-style pottery, and Cahokian prestige items, challenging the notion of the LIRV as a frontier region with a minimal number of isolated Mississippian settlements (Cook 1981, 1983; Delaney-Rivera 2000).

In this book, I consider that the proximity of the LIRV to Cahokia may have enabled certain political, economic, and social interactions that were not possible with more distant groups. Furthermore, these interactions may have resulted in major organizational changes to daily life for the inhabitants of the Audrey site. In the preceding chapters, I address these issues through an analysis of architecture and community organization, production and consumption of pottery, and lithic tool industries. To understand the nature of the culture contact dynamic in the LIRV and how it differed from that of northern hinterland groups, I also conducted a comprehensive comparative analysis of similar patterns from Greater Cahokia, the Central Illinois River Valley (CIRV), and Apple River Valley (ARV). Ultimately, my research shows that interactions between Audrey inhabitants and Cahokians did in fact result in more organizational changes at Audrey than have been observed in the northern hinterland. I also found that, similar to northern hinterland Mississippians, Audrey inhabitants maintained certain Woodland-era conventions and hybridized others, generating new Mississippian traditions in the process. Finally, this broad interregional analysis compiles evidence that the diverse groups of people living in the Illinois and Upper Mississippi valleys during the twelfth century were engaged in a network of interaction and exchange that was not dominated by Cahokia. I suggest that these interactions likely fueled the signaling of Mississippian identities and the making of Mississippian traditions in the north.

Discussion

What do the patterns presented in the previous chapters tell us about the bigger picture? What was life like for Audrey villagers? How does Audrey compare with other Mississippian groups? Can differences between the LIRV and northern hinterland be explained by relative distances from Cahokia? Were Audrey inhabitants involved in Cahokia's centralized political economy or were their economic activities locally organized in a less hierarchical fashion? If political-economic engagements were not the catalyst for Mississippianization outside of Greater Cahokia, how do we explain this process?

The analytical chapters of this book were organized by unit of analysis (rather than by topic) to facilitate a comprehensive interregional comparative analysis of specific patterns. In the following paragraphs, I hope to interpret and synthesize these patterns (summarized above) to address these questions. I begin with a discussion of the nature of social and community organization at the Audrey site in comparison to the hierarchically organized Greater Cahokia area and the less hierarchically organized practices of the northern hinterland Mississippian groups. I then address economic activities at Audrey and elsewhere, the organization of these activities, and the implications for limits to Cahokia's political and economic control and influence. Finally, I discuss evidence of interactions throughout the Mississippian world and the implications of these networks for the forging of new identities and the making of new Mississippian traditions.

Organizational Changes and Continuities

My analysis has shown that a close proximity to Cahokia resulted in major organizational changes occurring at Audrey that did not occur to the same degree in the northern hinterland. With regard to architecture and community organization, Audrey villagers participated in a Cahokian "architecture of power" where elite households were segregated by wall screens, and elites and administrators conducted religious practices and business dealings in large community buildings and sweat lodges. Moreover, the presence of a possible shrine complex at the site would not only indicate the adoption of Cahokian religious practices, but would also suggest a separation of the sacred from the profane, a pattern observed at Cahokian ceremonial nodes (Emerson et al. 2008).

Audrey's lithic assemblage supported these massive community-planning efforts. Indeed, Audrey inhabitants were engaged in the production of large chert bifaces that provide evidence of woodworking activities, suggesting the villagers were equipped to cut and shape wood consistent with architectural construction. Furthermore, Cahokia may have supported these efforts by supplying basalt celts for the felling of trees to be used in Audrey's impressive building activities; a geochemical analysis of Audrey's celts would be necessary to confirm this claim.

Other aspects of community and social organization at Audrey, however, were less influenced by interaction with Cahokia. For example, Audrey's inhabitants did not incorporate the level of ceremonialism in their foodways that has been observed in the Greater Cahokia area. A lower percentage of servingware at Audrey compared with Cahokia's many bowls, plates, bottles, and beakers suggests meals were not served with the same fanfare (Wilson et al. 2017). This pattern is even more pronounced in the northern hinterland, where they also lack Cahokian fineware vessels; only a small number of these were recovered from excavations at Audrey.

Another example of the maintenance of Woodland-era traditions is observed in the Audrey site architecture. While some of Audrey's buildings were constructed using a Cahokia-style wall-trench technique, one domestic structure (the only one for which we have detailed data) was built using a hybridized architectural technique of single-set posts within prepared wall trenches. Hybrid architecture has been observed at certain Richland Complex sites where traditional, Woodland-era methods of construction were combined with newer, Cahokian ways of creating space (Alt 2002a, 2006a). If future excavations at Audrey uncover additional hybrid houses, we might be able to say that Audrey inhabitants built their Cahokian village on a foundation of local traditions.

Decentralized Economic Activities

While the LIRV's proximity to Cahokia may have resulted in more organizational changes than are observed in the northern hinterland, the analyses presented in the previous chapters suggest that economies outside the Greater Cahokia area were neither tied into Cahokia's centralized political economy nor were they organized in the same complex hierarchical manner. First, the evidence presented here demonstrates that LIRV, CIRV, and ARV Mississippian groups were not actively involved in Cahokian craft-exchange networks in the way that Greater Cahokia groups were. Regardless of distance from the source, sites north of the American Bottom have negligible percentages of Mill Creek chert within their lithic assemblages. Second, there is little evidence to suggest northern groups engaged in the production of marine shell beads. Although both disk beads and Mill Creek hoes have been found in the LIRV, CIRV, and ARV, these were likely not acquired through Cahokia-sponsored economic activities.

A comparative analysis of basalt celts from the CIRV, LIRV, and Greater Cahokia area tell a slightly different story. While CIRV Mississippians produced celts locally using local materials, the basalt celts from Audrey resemble Cahokia-style celts, were not produced at the site, and may have been acquired through Cahokia's craft-exchange network. If Audrey inhabitants were directly tied into Cahokia's basalt celt network, we would see evidence of celt manufacture, as we do at Greater Cahokia settlements where craftworkers likely received the raw material in large cobbles through Cahokia's central political-administrative complex. Ultimately, Audrey's potentially Cahokian celts represent an exchange relationship that is not characteristic of Cahokia's centralized political-economic relationships.

Although Mississippian groups throughout the Midwest each engaged in their own Mississippian expedient flake tool industries (relying more on simple retouched flakes than formal bifaces for nonspecialized tasks), these economic activities generally lacked the complexity of Cahokia's centralized exploitation of the Crescent Hills Burlington chert quarries. For Audrey villagers, this decision may have been logical—with an outcrop of Burlington chert within a few kilometers of Audrey, it was probably more efficient to bring cores back to the village rather than to knap them into biface preforms at the raw-material site and distribute the preforms for finishing back at home. But the decentralized nature of Audrey's lithic tool industry is indicative of the broader social organization at the site; there was no complex administrative or social need for controlling tool production. Audrey's society was not structured by the same hierarchical social relationships that organized Cahokia's economy.

Further differentiating Audrey's economic activities from Cahokia's, Audrey's inhabitants hunted deer to a greater degree than was possible in the resource-depleted American Bottom, and it appears they also produced hides. While deer hunting was not a major economic focus in the Greater Cahokia area (Wilson and Kuehn 2011), there is even less evidence for hide working at the region's settlements (Hall 1967; Wilson 2015b). However, there is abundant evidence of deer hunting and hide working in the northern hinterland (Emerson et al. 2007; Finney 1993; Wilson 2015b). Perhaps Audrey's unique geographic position between Greater Cahokia and the northern hinterland encouraged Audrey villagers to diversify their economic strategies, enabling them to engage in both southern and northern networks. In this case, deer hides, which were likely a rare commodity in the American Bottom, would have been a valuable item for northern groups to exchange for the exotic materials and tools circulating within the Greater Cahokian networks (Bardolph and Wilson 2015: 145; Finney 1993: 16; Goldstein 1980). While the possibility of an interregional hide-exchange network is, at present, conjecture that requires further investigation, there are other lines of evidence to suggest that interactions were happening not only between Cahokia and Mississippianized groups, but also among these northern groups.

Interaction in the North

Deer hides may have been a trade item produced by northerners to facilitate interactions with neighboring or distant groups. But what evidence is there that these groups actually interacted? The exchange of culturally diagnostic pottery is one line of evidence. At Fred Edwards in the ARV, the Mississippian inhabitants of the site acquired Woodland-style pottery from groups in the surrounding area, suggesting a relatively healthy relationship with neighboring groups, Mississippian or otherwise (Finney 1993; 2013). Similarly, the presence of a Maples Mills, Mossville-phase jar from the Spoon River area of the CIRV at the Audrey site suggests either Late Woodland or early Mississippian interaction between groups in the LIRV and CIRV. Excavations of an elite household at Audrey also recovered fragments of a Holly Fine Engraved vessel which geochemical analysis confirmed originated from the Caddoan region of northeast Texas (Perttula 2002). These vessels, and emulated copies, are also found among Cahokian fineware. The presence of one of these pots at Audrey is suggestive of major external connections, which may or may not have been facilitated by political ties with Cahokia.

Interaction also appeared to be happening between northern neighbors independently of Cahokia. Indeed, exotic northern cherts were circulated throughout the Mississippian Midwest, yet there is no evidence that Cahokia controlled the distribution of any of these materials in these regions. By all indications, the materials were acquired through northern channels. The same may have been the case for the distribution of galena north of the

American Bottom, as sources of lead ore exist in both the Missouri Ozarks and the Upper Mississippi Valley (Walthall 1981: 55). While Cahokians may have obtained their galena (along with other important raw materials) from the Missouri Ozarks (Emerson 1991a: 235; Kelly and Brown 2012; Milner 1990), CIRV groups likely acquired galena through exchange relationships with ARV groups close to the northern source along the Apple River (Millhouse 2012: 316). Another interesting northern relationship to explore is the possible connection between Audrey and the Aztalan site in southeastern Wisconsin. Two identical cylindrical antler objects recovered from Feature 5's house basin resemble what Barrett (1933: Plate 65) identified as "antler punches" at Aztalan. The tools may have been used for indirect percussion flaking for the production of small chert tools, like projectile points. While antler punches appear to have been common at Aztalan, the tools are rare in the Greater Cahokia area (Koldehoff, personal communication 2016). Perhaps Audrey inhabitants obtained these objects, or the tradition of making them, through interactions with Aztalan or similar groups.

Why is it significant that these northern neighbors were interacting with each other? We have reason to suspect that, at least in the Illinois River Valley, intergroup conflicts in the region during the Late Woodland period hindered interaction between groups (Green and Nolan 2000: 369; Perino 1971; Wilson 2012b; see also VanDerwarker and Wilson 2016). Therefore, evidence of exchange between cultural groups in this region may be indicative of repaired intergroup relationships. This period of intensified interaction during the Terminal Late Woodland and early Mississippian periods has been documented not only in the Illinois Valley (Green and Nolan 2000: 372; McConaughy 1991; McConaughy et al. 1993), but also at the Shire site in the central Illinois prairie (Claflin 1991), the Fred Edwards site in the ARV (Finney 1993: 120–125; Finney and Stoltman 1991: 243), and of course, the American Bottom (Esarey 2000).

While there is not yet abundant archaeological evidence for interaction between these northern groups during the early Mississippian period, the patterns discussed here warrant further research into the possibility of a northern Mississippian exchange network. Intergroup interaction in the Upper Mississippi and Illinois River valleys was common during the Middle Woodland period, but there seems to have been a revitalization during the Terminal Late Woodland and Mississippian periods. It is possible that extraregional interactions in the north were facilitated by political alliances with Greater Cahokia, but I think it is important to describe these affiliations in a different manner: perhaps these renewed interactions were made easier by northerners choosing to signal Mississippian identities.

Igniting Interaction through Mississippian

Tradition Making

I am certainly not the first archaeologist to suggest that groups in contact with Cahokia developed some type of shared Mississippian identity. Hall (1991) characterized the development of Cahokian identity as involving ritual events through which fictive kin relationships were created. Alleen Betzenhauser (2011: 454–455) suggests similar identity negotiations were occurring in the early stages of Cahokia's expansion in the American Bottom, where commoners and elites asserted Cahokian connections by engaging in Cahokian practices and traditions; these efforts were mediated through nodal sites that acted as points of articulation for Cahokian interactions involved in the building of a "Cahokia Community." However, I think most contemporary Midwestern archaeologists would be hard pressed to describe northern Mississippian groups as part of the Cahokian community, given the host of material differences between these societies and their American Bottom neighbors. Indeed, Gregory Wilson (2011) proposed years ago that that the variations observed in Mississippian lifeways in the CIRV suggest these individuals embraced a Mississippian way of *being*, but not a Cahokian way of *belonging*. These are all valid and interesting ways of conceptualizing Mississippian identity, but I suggest there is more to be found in the process of identity formation, the reasons for it, and the consequences of enacting it.

My approach to these issues stems from Emerson's (1991a) call for archaeologists to look to the relationships and interactions between northern hinterland groups (rather than interactions with Cahokia) to better understand the Mississippian phenomenon. My comprehensive interregional analysis of architecture and community organization, pottery and foodways, and lithic tool industries has revealed both the wealth of diversity among Mississippian groups and the fact that this diversity was not a function of Cahokian economic control. Mississippian identities in the LIRV and northern hinterland were instead created through a renewed spirit of interaction burgeoning in the Mississippi Valley during the late eleventh and early twelfth centuries. But why? At the most simplistic end of the spectrum, as Wobst

(1977) would attest, shared identities are useful for determining trusted trade partners. On the less functional end, perhaps immigrants returning to their homelands from Cahokia encouraged their communities to be a part of the phenomenon unfolding there (Wilson et al. 2017; Wilson et al. 2020). Adopting a "Mississippian" way of life would have fulfilled both of these needs, but exploring the conditions and contexts surrounding Mississippianization in different regions should reveal more about the nature of the process and how it unfolded for various groups.

Recent work on social change in the American Southwest provides a useful framework for understanding interaction and identity in the context of pre-Columbian culture contact. In their research on social change and identity formation, White (2008) and Tilly (1978) have both suggested that, in building a collective identity, people must be linked through networks of interaction to facilitate the flow of information. Peeples (2018) builds on the relationship between interaction and the development of shared identity in his study of the Pueblo III to Pueblo IV transition in the Cibola region, suggesting that transformative social change is most likely to occur among groups of people who are both relationally connected and who share aspects of a categorical identity. He observes these relational connections in the evidence for interaction between groups, including the regional circulation of pottery and shared potting technology and domestic architectural practices. Categorical identification, on the other hand, occurs when individuals identify themselves and others as members of larger collective groups marked by boundaries and symbolism—such as public architecture and the decorative motifs on polychrome ceramics—rather than historical (relational) connections (Peeples 2018: 207). Under this framework, Peeples (2018: 217) ultimately concludes that social change in the Cibola region was marked by the regional consolidation of interaction networks, which allowed for the spread of new categorical identities.

Peeples's framework of social change is easily applied to the current study. For instance, the relational connections between hinterland groups can be observed in their exchange of Late Woodland pottery and exotic northern lithic material, in addition to their similarities in communally oriented domestic practices. The categorical identification, then, would be through the production of Cahokia-style material culture, the use of wall-trench architecture, and the planning of large nucleated settlements, to name a few correlates. In the end, this recipe of social interaction yielded a new Mississippian identity.

I argue, however, that this process is not linear; while the building of a shared Mississippian identity was made possible through networks of interaction, those shared identities simultaneously opened the door to interaction. Furthermore, there is variation in the nature and degree to which groups in contact were integrated (Neuzil 2008; Peeples 2018). Peeples (2018: 9) suggests that the strength of relational connections between groups can be evaluated in the degree of similarity in shared public expressions of identity. In the Mississippian case, the public expressions of identity can be used to evaluate relational connections between hinterland and Greater Cahokia groups, but also between groups in the north. For example, town planning and community organization that incorporates an architecture of power is observed throughout the American Bottom and eastern uplands, in addition to the Audrey site, suggesting strong relational connections between these groups. Yet while hinterland groups built "Cahokian" settlements using wall-trench architecture, only a handful of sites include the special-purpose buildings that publically express a Cahokian identity; this pattern suggests a lower degree of relational connection with Cahokia than is observed in the LIRV. Another example of a shared public expression of identity is the production of Ramey Incised pottery. This aspect of categorical Mississippian identity indeed links hinterland and Cahokia Mississippians, but the ways in which northern potters localized the expression of cosmological symbolism (Friberg 2018a) demonstrate a closer relational connection among northern groups than that between Cahokia and its hinterland.

Evaluating degrees of relation between groups is helpful for understanding the nature of Mississippian interactions and further characterizes the Mississippianization of the northern hinterland as a process that involved connections both between Cahokia and its hinterland, and among northern groups. Variation in the nature of interactions between these groups ultimately paved divergent paths to a shared Mississippian identity. To be sure, I think what the current study has demonstrated is that these ways of being Mississippian were diverse and particular to the communities who practiced them. It is clear that, from the fringes of the Cahokia polity to the distant reaches of the Upper Mississippi Valley, local people negotiating Mississippianization did so with reference to existing identities and traditions. Through this process of entangling, or hybridizing, new ideas and practices with those already familiar, these communities formed new Mississippian traditions.

One possible vehicle for signaling a "shared" Mississippian identity may have been the Ramey Incised jar. Embedded with cosmological symbolism, these pots would have acted as highly visible indictors of Mississippian religious ideologies. Importantly, northern hinterland groups produced more of these jars than did their Greater Cahokian counterparts, emphasizing the emulation of this particular aspect of Cahokian culture (Wilson et al. 2017). Hinterland Mississippians produced Ramey jars locally and in abundance, and they tended to decorate them with familiar, Woodland-derived motifs, organizing the designs based on local concepts of space (Friberg 2018a). Alt (2016) has described a similar transformation of vernacular architecture into Cahokian shrines; rather than leaping into unfamiliar religious practices, local people in the American Bottom uplands negotiated these changes by choosing to use familiar spaces through which to engage with newly introduced religious ideologies. Ceramic jars, much like houses, would have been an effective locus for ideological change, combining the familiar with the novel in a way that made sense to Woodland peoples. I see the emphasis of Ramey Incised pottery by northern hinterland groups, then, as a transformation of a quotidian object into a *vessel* for signaling Mississippian identity and experimenting with Cahokian religion. As northern potters produced these jars, they sought to emulate a Cahokian practice, but did so with reference to existing worldviews, entangling complex identities and forging new Mississippian traditions in the process.

Conclusion

The broader goal of this book was to facilitate a better understanding of how and why large and complex nonstate polities extend their influence over hinterland areas. To accomplish this, I believe we need to consider the inner workings of extensive social phenomena. It is useful, I think, to compare these social movements to the process of building a fire. The materials that fuel a fire include not only the logs that sustain the flames, but also the kindling, the network of sticks, twigs, and leaves that forms the interwoven cushion that catches the initial sparks; these tangible elements are further fed by the swirling of oxygen around them and tended by the human hands that set the whole thing in motion. For Cahokia's fire, I wonder, what produced the spark? Was it a particularly rainy season that made the maize grow in greater abundance? Or a group of charismatic individuals eager to achieve higher status? Or perhaps it was the spectacular supernova of AD 1054 that triggered a religious movement that quickly coalesced into the panregional phenomenon we recognize today. We may never know. I hope what this study makes clear is that the Mississippianization of the Midwest was made possible by the interaction and movement of diverse peoples, objects, and ideologies across the landscape. A renewed spirit of interaction was simultaneously supported by, and relied on, the negotiation of a shared Mississippian identity. And in signaling and enacting those identities, peoples in distant regions forged their own Mississippian traditions.

Notes

Chapter 2. Culture Contact and the Cahokia Phenomenon

1. Strontium isotope analysis of tooth enamel from individuals interred in diverse mortuary locations at Cahokia identified one-third of individuals as nonlocal in origin (Slater et al. 2014).

Chapter 4. Architecture and Community Organization

1. Even with the correction of the UCSB 2016 azimuths to true north, there seems to be a slight difference in orientation between the CAA and UCSB excavation grids. The reason for this is unclear and due to human error and thus cannot be corrected. These disparities, however, do not detract from the observation of two separate house orientations at Audrey.

2. Due to the limited availability of data from the CAA excavations of the Audrey site, features encountered during those excavations will not be included in the present analysis.

Chapter 5. Ceramic Traditions

1. While it would be interesting to consider rim curvature (RC) for the Audrey site ceramic assemblage, there are too few vessels with sufficiently intact rims and shoulders to be able to calculate RC, and thus the sample size is too small for comparison.

2. Without access to the proper documentation to isolate Mississippian features, Delaney-Rivera (2000) used a holistic method of combining ceramic analysis across occupations. For this reason, data from the Audrey ceramic assemblage of the CAA era are not used for comparative analysis.

Chapter 6. Lithic Tool Industries

1. Butler's (2014: 17) recent X-ray Fluorescence (pXRF) study of a large sample of American Bottom celts and raw materials suggests only 52 percent of the celts can be sourced to the Missouri Ozarks, while the remainder seem to align with Great Lakes sources (in the form of local glacial till). Although she questions the accuracy and ap-

plication of the pXRF method for elemental analysis of heterogeneous lithic material, Dymek and Kelly (2015) have drawn similar conclusions regarding the multiple sources for material used in the production of celts throughout the American Bottom.

2. Experimental research by Milner and colleagues (2010: 106) found that polish can develop on chert hoes within 30 minutes of the first use.

References Cited

Adler, Michael A.
1983   A Formal and Technological Analysis of Ceramics from the Audrey-North Site. Undergraduate thesis, Department of Anthropology, Princeton University.

Alt, Susan M.
2001   Cahokian Change and the Authority of Tradition. In *The Archaeology of Traditions: Agency and History Before and After Columbus,* edited by Timothy R. Pauketat, pp. 141–156. University Press of Florida, Gainesville.

2002a   Identities, Traditions, and Diversity in Cahokia's Uplands. *Midcontinental Journal of Archaeology* 27(2): 217–235.

2002b   The Knoebel Site: Tradition and Change in the Cahokian Suburbs. Master's thesis, Department of Anthropology, University of Illinois at Urbana–Champaign.

2006a   The Power of Diversity: The Roles of Migration and Hybridity in Culture Change. In *Leadership and Polity in Mississippian Society,* edited by Brian M. Butler and Paul D. Welch, pp. 289–308. Center for Archaeological Investigations Occasional Paper No. 33, Southern Illinois University–Carbondale.

2006b   Cultural Pluralism and Complexity: Analyzing a Cahokian Ritual Outpost. PhD dissertation, Department of Anthropology, University of Illinois at Urbana–Champaign.

2008   Unwilling Immigrants: Culture, Change, and the "Other." In *Invisible Citizens: Captives and their Consequences,* edited by Catherine M. Cameron, pp. 205–222. University of Utah Press, Salt Lake City.

2016   Building Cahokia: Transformation through Tradition. In *Vernacular Architecture in the Pre-Columbian Americas,* edited by Christina T. Halperin and Lauren E. Schwartz, pp. 139–157. Routledge, London and New York.

2018   *Cahokia's Complexities: Ceremonies and Politics of the First Mississippian Farmers.* University of Alabama Press, Tuscaloosa.

Alt, Susan M., and Timothy R. Pauketat
2007   Sex and the Southern Cult. In *Southeastern Ceremonial Complex: Chronology, Content, Context,* edited by Adam King, pp. 232–250. University of Alabama Press, Tuscaloosa.

2011   Why Wall Trenches? *Southeastern Archaeology* 30(1): 108–122.

2017 Cahokia and the Mississippian World: Shrines Near Cahokia. *Illinois Archaeology* 29: 1–26.

Anderson, David G.

1994 *The Savannah River Chiefdoms.* University of Alabama Press, Tuscaloosa.

1997 The Role of Cahokia in the Evolution of Southeastern Mississippian Society. In *Cahokia: Domination and Ideology in the Mississippian World,* edited by Timothy R. Pauketat and Thomas E. Emerson, pp. 248–268. University of Nebraska Press, Lincoln.

Armstrong, Douglas V.

1998 Cultural Transformation within Enslaved Laborer Communities in the Caribbean. In *Studies in Culture Contact: Interaction, Culture Change, and Archaeology,* edited by James G. Cusick, pp. 378–401. Center for Archaeological Investigations Occasional Paper No. 25, Southern Illinois University–Carbondale.

Baires, Sarah E.

2014 Cahokia's Origins: Religion, Complexity, and Ridge-top Mortuaries in the Mississippi River Valley. PhD dissertation, Department of Anthropology, University of Illinois at Urbana–Champaign.

Baires, Sarah E., Melissa R. Baltus, and Elizabeth Watts Malouchos

2017 Exploring New Cahokian Neighborhoods: Structure Density Estimates from the Spring Lake Tract, Cahokia. *American Antiquity* 82(4): 742–760.

Baltus, Melissa R., and Sarah E. Baires

2012 Elements of Ancient Power in the Cahokian World. *Journal of Social Archaeology* 12(2): 167–192.

2017 Defining Diaspora: A View from the Cahokia Homeland. Paper presented at the 74th Annual Meeting of the Southeastern Archaeological Conference, Tulsa, Oklahoma.

Bardolph, Dana N.

2014 Evaluating Cahokian Contact and Mississippian Identity Politics in the Late Prehistoric Central Illinois River Valley. *American Antiquity* 79(1): 69–89.

2015 Lamb Site Features: Clues to Cooking and Community Organization in the Central Illinois River Valley. *Illinois Archaeology* 27: 150–173.

Bardolph, Dana N., and Gregory D. Wilson

2015 The Lamb Site (11SC24): Evidence of Cahokian Contact and Mississippianization in the Central Illinois River Valley. *Illinois Archaeology* 27: 138–149.

Bareis, Charles J., and James W. Porter (editors)

1984 *American Bottom Archaeology.* University of Illinois Press, Urbana.

Barrett, Samuel Alfred

1933 *Ancient Aztalan.* Greenwood, Westport, Connecticut.

Barrier, Casey R, and Timothy J Horsley

2014 Shifting Communities: Demographic Profiles of Early Village Population Growth and Decline in the Central American Bottom. *American Antiquity* 79(2): 295–313.

Benn, David W.

1995 Woodland People and the Roots of the Oneota. In *Oneota Archaeology: Past,*

Present, and Future, edited by William Green, pp. 91–139. Report 20. Office of the State Archaeologist, University of Iowa, Iowa City.

1997   Who Met the Mississippians at the Mouth of the Apple River? *Illinois Archaeology* 9(1–2): 1–35.

Benn, David W., and William Green

2000   Late Woodland Cultures in Iowa. In *Late Woodland Tradition and Transformation across the Midcontinent,* edited by Thomas E. Emerson, pp. 429–496. University of Nebraska Press, Lincoln.

Bennett, John W.

1945   *Archaeological Explorations in Jo Daviess County, Illinois.* University of Chicago Press, Chicago, Illinois.

Betzenhauser, Alleen

2008   Timing the Terminal Late Woodland to Mississippian Transition in the Southern American Bottom: Preliminary Results from the Washausen Site (11MO305). Paper presented at the 54th Annual Meeting of the Midwest Archaeological Conference, Milwaukee, Wisconsin.

2011   Creating the Cahokian Community: The Power of Place in Early Mississippian Sociopolitical Dynamics. PhD dissertation, Department of Anthropology, University of Illinois at Urbana–Champaign.

2017   Cahokia's Beginnings: Mobility, Urbanization, and the Cahokian Political Landscape. In *Mississippian Beginnings,* edited by Gregory D. Wilson, pp. 71–96. University of Florida Press, Gainesville.

Binford, Lewis R.

1967   Smudge Pits and Hide Smoking: The Use of Analogy in Archaeological Reasoning. *American Antiquity* 32(1): 1–12.

Binford, Lewis R., Sally R. Binford, Robert Whallon, and Margaret Ann Hardin

1970   *Archaeology at Hatchery West.* Memoir No. 24. Society for American Archaeology, Washington, DC.

Birmingham, Robert A., and Lynne Goldstein

2005   *Aztalan: Mysteries of an Ancient Indian Town.* Wisconsin Historical Society, Madison.

Bronk Ramsey, Christopher

2017   OxCal Program, Version 4.3. *Oxford Radiocarbon Unit:* University of Oxford.

Brown, James A.

2003   The Cahokia Mound 72-Sub 1 Burials as Collective Representation. *Wisconsin Archeologist* 84(1&2): 83–99.

2006   Where's the Power in Mound Building? An Eastern Woodlands Perspective. In *Leadership and Polity in Mississippian Society,* edited by Brian M. Butler and Paul D. Welch, pp. 197–213. Center for Archaeological Investigations Occasional Paper No. 33, Southern Illinois University–Carbondale.

2007   On the Identity of the Birdman within Mississippian Period Art and Iconography. In *Ancient Objects and Sacred Realms: Interpretations of Mississippian Iconography,* edited by F. Kent Reilly III and James F. Garber, pp. 56–106. University of Texas Press, Austin.

Brown, James A., and John E. Kelly
2000   Cahokia and the Southeastern Ceremonial Complex. In *Mounds, Modoc, and Mesoamerica: Papers in Honor of Melvin Fowler,* edited by Steven R. Ahler, pp. 464–510. Scientific Papers 28. Illinois State Museum, Springfield.

Brown, James A., Richard A. Kerber, and Howard D. Winters
1990   Trade and the Evolution of Exchange Relations at the Beginning of the Mississippian Period. In *Mississippian Emergence: The Evolution of Ranked Agricultural Societies in Eastern North America,* edited by Bruce D. Smith, pp. 251–280. Smithsonian Institution Press, Washington, DC.

Butler, Amanda Jo
2014   The Siren's Song of Portable X-ray Fluorescence: Lessons Learned and What All Archaeologists Need to Know. Master's thesis, Department of Anthropology, University of Illinois at Urbana–Champaign.

Champion, Timothy (editor)
1989   *Centre and Periphery: Comparative Studies in Archaeology.* Urwin Hyman, London.

Chase-Dunn, Christopher, and Thomas D. Hall
1991   *Core/Periphery Relations in Precapitalist Worlds.* Westview Press, Boulder, Colorado.

Claflin, John
1991   The Shire Site: Mississippian Outpost in the Central Illinois Prairie. In *New Perspectives on Cahokia: Views from the Periphery,* edited by James B. Stoltman, pp. 155–176. Monographs in World Archaeology, Vol. 2. Prehistory Press, Madison, Wisconsin.

Clark, Jeffrey J.
2001   *Tracking Prehistoric Migrations: Pueblo Settlers among the Tonto Basin Hohokam.* Anthropological Papers, University of Arizona, Tucson.

Cobb, Charles R.
1989   An Appraisal of the Role of Mill Creek Chert Hoes in Mississippian Exchange Systems. *Southeastern Archaeology* 8(2): 79–92.

1991   One Hundred Years of Investigations at the Linn Site in Southern Illinois. *Illinois Archaeology* 3(1): 56–76.

1996   Specialization, Exchange, and Power in Small-Scale Societies and Chiefdoms. *Research in Economic Anthropology* 18: 251–294.

2000   *From Quarry to Cornfield: The Political Economy of Mississippian Hoe Production.* University of Alabama Press, Tuscaloosa.

2003   Mississippian Chiefdoms: How Complex? *Annual Review of Anthropology* 32: 63–84.

Collins, James M.
1990   *The Archaeology of the Cahokia Mounds ICT-II: Site Structure.* Illinois Cultural Resources Study No. 10, Illinois Historic Preservation Agency, Springfield.

1997   Cahokia Settlement and Social Structure as Viewed from the ICT-II. In *Cahokia: Domination and Ideology in the Mississippian World,* edited by Timothy

R. Pauketat and Thomas E. Emerson, pp. 124–140. University of Nebraska Press, Lincoln.

Conrad, Lawrence A.

1991   The Middle Mississippian Cultures of the Central Illinois Valley. In *Cahokia and the Hinterlands: Middle Mississippian Cultures of the Midwest,* edited by Thomas E. Emerson, pp. 119–156. University of Illinois Press, Urbana.

1993   Two Elaborate Middle Mississippian Graves from the Kingston Lake Site, Peoria County, Illinois. In *Highways to the Past: Essays on Illinois Archaeology in Honor of Charles J. Bareis, Illinois Archaeology,* Vol. 5, edited by Thomas E. Emerson, Andrew C. Fortier, and Dale L. McElrath, pp. 297–314. Illinois Archaeological Society, Springfield.

Cook, Thomas Genn

1981   *A Summary of Research through 1981: Special Report for Alumni.* Center for American Archaeology, Kampsville, Illinois.

1983   *The Audrey Site: A Summary of Research through 1982.* Center for American Archaeology, Kampsville, Illinois.

Crown, Patricia L., Thomas E. Emerson, Jiyan Gu, W. Jeffrey Hurst, Timothy R. Pauketat, and Timothy Ward

2012   Ritual Black Drink Consumption at Cahokia. *Proceedings of the National Academy of Sciences* 109: 13944–13949.

Cusick, James G. (editor)

1998   *Studies in Culture Contact: Interaction, Culture Change, and Archaeology.* Center for Archaeological Investigations Occasional Paper No. 25, Southern Illinois University–Carbondale.

Cusick, James G.

1998   Historiography of Acculturation: An Evaluation of Concepts and Their Application in Archaeology. In *Studies in Culture Contact: Interaction, Culture Change, and Archaeology,* edited by James G. Cusick, pp. 126–145. Occasional Paper No. 25, Center for Archaeological Investigations, Southern Illinois University–Carbondale.

Daniels, Stephanie

2007   Lithic Artifacts. In *The Archaeology of the East St. Louis Mound Center Part II: The Northside Excavations,* edited by Andrew C. Fortier, pp. 715–746. Transportation Archaeological Research Reports No. 22. University of Illinois at Urbana–Champaign.

Deagan, Kathleen

1998   Transculturation and Spanish American Ethnogenesis: The Archaeological Legacy of the Quincentenary. In *Studies in Culture Contact: Interaction, Culture Change, and Archaeology,* edited by James G. Cusick, pp. 23–43. Center for Archaeological Investigations Occasional Paper No. 25, Southern Illinois University–Carbondale.

2004   Reconsidering Taino Social Dynamics after Spanish Conquest: Gender and Class in Culture Contact. *American Antiquity* 69(4): 597–626.

2013   Hybridity, Identity, and Archaeological Practice. In *The Archaeology of Hybrid*

Material Culture, edited by Jeb J. Card, pp. 260–276. Center for Archaeological Investigations Occasional Paper No. 39, Southern Illinois University–Carbondale.

DeBoer, Warren R.

1988   Subterranean Storage and the Organization of Surplus: The View from Eastern North America. *Southeastern Archaeology* 26: 1–20.

Delaney-Rivera, Colleen

2000   Mississippian and Late Woodland Cultural Interaction and Regional Dynamics: A View from the Lower Illinois River Valley. PhD dissertation, Department of Anthropology, University of California, Los Angeles.

2004   From Edge to Frontier: Early Mississippian Occupation of the Lower Illinois River Valley. *Southeastern Archaeology* 23(1): 41–56.

2007   Examining Interaction and Identity in Prehistory: Mortuary Vessels from the Schild Cemetery. *North American Archaeologist* 28(4): 295–331.

Dietler, Michael

2010   *Archaeologies of Colonialism: Consumption, Entanglement, and Violence in Ancient Mediterranean France.* University of California Press, Berkeley.

Douglas, John Goodwin

1976   Collins: A Late Woodland Ceremonial Complex in the Woodfordian Northeast. PhD dissertation, Department of Anthropology, University of Illinois at Urbana–Champaign.

Droessler, Judith

1981   *Craniometry and Biological Distance: Biocultural Continuity and Change in the Late Woodland–Mississippian Interface.* Research Series 1. Center for American Archaeology at Northwestern University, Evanston, Illinois.

Dymek, Robert F., and John E. Kelly

2015   Recent Sourcing and Analyses of Basaltic Materials from Mississippian Contexts in the Cahokia Region. Presented at the 61st Annual Meeting of the Midwest Archaeological Conference, Milwaukee, Wisconsin.

Edwards, Tai S.

2010   Osage Gender: Continuity, Change, and Colonization, 1720s–1820s. PhD dissertation, Department of History, University of Kansas, Lawrence.

Emberling, Geoff

1997   Ethnicity in Complex Societies: Archaeological Perspectives. *Journal of Archaeological Research* 5(4): 295–344.

Emerson, Thomas E.

1984   Stirling Phase Occupation. In *The BBB Motor Site,* edited by Thomas E. Emerson and Douglas K. Jackson, pp. 197–345. American Bottom Archaeology FAI-270 Site Reports, Vol. 17. University of Illinois Press, Urbana.

1989   Water, Serpents, and the Underworld: An Exploration into Cahokia Symbolism. In *Southeastern Ceremonial Complex: Artifacts and Analysis,* edited by Patricia K. Galloway, pp. 45–95. University of Nebraska Press, Lincoln.

1991a   Some Perspectives on Cahokia and the Northern Mississippian Expansion. In *Cahokia and the Hinterlands: Middle Mississippian Cultures of the Midwest,* edited by Thomas E. Emerson and R. Barry Lewis, pp. 221–236. University of Illinois Press, Urbana.

1991b   The Apple River Mississippian Culture of Northwestern Illinois. In *Cahokia and the Hinterlands: Middle Mississippian Cultures of the Midwest,* edited by Thomas E. Emerson and R. Barry Lewis, pp. 164–182. University of Illinois Press, Urbana.

1997a   *Cahokia and the Archaeology of Power.* University of Alabama Press, Tuscaloosa.

1997b   Elite Ideology and the Mississippian Cosmos. In *Cahokia: Domination and Ideology in the Mississippian World,* edited by Timothy R. Pauketat and Thomas E. Emerson, pp. 190–228. University of Nebraska Press, Lincoln.

1997c   Reflections on Cahokian Hegemony. In *Cahokia: Domination and Ideology in the Mississippian World,* edited by Timothy R. Pauketat and Thomas E.E merson, pp. 167–189. University of Nebraska Press, Lincoln.

Emerson, Thomas E., Susan M. Alt, and Timothy R. Pauketat

2008   Locating American Indian Religion at Cahokia and Beyond. In *Religion, Archaeology, and the Material World,* edited by Lars Fogelin, pp. 216–236. Center for Archaeological Investigations Occasional Paper No. 36, Southern Illinois University–Carbondale.

Emerson, Thomas E., and Kristin M. Hedman

2016   The Dangers of Diversity: The Consolidation and Dissolution of Cahokia, Native North America's First Urban Polity. In *Beyond Collapse: Archaeological Perspectives on Resilience, Revitalization, and Transformation in Complex Societies,* edited by Ronald K. Faulseit, pp. 147–175. Center for Archaeological Investigations Occasional Paper No. 42. Southern Illinois University Press, Carbondale.

Emerson, Thomas E., Kristin M. Hedman, Tamira K. Brennan, and Timothy R. Pauketat

2017   Contextualizing Diaspora within an Urbanized Cahokia. Paper presented at the 74th Annual Meeting of the Southeastern Archaeological Conference, Tulsa, Oklahoma.

Emerson, Thomas E., and Randall E. Hughes

2000   Figurines, Flint Clay Sourcing, the Ozark Highlands, and Cahokian Acquisition. *American Antiquity* 65(1): 79–101.

Emerson, Thomas E., Randall E. Hughes, Mary R. Hynes, and Sarah U. Wisseman

2002   Implications of Sourcing Cahokia-style Flint Clay Figures in the American Bottom and the Upper Mississippi Valley. *Midcontinental Journal of Archaeology* 27(2): 309–338.

Emerson, Thomas E., and Douglas K. Jackson (editors)

1984   *The BBB Motor Site.* American Bottom Archaeology FAI-270 Site Reports, Vol. 17. University of Illinois Press, Urbana and Chicago.

Emerson, Thomas E., and R. Barry Lewis (editors)

1991   *Cahokia and the Hinterlands: Middle Mississippian Cultures of the Midwest.* University of Illinois Press, Urbana.

Emerson, Thomas E., Phillip G. Millhouse, and Marjorie B. Schroeder

2007   The Lundy Site and the Mississippian Presence in the Apple River Valley. *Wisconsin Archeologist* 88(2): 1–123.

Emerson, Thomas E., and Timothy R. Pauketat
2008   Historical-Processual Archaeology and Culture Making: Unpacking the Southern Cult and Mississippian Religion. In *Belief in the Past: Theoretical Approaches to the Archaeology of Religion,* edited by David S. Whitely and Kelley Hays-Gilpin, pp. 167–188. Left Coast Press, Walnut Creek, California.

Esarey, Duane
2000   Late Woodland Maples Mills and Mossville Phase Sequence in the Central Illinois River Valley. In *Late Woodland Tradition and Transformation across the Midcontinent,* edited by Thomas E. Emerson, Dale L. McElrath, and Andrew C. Fortier, pp. 387–410. University of Nebraska Press, Lincoln.

Esarey, Duane, and Timothy R Pauketat
1992   *The Lohmann Site: An Early Mississippian Center in the American Bottom (11-S-49).* American Bottom Archaeology FAI-270 Site Reports, Vol. 25. University of Illinois Press, Urbana.

Farnsworth, Kenneth B., and Thomas E. Emerson
1989   The Macoupin Creek Figure Pipe and Its Archaeological Context: Evidence for Late Woodland–Mississippian Interaction Beyond the Northern Border of Cahokian Settlement. *Midcontinental Journal of Archaeology* 14(1): 18–37.

Farnsworth, Kenneth B., Thomas E. Emerson, and Rebecca Miller Glenn
1991   Patterns of Late Woodland/Mississippian Interaction in the Lower Illinois Valley Drainage: A View from Starr Village. In *Cahokia and the Hinterlands: Middle Mississippian Cultures of the Midwest,* edited by Thomas E. Emerson and R. Barry Lewis, pp. 83–118. University of Illinois Press, Urbana.

Finney, Fred A.
1985   *The Carbon Dioxide Site (11-Mo-594).* American Bottom Archaeology FAI-270 Site Reports, Vol. 11. University of Illinois Press, Urbana.
1993   Cahokia's Northern Hinterland as Viewed from the Fred Edwards Site in Southwest Wisconsin: Intrasite and Regional Evidence for Production, Consumption, and Exchange. PhD dissertation, Department of Anthropology, University of Wisconsin–Madison.
2013   Intrasite and Regional Perspectives on the Fred Edwards Site and the Stirling Horizon in the Upper Mississippi Valley. *Wisconsin Archeologist* 94: 3–248.

Finney, Fred A., and James B. Stoltman
1991   The Fred Edwards Site: A Case of Stirling Phase Culture Contact in Southwestern Wisconsin. In *New Perspectives on Cahokia: Views from the Periphery,* edited by James B. Stoltman, pp. 229–252. Monographs in World Archaeology No. 2. Prehistory Press, Madison, Wisconsin.

Fishel, Richard L. (editor)
2018   *Archaeological Investigations at the Eileen Cunningham Site: Woodland and Mississippian Habitations in the Lower Illinois Valley of Greene County, Illinois.* Illinois State Archaeological Survey, Prairie Research Institute, Technical Report No. 185, University of Illinois at Urbana–Champaign.

Fortier, Andrew C.
1985   *The Robert Schneider Site (11-Ms-1177).* American Bottom Archaeology FAI-270 Site Report, Vol. 11. University of Illinois Press, Urbana.

Fortier, Andrew C., Richard B. Lacampagne, and Fred A. Finney
1984   *The Fish Lake Site (11-Mp-608).* American Bottom Archaeology FAI-270 Site Reports, Vol. 8. University of Illinois Press, Urbana.

Fowler, Melvin L.
1971   Agriculture and Village Settlement in the North American East: The Central Mississippi Valley Area, A Case History. In *Prehistoric Agriculture,* edited by Stuart Struever, pp. 391–403. Natural History Press, Garden City, New York.

1978   Cahokia and the American Bottom: Settlement Archeology. In *Mississippian Settlement Patterns,* edited by Bruce D. Smith, pp. 455–478. Academic Press, New York.

1991   Mound 72 and Early Mississippian at Cahokia. In *New Perspectives on Cahokia: Views from the Periphery,* edited by James B. Stoltman, pp. 1–28. Monographs in World Archaeology No. 2. Prehistory Press, Madison.

1997   *The Cahokia Atlas: A Historical Atlas of Cahokia Archaeology.* University of Illinois Press, Urbana.

Fowler, Melvin L., Jerome Rose, Barbara Vander Leest, and Steven A. Ahler
1999   *The Mound 72 Area: Dedicated and Sacred Space in Early Cahokia.* Illinois State Museum, Reports of Investigations No. 54, Springfield.

Frank, Andre Gunder
1993   Bronze Age World System Cycles. *Current Anthropology* 34(4): 383–429.

Frankenstein, Susan, and Michael J. Rowlands
1978   The Internal Structure and Regional Context of Early Iron Age Society in Southwest Germany. *University of London Institute of Archaeology Bulletin* 15: 73–112.

Friberg, Christina M.
2018a   Cosmic Negotiations: Cahokian Religion and Ramey Incised Pottery in the Northern Hinterland. *Southeastern Archaeology* 37(1): 39–57.

2018b   Igniting Interaction through Mississippian Tradition-making: An Interregional Analysis at the Audrey Site (11GE20). PhD dissertation, Department of Anthropology, University of California, Santa Barbara.

Friberg, Christina M., and Gregory D. Wilson
2015   Cahokia's Western Frontier: Consolidation and Collapse as Viewed from the Big River Valley, Missouri. Paper presented at the 80th Annual Meeting of the Society for American Archaeology, San Francisco, California.

Friedman, Jonathan A., and Michael J. Rowlands
1977   Notes towards an Epigenetic Model of the Evolution of Civilization. In *The Evolution of Social Systems,* edited by Jonathan A. Friedman and Michael Rowlands, pp. 201–276. University of Pittsburgh Press, Pittsburgh, Pennsylvania.

Frison, George C.
1978   *Prehistoric Hunters of the High Plains,* Vol. 1. Academic Press, Cambridge, Massachusetts.

Galloway, Patricia (editor)

1989   *The Southeastern Ceremonial Complex: Artifacts and Analysis.* University of Nebraska Press, Lincoln.

Gibbons, Guy E., and Clark A. Dobbs

1991   The Mississippian Presence in the Red Wig Area, Minnesota. In *New Perspectives on Cahokia: Views from the Periphery,* edited by James B. Stoltman, pp. 281–305. Monographs in World Archaeology No. 2. Prehistory Press, Madison, Wisconsin.

Goldstein, Lynne

1980   *Mississippian Mortuary Practices: A Case Study of Two Cemeteries in the Lower Illinois Valley.* Northwestern University Archaeological Program Scientific Papers 4. Evanston, Illinois.

1982   *Archaeology in the Southeastern Wisconsin Glaciated Region: Phase 1,* No. 64. University of Wisconsin–Milwaukee, Archaeological Research Laboratory.

Goldstein, Lynne, and John D. Richards

1991   Ancient Aztalan: The Cultural and Ecological Context of a Late Prehistoric Site in the Midwest. In *Cahokia and the Hinterlands: Middle Mississippian Cultures of the Midwest,* edited by Thomas E. Emerson, pp. 193–206. University of Illinois Press–Urbana.

Green, William, and David J. Nolan

2000   Late Woodland Peoples in West-Central Illinois. In *Late Woodland Tradition and Transformation across the Midcontinent,* edited by Thomas E. Emerson, pp. 345–386. University of Nebraska Press, Lincoln.

Green, William, and Roland L. Rodell

1994   The Mississippian Presence and Cahokia Interaction at Trempealeau, Wisconsin. *American Antiquity* 59(2): 334–359.

Gregg, Michael L.

1975   A Population Estimate for Cahokia. In *Perspectives in Cahokia Archaeology,* pp. 126–136. Illinois Archaeological Survey Bulletin No. 10, Urbana.

Griffin, James B.

1949   The Cahokia Ceramic Complexes. In *Proceedings of the Fifth Plains Conference for Archaeology,* edited by J. L. Campe, pp. 44–58. University of Nebraska–Lincoln.

1960   A Hypothesis for the Prehistory of the Winnebago. In *Culture in History: Essays in Honor of Paul Radin,* edited by S. Diamond, pp. 809–868. Columbia University Press, New York.

1961   Lake Superior Copper and the Indians: Miscellaneous Studies of Great Lakes Prehistory. Manuscript on file, Department of Anthropology, University of Michigan–Ann Arbor.

Griffin, James B, and Albert C Spaulding

1951   The Central Mississippi Valley Archaeological Survey, Season 1950—A Preliminary Report. *Journal of the Illinois State Archaeological Society* 1(3): 75–84.

Hall, Robert L.

1967   The Mississippian Heartland and Its Plains Relationship. *Plains Anthropologist* 12(36): 175–183.

1975   Chronologies and Phases at Cahokia. In *Chronologies and Phases at Cahokia*, pp. 15–31. Illinois Archaeological Survey Bulletin No. 10, Urbana.

1991   Cahokia Identity and Interaction Models of Cahokia Mississippian. In *Cahokia and the Hinterlands: Middle Mississippian Cultures of the Midwest*, edited by Thomas E. Emerson, pp. 3–34. University of Illinois Press, Urbana.

1997   *An Archaeology of the Soul: North American Indian Belief and Ritual.* University of Illinois Press, Urbana.

Hally, David J.

1986   The Identification of Vessel Function: A Case Study from Northwest Georgia. *American Antiquity* 51: 267–295.

1993   The Territorial Size of Mississippian Chiefdoms. In *Archaeology of Eastern North America: Papers in Honor of Stephen Williams,* edited by James B. Stoltman, pp. 143–168. Mississippi Department of Archives and History, Jackson.

Hally, David J., Marvin T. Smith, and James B. Langford, Jr.

1990   The Archaeological Reality of DeSoto's Coosa. In *Columbian Consequences: Archaeology and Historical Perspectives on the Spanish Borderlands East,* edited by David Hurst Thomas, pp. 121–138. Smithsonian Institution Press, Washington, DC.

Hammerstedt, Scott W., and Erin R. Hughes

2015   Mill Creek Chert Hoes and Prairie Soils: Implications for Cahokian Production and Expansion. *Midcontinental Journal of Archaeology* 40: 149–165.

Hanenberger, Ned H.

1990   The Karol Rekas Site (11-Ms-1255). In *Selected Early Mississippian Household Sites in the American Bottom,* edited by Douglas K. Jackson and Ned H. Hanenberger, pp. 425–509. American Bottom Archaeology FAI-270 Site Reports, Vol. 22. University of Illinois Press, Urbana.

2003   *The Range Site 3: Mississippian and Oneota Occupations.* Transportation Archaeology Research Reports 17. Illinois Transportation Archaeology Research Program, Urbana.

Harn, Alan D.

1975   Cahokia and the Mississippian Emergence in the Spoon River Area of Illinois. *Transactions of the Illinois State Academy of Sciences* 68(4): 414–434.

1991   The Eveland Site: Inroad to Spoon River Mississippian Society. In *New Perspectives on Cahokia: Views from the Periphery,* edited by James B. Stoltman, pp. 129–153. Monographs in World Archaeology No. 2. Prehistory Press, Madison, Wisconsin.

Harris, Wendy G.

1996   Form and Function of Crab Orchard Tradition Pit Features in the Big Muddy River Drainage of Southern Illinois. Master's thesis, Department of Anthropology, Southern Illinois University–Carbondale.

Hassig, Ross

1985   *Trade, Tribute, and Transportation: The Sixteenth-century Political Economy of the Valley of Mexico.* University of Oklahoma Press, Norman.

Hastorf, Christine

1988   The Use of Paleoethnobotanical Data in Prehistoric Studies of Crop Production, Processing, and Consumption. In *Current Paleoethnobotany: Analytical Methods and Cultural Interpretations of Archaeological Plant Remains,* edited by Christine Hastorf and Virginia Popper, pp. 119–144. University of Chicago Press, Chicago, Illinois.

Helms, Mary W.

1992   Long Distance Contacts, Elite Aspirations, and the Age of Discovery in Cosmological Context. In *Resources, Power, and Interregional Interaction,* edited by Edward M. Schortman and Patricia A. Urban, pp. 157–174. Plenum Press, New York.

Henning, Dale R.

1967   Mississippian Influences on the Eastern Plains Border: An Evaluation. *Plains Anthropologist* 12: 184–193.

Hodder, Ian

2012   *Entangled: An Archaeology of the Relationships Between Humans and Things.* Wiley, Oxford, UK.

Holley, George R.

1989   *The Archaeology of Cahokia Mounds ICT-II: Ceramics.* Illinois Cultural Resources Study 11. Illinois Historic Preservation Agency, Springfield.

1995   Microliths and the Kunnemann Tract: An Assessment of Craft Production at the Cahokia Site. *Illinois Archaeology* 7: 1–68.

2008   The Red Wing Locality Late Prehistoric Ceramic Sequence. Manuscript on file, Department of Anthropology, Minnesota State University–Moorhead.

Holley, George R., Kathryn E. Parker, Harold W. Watters, Julie N. Harper, Mikels Skele, and Jennifer E. Ringberg

2001   *The Lembke Locality, Scott Joint-Use Archaeological Project.* Office of Contract Archaeology, Southern Illinois University, Edwardsville.

Holmes, William H.

1903   *Aboriginal Pottery of the Eastern United States.* Government Printing Office, Washington, DC.

Holt, Julie Z.

1996   AG Church Site Features and Community Organization. *Illinois Archaeology* 8(1 & 2): 58–84.

Ingram, J. K.

1885   Political Economy. *Encycolpaedia Britannica.* Scribner's.

Iseminger, William

2010   *Cahokia Mounds, America's First City.* History Press, Charleston, South Carolina.

Jackson, Douglas K.

1984   *The Determann Borrow Site, Madison County, Illinois. Research* Reports, 14, Resource Investigation Program, University of Illinois, Urbana.

1990   The Esterlein Site (11-Ms-598). In *Selected Early Mississippian Household Sites in the American Bottom,* edited by Douglas K. Jackson and Ned H. Hanenberger, pp. 91–216. American Bottom Archaeology FAI-270 Site Reports, Vol. 22. University of Illinois Press, Urbana.

2014   *Hawkins Hollow : A Late Mississippian Household in the Southern American Bottom.* Illinois State Archaeological Survey, Prairie Research Institute, Technical Report No. 159, University of Illinois at Urbana–Champaign.

Jackson, Douglas K., Andrew C. Fortier, and Joyce A. Williams

1992   *The Sponemann Site 2 (11-MS-517): The Mississippian and Oneota Occupations.* American Bottom Archaeology, FAI-270 Site Reports No. 24, University of Illinois Press, Urbana.

Jackson, Douglas K., and Ned H. Hanenberger (editors)

1990   *Selected Early Mississippian Household Sites in the American Bottom.* American Bottom Archaeology FAI-270 Site Reports, Vol. 22. University of Illinois Press, Urbana.

Jackson, Douglas K., and Phillip G. Millhouse

2003   *The Vaughn Branch and Old Edwardsville Road Sites: Late Stirling and Early Moorehead Phase Mississippian Occupations in the Northern American Bottom.* Transportation Archaeological Research Reports No. 16. University of Illinois at Urbana–Champaign.

Keeley, Lawrence H.

1980   *Experimental Determination of Stone Tools Uses: A Microwear Analysis.* University of Chicago Press, Chicago, Illinois.

Kelly, John E.

1982   Formative Developments at Cahokia and the Adjacent American Bottom: A Merrell Tract Perspective. PhD dissertation, Department of Anthropology, University of Wisconsin–Madison.

1984   Late Bluff Chert Utilization on the Merrel Tract, Cahokia. In *Prehistoric Chert Exploitation: Studies from the Midcontinent,* edited by Brian Butler and Ernest E. May, pp. 23–44. Center for Archaeological Investigations Occasional Paper No. 2, Southern Illinois University–Carbondale.

1990   Range Phase Features. In *The Range Site 2: The Emergent Mississippian Dohack and Range Phase Occupations,* edited by John E. Kelly, Steven J. Ozuk, and Joyce A. Williams, pp. 313–386. American Bottom Archaeology FAI-270 Site Reports, Vol. 20. University of Illinois Press, Urbana.

1991a   Cahokia and Its Role as a Gateway Center in Interregional Exchange. In *Cahokia and the Hinterlands: Middle Mississippian Cultures of the Midwest,* edited by Thomas E. Emerson and R. Barry Lewis, pp. 61–80. University of Illinois Press, Urbana.

1991b   The Evidence for Prehistoric Exchange and Its Implications for the Development of Cahokia. In *New Perspectives on Cahokia: Views from the Periphery,* edited by James B. Stoltman, pp. 65–92. Monographs in World Archaeology No. 2. Prehistory Press, Madison, Wisconsin.

1997   Stirling-Phase Sociopolitical Activity at East St. Louis and Cahokia. In *Cahokia: Domination and Ideology in the Mississippian World,* edited by Timothy R. Pauketat and Thomas E. Emerson, pp. 141–166. University of Nebraska Press, Lincoln.

2000   Introduction. In *The Cahokia Mounds,* edited by John E. Kelly, pp. 1–48. University of Alabama Press, Tuscaloosa.

2002   The Pulcher Tradition and the Ritualization of Cahokia: A Perspective from Cahokia's Southern Neighbor. *Southeastern Archaeology* 21(2): 136–148.

2008   The Geological and Cultural Contexts of Basalt in the St. Louis Region during the Emergent Mississippian and Early Mississippian. Paper presented at the Ozark Lithic Symposium of the Missouri Archaeological Society, Sullivan, Missouri.

Kelly, John E., and James A. Brown

2012   In Search of Cosmic Power: Contextualizing Spiritual Journeys between Cahokia and the St. Francois Mountains. In *Archaeology of Spiritualities,* edited by Kathryn Roundtree, Christine Morris, and Alan A. D. Peatfield, pp. 107–129. Springer Science + Business Media, New York.

Kelly, John E., Fred A. Finney, Dale L. McElrath, and Steven J. Ozuk

1984   Late Woodland Period. In *American Bottom Archaeology,* edited by Charles J. Bareis and James W. Porter, pp. 104–127. University of Illinois Press, Urbana.

Kelly, John E., Andrew C. Fortier, Steven J. Ozuk, and Joyce A. Williams

1987   *The Range Site.* American Bottom Archaeology FAI-270 Site Reports, Vol. 16. University of Illinois Press, Urbana.

Kelly, John E., Steven J. Ozuk, Douglas K. Jackson, Dale L. McElrath, Fred A. Finney, and Duane Esarey

1984   Emergent Mississippian Period. In *American Bottom Archaeology,* edited by Charles J. Bareis and James W. Porter, pp. 128–157. University of Illinois Press, Urbana.

Kelly, John E., Steven J. Ozuk, and Joyce A. Williams (editors)

1990   *The Range Site 2: The Emergent Mississippian Dohack and Range Phase Occupations.* American Bottom Archaeology FAI-270 Site Reports, Vol. 20. University of Illinois Press, Urbana.

Kelly, Lucretia S.

1979   *Animal Resource Exploitation by Early Cahokia Populations on the Merrell Tract.* Circular Number Four, Illinois Archaeological Survey, Urbana.

1997   Patterns of Faunal Exploitation at Cahokia. In *Cahokia: Domination and Ideology in the Mississippian World,* edited by Timothy R. Pauketat and Thomas E. Emerson, pp. 69–88. University of Nebraska Press, Lincoln.

King, Adam (editor)

2007   *Southeastern Ceremonial Complex: Chronology, Content, Context.* University of Alabama Press, Tuscaloosa.

Knight, Vernon James, Jr.

1986 The Institutional Organization of Mississippian Religion. *American Antiquity* 51(4) 675–687.

1989 Some Speculations on Mississippian Monsters. In *The Southeastern Ceremonial Complex: Artifacts and Analysis,* edited by Adam King, pp. 205–210. University of Nebraska Press, Lincoln.

2006 Farewell to the Southeastern Ceremonial Complex. *Southeastern Archaeology* 25(1): 129–141.

Knight, Vernon James Jr., James A. Brown, and George E. Lankford

2001 On the Subject Matter of Southeastern Ceremonial Complex Art. *Southeastern Archaeology* 20(2): 129–141.

Koldehoff, Brad

1985 Southern Illinois Cherts: A Guide to Silicious Materials Exploited by Prehistoric Populations in Southern Illinois. Manuscript on file, Center for Archaeological Investigations, Southern Illinois University–Carbondale.

1987 The Cahokia Flake Tool Industry: Socioeconomic Implications for Late Prehistory in the Central Mississippi Valley. In *The Organization of Core Technology,* edited by Jay K. Johnson and Carol A. Morrow, pp. 151–185. Westview Press, Boulder, Colorado, and London.

1995 Lithic Analysis. In *The Sand Prairie Phase Occupation of the Merrel Tract, Cahokia,* edited by John E. Kelly, pp. 50–73. Central Mississippi Valley Archaeological Research Institute, Collinsville, Illinois.

2002 Appendix B: Chipped-Stone Resources of Alexander and Union Counties. In *The Archaeology and History of Horseshoe Lake, Alexander County, Illinois,* edited by Brad Koldehoff and Mark J. Wagner, pp. 135–139. Center for Archaeological Investigations Research Paper No. 60, Southern Illinois University–Carbondale.

2006 Chipped-Stone Resources of Monroe County. In *Late Woodland Frontiers: Patrick Phase Settlements along the Kaskaskia Trail, Monroe County, Illinois,* edited by Brad Koldehoff and Joseph M. Galloy, pp. 367–376. Transportation Archaeological Research Reports No. 23. University of Illinois at Urbana–Champaign.

Koldehoff, Brad, and Tamira Brennan

2010 Exploring Mississippian Polity Interaction and Craft Specialization with Ozark Chipped-Stone Resources. *Missouri Archaeologist* 71.

Koldehoff, Brad, and Ronald Kearns

1993 Using Stone Tools to Detect Mississippian Homesteads. *Illinois Antiquity* 28(3): 4–8.

Koldehoff, Brad, and Gregory D. Wilson

2010 Mississippian Celt Production and Resource Extraction in the Upper Big River Valley of St. Francois County, Missouri. *Missouri Archaeologist* 71: 217–248.

Kruchten, Jeffery D.

2012 Recent Investigations at the Knoebel Site, St. Clair County, IL. *Illinois Archaeology* 24: 1–25.

Kuehn, Steven R.

2017   Audrey North (11GE20) Faunal Analysis Greene County, Illinois. Unpublished manuscript, Illinois State Archaeological Survey, Prairie Research Institute, University of Illinois–Urbana.

Lankford, George E.

2004   World on a String: Some Cosmological Components of the Southeastern Ceremonial Complex. In *Hero, Hawk, and Open Hand: American Indian Art of the Ancient Midwest and South,* edited by Richard F. Townsend, pp. 207–218. Art Institute of Chicago, Yale University Press, New Haven, Connecticut.

2007   The Great Serpent in Eastern North America. In *Ancient Objects and Sacred Realms: Interpretations of Mississippian Iconography,* edited by F. Kent Reilly III, and James F. Garber, pp. 107–135. University of Texas Press, Austin.

Lankford, George E., F. Kent Reilly III, and James F. Garber

2011   *Visualizing the Sacred: Cosmic Visions, Regionalism, and the Art of the Mississippian World,* edited by George E. Lankford, F. Kent Reilly III, and James F. Garber. University of Texas Press, Austin.

Lidberg, George A.

1940   Thompson Village (40HY5). Field Notes on File at the Frank H. McClung Museum, University of Tennessee–Knoxville.

Liebmann, Matthew, and Melissa S. Murphy (editors)

2011   *Enduring Conquests: Rethinking the Archaeology of Resistance to Spanish Colonialism in the Americas.* School for Advanced Research Press, Santa Fe, New Mexico.

Liebmann, Matthew, and Melissa S. Murphy

2011   Rethinking the Archaeology of "Rebels, Backsliders, and Idolaters." In *Enduring Conquests: Rethinking the Archaeology of Resistance to Spanish Colonialism in the Americas,* edited by Matthew Liebmann and Melissa S. Murphy, pp. 3–18. School for Advanced Research Press, Santa Fe, New Mexico.

Lightfoot, Kent G., and Antoinette Martinez

1995   Frontiers and Boundaries in Archaeological Perspective. *Annual Review of Anthropology* 24: 471–492.

Lopinot, Neal H.

1997   Cahokian Food Production Reconsidered. In *Cahokia: Domination and Ideology in the Mississippian World,* edited by Timothy R. Pauketat and Thomas E. Emerson, pp. 52–68. University of Nebraska Press, Lincoln.

Lyons, Claire L., and John K. Papadopoulos (editors)

2002   *The Archaeology of Colonialism.* Getty, Los Angeles, California.

Lyons, Patrick D.

2003   *Ancestral Hopi Migrations.* Anthropological Papers of the University of Arizona No. 68, Tucson.

Marshall, John B.

1992   The St. Louis Mound Group. *Missouri Archaeologist* 53: 23–46.

Mason, Ronald J., and Gregory Perino

1961   Microblades at Cahokia, Illinois. *American Antiquity* 26(4): 553–557.

McConaughy, Mark A

1991   The Rench Site Late Late Woodland/Mississippian Farming Hamlet from the Central Illinois River Valley: Food for Thought. In *New Perspectives on Cahokia: Views from the Periphery,* edited by James B. Stoltman, pp. 101–128. Monographs in World Archaeology No. 2. Prehistory Press, Madison, Wisconsin.

McConaughy, Mark A, Terrance J. Martin, and Frances B. King

1993   Late Late Woodland/Mississippian Component. In *Rench: A Stratified Site in the Central Illinois River Valley,* edited by Mark A. McConaughy, pp. 76–130. Illinois State Museum, Reports of Investigations No. 49, Springfield.

McCullough, Robert B., B. Jacob Skousen, Steven R. Kuehn, Adam Tufano, Alexy Zelin, and Katie Parker

2017   *Archaeological Investigations of the Mississippian Component at the Lillie Site (11MS662) in the Northern American Bottom, Madison County, Illinois.* Illinois State Archaeological Survey, Prairie Research Institute, Report No. 481, Urbana, Illinois.

McElrath, Dale L., Fred A. Finney, Marlene Moshage, Sissel Johannessen, Paula G. Cross, Charles Bareis, and James W. Porter

1987   *The George Reeves Site,* edited by Dale L. McElrath and Fred A. Finney. FAI-270 Si. University of Illinois Press, Urbana.

McGuire, Randall H.

1983   Breaking Down Cultural Complexity: Inequality and Heterogeneity. In *Advances in Archaeological Method and Theory,* Vol. 6, edited by Michael B. Schiffer, pp. 91–142. Academic Press, Orlando, Florida.

Mehrer, Mark W.

1995   *Cahokia's Countryside: Household Archaeology, Settlement Patterns, and Social Power.* Northern Illinois University Press, DeKalb.

Mehta, Jayur Madhusudan

2007   A Study of Sweat Lodges in the Southeastern United States. Master's thesis, Department of Anthropology, University of Alabama, Tuscaloosa.

Meinkoth, Michael C.

1993   Middle Mississippian Households in the Central Illinois River Valley: Examples from the Tree Row and Baker-Preston Sites. In *Highways to the Past:* Essays on Illinois Archaeology in Honor of Charles J. Bareis, Illinois Archaeology, Vol. 5, edited by Thomas E. Emerson, Andrew C. Fortier, and Dale L. McElrath, pp. 315–330. Illinois Archaeological Society, Springfield.

Meyers, Thomas J.

1970   *Chert Resources of the Lower Illinois Valley.* Illinois State Museum, Springfield.

Miller, Jessica R.

2015   Interior Carbonization Patterns as Evidence of Ritual Drink Preparation in Powell Plain and Ramey Incised Vessels. *American Antiquity* 80(1): 170–183.

Millhouse, Phillip G.

2012   The John Chapman Site and Creolization on the Northern Frontier of the Mississippian World. PhD dissertation, Department of Anthropology, University of Illinois at Urbana–Champaign.

Milner, George R.

1983   *The East St. Louis Stone Quarry Site Cemetery.* American Bottom Archaeology FAI-270 Site Reports, Vol. 1. University of Illinois Press, Urbana.

1984   Social and Temporal Implications of Variation among American Bottom Mississippian Cemeteries. *American Antiquity* 49(3): 468–488.

1990   Late Prehistoric Cultural Systems of the Mississippi River Valley: Foundations, Florescence, and Fragmentation. *Journal of World Prehistory* 4(1): 1–43.

1998   *The Cahokia Chiefdom: The Archaeology of a Mississippian Society.* Smithsonian Institution Press, Washington, DC.

Milner, George R. (editor)

1984   *The Julien Site,* edited by George R. Milner. FAI-270 Site. University of Illinois Press, Urbana.

Milner, George R., Thomas E. Emerson, Mark W. Mehrer, Joyce A. Williams, and Duane Esarey

1984   Mississippian and Oneota Period. In *American Bottom Archaeology,* edited by Charles J. Bareis and James W. Porter, pp. 158–186. University of Illinois Press, Urbana.

Milner, George R., Scott W. Hammerstedt, and Kirk D. French

2010   Chert Hoes as Digging Tools. *Antiquity* 84: 103–113.

Mollerud, Katy J.

2005   Messages, Meanings and Motifs: An Analysis of Ramey Incised Ceramics at the Aztalan Site. Master's thesis, Department of Anthropology, University of Wisconsin–Milwaukee.

Moorehead, Warren K.

[1929] 2000 *The Cahokia Mounds.* Edited by John E. Kelly. University of Alabama Press, Tuscaloosa.

Morse, Dan, George Schoenbeck, and Dan F. Morse

1953   Fiedler Site. *Journal of the Illinois State Archaeological Society* 3(2): 35–46.

Muller, Jon

1997   *Mississippian Political Economy.* Plenum Press, New York.

Neuzil, Anna A.

2008   *In the Aftermath of Migration: Renegotiating Ancient Identity in Southeastern Arizona.* Anthropological Papers of the University of Arizona No. 73, Tucson.

Pauketat, Timothy R

1993   *Temples for Cahokian Lords: Preston Holder's 1995–1956 Excavations of Kunnemann Mound.* Memoirs No. 26. University of Michigan, Museum of Anthropology, Ann Arbor.

1994   *The Ascent of Chiefs: Cahokia and Mississippian Politics in Native North America.* University of Alabama Press, Tuscaloosa.

1997a   Specialization, Political Symbols, and the Crafty Elite of Cahokia. *Southeastern Archaeology* 16(1): 1–15.

1997b   Cahokia Political Economy. In *Cahokia: Domination and Ideology in the Mississippian World,* edited by Timothy R. Pauketat and Thomas E. Emerson, pp. 30–51. University of Nebraska Press, Lincoln.

1998a   Refiguring the Archaeology of Greater Cahokia. *Journal of Archaeological Research* 6(1): 45–89.

1998b   *The Archaeology of Downtown Cahokia: The Tract-15A and Dunham Tract Excavations.* Studies in Archaeology No. 1. Illinois Transportation Archaeological Research Program, University of Illinois at Urbana–Champaign.

2001a   Practice and History in Archaeology: An Emerging Paradigm. *Anthropological Theory* 1(1): 73–98.

2001b   Concluding Thoughts on Tradition, History, and Archaeology. In *The Archaeology of Traditions: Agency and History Before and After Columbus,* edited by Timothy R. Pauketat, pp. 253–256. University of Florida Press, Gainesville.

2003   Resettled Farmers and the Making of a Mississippian Polity. *American Antiquity* 68: 39–66.

2004   *Ancient Cahokia and the Mississippians.* Cambridge University Press, Cambridge, UK.

2005   *The Archaeology of the East St. Louis Mound Center: Part I: The Southside Excavations.* Illinois Transportation Archaeological Research Reports No. 21. University of Illinois–Urbana.

2007   *Chiefdoms and Other Archaeological Delusions.* AltaMira Press, Lanham, Maryland.

2010   Of Leaders and Legacies in Native North America. In *The Evolution of Leadership and Complexity,* edited by John Kantner, Kevin J. Vaughn, and Jelmer Eerkins, pp. 169–192. School for Advanced Research Press, Santa Fe, New Mexico.

2013   *An Archaeology of the Cosmos: Rethinking Agency and Religion in Ancient America.* Routledge, London.

Pauketat, Timothy R. (editor)

2001   *The Archaeology of Traditions: Agency and History Before and After Columbus.* University of Florida Press, Gainesville.

Pauketat, Timothy R., and Susan M. Alt

2004   The Making and Meaning of a Mississippian Axe-head Cache. *Antiquity* 78: 779–797.

2005   Agency in a Postmold? Physicality and the Archaeology of Culture-Making. *Journal of Archaeological Method and Theory* 12(3): 213–236.

2015   Water and Shells in Bodies and Pots. In *Relational Identities and Other-than-human Agency in Archaeology,* edited by Eleanor Harrison-Buck and Julia A. Hendon, pp. 72–99. University Press of Colorado, Louisville.

Pauketat, Timothy R., Susan M. Alt, and Jeffery D. Kruchten

2017   The Emerald Acropolis: Elevating the Moon and Water in the Rise of Cahokia. *Antiquity* 91(355): 207–222.

Pauketat, Timothy R., and Thomas E. Emerson

1991   The Ideology of Authority and the Power of the Pot. *American Anthropologist* 93(4): 919–941.

1997   Introduction: Domination and Ideology in the Mississippian World. In *Cahokia: Domination and Ideology in the Mississippian World,* edited by Timothy

R. Pauketat and Thomas E. Emerson, pp. 1–29. University of Nebraska Press, Lincoln.

Pauketat, Timothy R., and Thomas E. Emerson (editors)

1997   *Cahokia: Domination and Ideology in the Mississippian World.* University of Nebraska Press, Lincoln.

Pauketat, Timothy R., Andrew C. Fortier, Susan M. Alt, and Thomas E. Emerson

2013   A Mississippian Conflagration at East St. Louis and Its Political-historical Implications. *Journal of Field Archaeology* 38(3): 210–226.

Pauketat, Timothy R., Jeffery D. Kruchten, Melissa R. Baltus, Kathryn E. Parker, and Elizabeth Kassly

2012   An Ancient Medicine Lodge in the Richland Complex. *Illinois Archaeology* 24: 1–25.

Pauketat, Timothy R., and Neal H. Lopinot

1997   Cahokia Population Dynamics. In *Cahokia: Domination and Ideology in the Mississippian World,* edited by Timothy R. Pauketat and Thomas E. Emerson, pp. 103–123. University of Nebraska Press, Lincoln.

Pauketat, Timothy R., and William I. Woods

1986   Middle Mississippian Structure Analysis: The Lawrence Primas Site in the American Bottom. *Wisconsin Archeologist* 67(2): 104–127.

Pauketat, Timothy R, Robert F Boszhardt, and Danielle M. Benden

2015   Trempealeau Entanglements: An Ancient Colony's Causes and Effects. *American Anthropologist* 80(2): 260–289.

Pauketat, Timothy R., Lucretia S. Kelly, Gayle J. Fritz, Neal H. Lopinot, Scott Elias, and Eve Hargrave

2002   The Residues of Feasting and Public Ritual at Early Cahokia. *American Antiquity* 67(2): 257–279.

Peebles, Christopher S.

1978   Determinants of Settlement Size and Location in the Moundville Phase. In *Mississippian Settlement Patterns,* edited by Bruce D. Smith, pp. 369–416. Academic Press, New York.

Peeples, Matthew A.

2018   *Connected Communities: Networks, Identity, and Social Change in the Ancient Cibola World.* University of Arizona Press, Tucson.

Perino, Gregory

1971   The Mississippian Component at the Schild Site (No. 4), Greene County, Illinois. Mississippian Archaeology in Illinois I: Site Reports from the St. Louis and Chicago Areas. *Illinois Archaeological Survey Bulletin* 8: 1–148.

Perttula, Timothy K.

2002   Archaeological Evidence for the Long-Distance Exchange of Caddo Indian Ceramics in the Southern Plains, Midwest, and Southeastern United States. In *Geochemical Evidence for Long-Distance Exchange,* edited by Michael D. Glascock, pp. 89–107. Bergin & Garvey, Westport, Connecticut.

Phillips, Phillip, and James A. Brown
1984   Pre-Columbian Shell Engravings from the Craig Mound at Spiro, Oklahoma. Pea-
        body Museum Press, Cambridge, Massachusetts.
Porter, James W.
1974   Cahokia Archaeology as Viewed from the Mitchell Site: A Satellite Community
        at A.D. 1150–1200. University of Wisconsin–Milwaukee.
1977   The Mitchell Site and Prehistoric Exchange Systems at Cahokia: A.D. 1000 +300.
        In Explorations into Cahokia Archaeology, edited by Melvin L. Fowler, pp. 137–
        164. Illinois Archaeological Survey Bulletin 7. Urbana.
Reilly, F. Kent III
2004   Visualizing the Sacred in Native American Art of the Mississippian Period. In
        Hero, Hawk, and Open Hand: American Indian Art of the Ancient Midwest and
        South, edited by Richard F. Townsend, pp. 125–137. Art Institute of Chicago, Yale
        University Press, New Haven, Connecticut.
Reimer, Paula J., Edouard Bard, Alex Bayliss, J. Warren Beck, Paul G. Blackwell, Chris-
topher Bronk Ramsey, Caitlin E. Buck, Hai Cheng, R. Lawrence Edwards, Michael
Friedrich, Pieter M. Grootes, Thomas P. Guilderson, Haflida Haflidason, Irka Hajdas,
Christine Hatte, Timothy J. Heaton, Dirk L. Hoffman, Alan G. Hogg, Konrad A. Hughen,
K. Felix Kaiser, Bernd Kromer, Stuart W. Manning, Mu Niu, Ron W. Reimer, David A.
Richards, Marian Scott, John R. Southon, Richard A. Staff, Christian S. M. Turney, and
Johannes van der Plicht
2013   IntCal13 and Marine13 Radiocarbon Age Calibration Curves 0–50,000 Years Cal
        BP. Radiocarbon 55: 1869–1887.
Reynolds, Austin W., Jennifer A. Raff, Deborah A. Bolnick, Delia C. Cook, and Frederika
A. Kaestle
2015   Ancient DNA from the Schild Site in Illinois: Implications for the Mississip-
        pian Transition in the Lower Illinois River Valley. American Journal of Physical
        Anthropology 156(3): 434–448.
Richards, John D.
1992   Ceramics and Culture at Aztalan, A Late Prehistoric Village in Southeast Wis-
        consin. PhD dissertation, Department of Anthropology, University of Wiscon-
        sin–Milwaukee.
Rodell, Roland L.
1991   The Diamond Bluff Complex and Cahokia Influence in the Red Wing Locality.
        In New Perspectives on Cahokia: Views from the Periphery, edited by James B.
        Stoltman, pp. 253–280. Prehistory Press, Madison, Wisconsin.
Rye, Owen S.
1981   Pottery Technology: Principles and Reconstruction. Taraxacum, Washington, DC.
Sampson, Kelvin W.
1988   Conventionalized Figures on Late Woodland Ceramics. Wisconsin Archaeologist
        69(3): 163–188.
Schilling, Timothy
2010   An Archaeological Model of the Construction of Monks Mound and Implica-
        tions for the Development of the Cahokian Society (800–1400 A.D.). PhD dis-

sertation, Department of Anthropology, Washington University in St. Louis, Missouri.

Schortman, Edward M., and Patricia A. Urban

1998   Culture Contact Structure and Process. In *Studies in Culture Contact: Interaction, Culture Change, and Archaeology,* edited by James G. Cusick, pp. 102–125. Center for Archaeological Investigations Occasional Paper No. 25, Southern Illinois University–Carbondale.

Silliman, Stephen W.

2005   Culture Contact or Colonialism? Challenges in the Archaeology of Native North America. *American Antiquity* 70(1): 55–74.

2009   Change and Continuity, Practice and Memory: Native American Persistence in Colonial New England. *American Antiquity* 74(2): 211–230.

Sinopoli, Carla M.

1991   *Approaches to Archaeological Ceramics.* Plenum Press, New York.

Skousen, B. Jacob

2016   Pilgrimage and the Construction of Cahokia: A View from the Emerald Site. University of Illinois at Urbana–Champaign.

2018   Dugan Airfield Site Lithics. In *Early Mississippian Settlement Along the Kaskaskia Trail: The Dugan Airfield and Booster Station Sites,* edited by B. Jacob Skousen. Illinois State Archaeological Survey, Prairie Research Institute, Technical Report No. 96, University of Illinois at Urbana–Champaign.

Skousen, B. Jacob (editor)

2018   *Early Mississippian Settlement Along the Kaskaskia Trail: The Dugan Airfield and Booster Station Sites.* Illinois State Archaeological Survey, Prairie Research Institute, Technical Report No. 96, University of IllinoisUrbana.

Slater, Philip A., Kristin M. Hedman, and Thomas E. Emerson

2014   Immigrants at the Mississippian Polity of Cahokia: Strontium Isotope Evidence for Population Movement. *Journal of Archaeological Science* 44(1): 117–127.

Smith, Stuart Tyson

2007   Ethnicity and Culture. In *The Egyptian World,* edited by Toby Wilkinson, pp. 218–241. Routledge, London.

Stahl, Anne B.

1985   *The Dohak Site (11-S-642).* American Bottom Archaeology FAI-270 Site Reports, Vol. 12. University of Illinois Press, Urbana.

Steadman, Dawnie Wolfe

2001   Mississippians in Motion? A Population Genetic Analysis of Interregional Gene Flow in West-Central Illinois. *American Journal of Physical Anthropology* 114(1): 61–73.

Stein, Gill J.

2002   From Passive Periphery to Active Agents: Emerging Perspectives in the Archaeology of Interregional Interaction: Archaeology Division Distinguished Lecture AAA Annual Meeting, Philadelphia, December 5, 1998. *American Antiquity* 104(3): 903–916.

2005   Introduction: The Comparative Archaeology of Colonial Encounters. In *The*

Archaeology of Colonial Encounters: Comparative Perspectives, edited by Gill J. Stein, pp. 1–29. School of American Research Press, Santa Fe, New Mexico.

Stoltman, James B.

1991   Ceramic Petrography as a Technique for Documenting Cultural Interaction: An Example from the Upper Mississippi Valley. *American Antiquity* 56(1): 103–120.

2001   The Role of Petrography in the Study of Archaeological Ceramics. In *Earth Sciences in Archaeology,* edited by Paul Goldberg, Vance Holliday, and Reid Ferring, pp. 297–326. Kluwer Academic Plenum, New York.

Stoltman, James B. (editor)

1991   *New Perspectives on Cahokia: Views from the Periphery.* Monographs in World Archaeology, Vol. 2. Prehistory Press, Madison, Wisconsin.

Struever, Stuart

1968   A Re-examination of Hopewell in Eastern North America. University of Chicago, Chicago, Illinois.

Studenmund, Sarah

2000   Late Woodland Occupation in the Lower Illinois Valley: Research Questions and Data Sets. In *Late Woodland Tradition and Transformation across the Midcontinent,* edited by Thomas E. Emerson, pp. 301–343. University of Nebraska Press, Lincoln.

Sullivan, Lynne P.

2007   A WPA Déjà Vu on Mississippian Architecture. In *Architectural Variability in the Southeast: Comprehensive Case Studies of Mississippian Structures,* pp. 117–135, edited by Cameron H. Lacquement. University of Alabama Press, Tuscaloosa.

Swanton, John R.

1946   *The Indians of the Southeastern United States.* Smithsonian Institution, Bureau of American Ethnology Bulletin 137. Washington, DC.

Tilly, Charles

1978   *From Mobilization to Revolution.* Addison-Wesley, Reading, Masssachusetts.

Townsend, Richard F. (editor)

2004   *Hero, Hawk, and Open Hand: American Indian Art of the Ancient Midwest and South.* Art Institute of Chicago; Yale University Press, New Haven.

Trubitt, Mary Beth D.

2000   Mound Building and Prestige Goods Exchange: Changing Strategies in the Cahokia Chiefdom. *American Antiquity* 65(4): 669–690.

VanDerwarker, Amber M., and Gregory D. Wilson

2016   War, Food, and Structural Violence in the Mississippian Central Illinois Valley. In *The Archaeology of Food and Warfare: Food Insecurity in Prehistory,* edited by Amber M. VanDerwarker and Gregory D. Wilson, pp. 75–106. Springer, New York.

VanDerwarker, Amber M., Gregory D. Wilson, and Dana N. Bardolph

2013   Maize Adoption and Intensification in the Central Illinois River Valley: An Analysis of Archaeobotanical Data from the Late Woodland to Early Mississippian Periods (A.D. 600–1200). *Southeastern Archaeology* 32(2): 147–168.

Vogel, Joseph O.

1964   *A Preliminary Report on the Analysis of Ceramics from the Cahokia Area at the Illinois State Museum.* Preliminary Reports of Investigations No. 6. Illinois State Museum, Springfield.

1975   Trends in Cahokia Ceramics: Preliminary Study of the Collections from Tracts 15A and 15B. In *Perspectives in Cahokia Archaeology,* pp. 32–125. Illinois Archaeological Survey Bulletin No. 10, Urbana.

Voss, Barbara

2008   *The Archaeology of Ethnogenesis: Race and Sexuality in Colonial San Francisco.* University of California Press, Berkeley and Los Angeles.

Wallerstein, Immanuel

[1974] 1991 *The Modern Word System: Capitalist Agriculture and the Origin of the European World-Economy in the Sixteenth Century.* Academic Press, New York.

Walthall, John A.

1981   *Galena and Aboriginal Trade in Eastern North America.* Scientific Papers 17. Illinois State Museum, Springfield.

Waring, Antonio J., and Preston Holder

1945   A Prehistoric Ceremonial Complex in the Southeastern United States. *American Anthropologist* 47(1): 1–34.

Welch, Paul D.

1991   *Moundville's Economy.* University of Alabama Press, Tuscaloosa.

Wernke, Steven A.

2011   Convergences: Producing Early Colonial Hybridity at a Doctrina in Highland Peru. In *Enduring Conquests: Rethinking the Archaeology of Resistance to Spanish Colonialism in the Americas,* edited by Matthew Liebmann and Melissa S. Murphy, pp. 77–102. School for Advanced Research Press, Santa Fe, New Mexico.

White, Harrison C.

2008   *Identity and Control: How Social Formations Emerge.* Princeton University Press, Princeton, New Jersey.

Wilkie, Laurie A., and Paul Farnsworth

1999   Trade and the Construction of Bahamian Identity: A Multiscalar Exploration. *International Journal of Historical Archaeology* 3(4): 238–320.

Williams, Stephen, and John M. Goggin

1956   The Long Nosed God Mask in Eastern United States. *The Missouri Archaeologist* 18(3): 4–72.

Wilson, Gregory D.

1996   Insight through Icons. *Illinois Archaeology* 8(1&2): 23–37.

1998   An Investigation of Early Mississippian Resistance in the American Bottom. Master's thesis, Department of Anthropology, University of Oklahoma, Norman.

1999   The Production and Consumption of Mississippian Fineware Vessels in the American Bottom. *Southeastern Archaeology* 18(2): 98–109.

2001   Crafting Control and the Control of Crafts: Rethinking the Moundville Greenstone Industry. *Southeastern Archaeology* 20(2): 118–128.

2011   Post-Cahokian Contact in the Central Illinois River Valley. Paper presented at the 76th Annual Society for American Archaeology Conference, Sacramento, California.

2012a   Merchants, Missionaries, or Militants? A Critical Evaluation of Cahokian Contact Scenarios in the Central Illinois River Valley. At the 77th Annual Society for American Archaeology Conference. Memphis, Tennessee.

2012b   Living with War: The Impact of Chronic Violence in the Mississippian-Period Central Illinois River Valley. In *The Oxford Handbook of North American Archaeology,* edited by Timothy R. Pauketat, pp. 522–533. Oxford University Press, Oxford.

2015a   Lamb Site Ceramics: Mississippianization in the Central Illinois River Valley. *Illinois Archaeology* 27: 174–200.

2015b   Lamb Site Lithics: Early Mississippian Stone-Tool Technology in the Central Illinois River Valley. *Illinois Archaeology* 27: 201–214.

2018   Dugan Airfield Site Ceramics. In *Early Mississippian Settlement Along the Kaskaskia Trail: The Dugan Airfield and Booster Station Sites,* edited by B. Jacob Skousen, pp. 125–164. Illinois State Archaeological Survey, Prairie Research Institute, Technical Report No. 96, University of Illinois–Urbana.

Wilson, Gregory D. (editor)

2017   *Mississippian Beginnings.* University of Florida Press, Gainesville.

Wilson, Gregory D., Dana N. Bardolph, Duane Esarey, and Jeremy Wilson

2020   Transregional Social Fields of the Early Mississippian Midcontinent. *Journal of Archaeological Method and Theory.* https://doi.org/10.1007/s10816-019-09440-y.

Wilson, Gregory D., Mallory A. Melton, and Amber M. VanDerwarker

2018   Reassessing the Chronology of the Mississippian Central Illinois River Valley using Bayesian Analysis. Southeastern Archaeology 37(1): 22–38.

Wilson, Gregory D., Colleen M. Delaney, and Phillip G. Millhouse

2017   The Mississippian of the Illinois and Apple River Valleys. In *Mississippian Beginnings,* edited by Gregory D. Wilson, pp. 97–129. University of Florida Press, Gainesville.

Wilson, Gregory D., and Brad Koldehoff

1998   The Miller Farm Sites: Early Mississippian Occupations on Turkey Hill. *Illinois Antiquity* 33(2): 4–9.

2009   Organizational Variation among Mississippian Groundstone Celt Industries. Paper presented at the 47th Annual Meeting of the Southeastern Archaeological Conference, Mobile, Alabama.

Wilson, Gregory D., and Steven R. Kuehn

2011   Hunting, Warring, and Resource Depression in the Mississippian Midwest. Paper presented at the 57th Annual Meetings of the Midwest Archaeological Conference, La Crosse, Wisconsin.

Wilson, Gregory D., Jon Marcoux, and Brad Koldehoff

2006   Square Pegs in Round Holes: Organizational Diversity Between Early Moundville and Cahokia. In *Leadership and Polity in Mississippian Society,* edited by

Brian M. Butler and Paul D. Welch, pp. 43–72. Center for Archaeological Investigations Occasional Paper No. 33, Southern Illinois University–Carbondale.

Wilson, Gregory D., and Lynne P. Sullivan

2017   Mississippian Origins: From Emergence to Beginnings. In *Mississippian Beginnings,* edited by Gregory D. Wilson, pp. 1–28. University of Florida Press, Gainesville.

Wilson, Gregory D., and Amber M. VanDerwarker

2015   The Functional Dimensions of Earth Oven Cooking: An Analysis of an Accidently Burned Maize Roast at the C. W. Cooper Site in West-Central Illinois. *Journal of Field Archaeology* 40(2): 165–174.

Wobst, Martin H.

1977   Stylistic Behavior and Information Exchange. In *For the Director: Research Essays in Honor of James B. Griffin,* edited by Charles E. Cleland, pp. 317–342. University of Michigan Museum of Anthropology, Ann Arbor.

Yerkes, Richard W.

1983   Microwear, Microdrills, and Mississippian Craft Specialization. *American Antiquity* 48(3): 499–518.

1989   Mississippian Craft Specialization on the American Bottom. *Southeastern Archaeology* 8(2): 93–106.

Yoffee, Norman

2005   *Myths of the Archaic State: Evolution of the Earliest Cities, States, and Civilizations.* Cambridge University Press, Cambridge, UK.

Zych, Thomas J.

2013   The Construction of a Mound and a New Community: An Analysis of the Ceramic and Feature Assemblages from the Northeast Mound at the Aztalan Site. Master's thesis, Department of Anthropology, University of Wisconsin, Milwaukee.

Index

CHRISTINA M. FRIBERG is postdoctoral research fellow in the Department of Earth and Atmospheric Sciences at Indiana University, Bloomington. Her research interests include culture contact, identity, craft production, and archaeologies of materiality in the Mississippian-period southeastern and midwestern United States. Dr. Friberg has codirected archaeological excavations and geophysical surveys at multiple sites in both the Illinois River Valley and St. Catherines Island, Georgia. She is the author of "Cosmic Negotiations: Ramey Incised Pottery and the Mississippianization of Cahokia's Northern Hinterlands," in *Southeastern Archaeology*.

Bioarchaeology of Spanish Florida: The Impact of Colonialism, edited by Clark Spencer Larsen (2001)

Archaeological Studies of Gender in the Southeastern United States, edited by Jane M. Eastman and Christopher B. Rodning (2001)

The Archaeology of Traditions: Agency and History Before and After Columbus, edited by Timothy R. Pauketat (2001)

Foraging, Farming, and Coastal Biocultural Adaptation in Late Prehistoric North Carolina, by Dale L. Hutchinson (2002)

Windover: Multidisciplinary Investigations of an Early Archaic Florida Cemetery, edited by Glen H. Doran (2002)

Archaeology of the Everglades, by John W. Griffin (2002; first paperback edition, 2017)

Pioneer in Space and Time: John Mann Goggin and the Development of Florida Archaeology, by Brent Richards Weisman (2002)

Indians of Central and South Florida, 1513–1763, by John H. Hann (2003)

Presidio Santa María de Galve: A Struggle for Survival in Colonial Spanish Pensacola, edited by Judith A. Bense (2003)

Bioarchaeology of the Florida Gulf Coast: Adaptation, Conflict, and Change, by Dale L. Hutchinson (2004; first paperback edition, 2020)

The Myth of Syphilis: The Natural History of Treponematosis in North America, edited by Mary Lucas Powell and Della Collins Cook (2005)

The Florida Journals of Frank Hamilton Cushing, edited by Phyllis E. Kolianos and Brent R. Weisman (2005)

The Lost Florida Manuscript of Frank Hamilton Cushing, edited by Phyllis E. Kolianos and Brent R. Weisman (2005)

The Native American World Beyond Apalachee: West Florida and the Chattahoochee Valley, by John H. Hann (2006)

Tatham Mound and the Bioarchaeology of European Contact: Disease and Depopulation in Central Gulf Coast Florida, by Dale L. Hutchinson (2007)

Taíno Indian Myth and Practice: The Arrival of the Stranger King, by William F. Keegan (2007)

An Archaeology of Black Markets: Local Ceramics and Economies in Eighteenth-Century Jamaica, by Mark W. Hauser (2008; first paperback edition, 2013)

Mississippian Mortuary Practices: Beyond Hierarchy and the Representationist Perspective, edited by Lynne P. Sullivan and Robert C. Mainfort Jr. (2010; first paperback edition, 2012)

Bioarchaeology of Ethnogenesis in the Colonial Southeast, by Christopher M. Stojanowski (2010; first paperback edition, 2013)

French Colonial Archaeology in the Southeast and Caribbean, edited by Kenneth G. Kelly and Meredith D. Hardy (2011; first paperback edition, 2015)

Late Prehistoric Florida: Archaeology at the Edge of the Mississippian World, edited by Keith Ashley and Nancy Marie White (2012; first paperback edition, 2015)

Early and Middle Woodland Landscapes of the Southeast, edited by Alice P. Wright and Edward R. Henry (2013; first paperback edition, 2019)

Trends and Traditions in Southeastern Zooarchaeology, edited by Tanya M. Peres (2014)

New Histories of Pre-Columbian Florida, edited by Neill J. Wallis and Asa R. Randall (2014; first paperback edition, 2016)

Discovering Florida: First-Contact Narratives from Spanish Expeditions along the Lower Gulf Coast, edited and translated by John E. Worth (2014; first paperback edition, 2016)

Constructing Histories: Archaic Freshwater Shell Mounds and Social Landscapes of the St. Johns River, Florida, by Asa R. Randall (2015)

Archaeology of Early Colonial Interaction at El Chorro de Maíta, Cuba, by Roberto Valcárcel Rojas (2016)

Fort San Juan and the Limits of Empire: Colonialism and Household Practice at the Berry Site, edited by Robin A. Beck, Christopher B. Rodning, and David G. Moore (2016)